Study skills

Writing *and* Presenting
Research

Angela Thody

SAGE Publications
London ● Thousand Oaks ● New Delhi

Contents Overview

Writing *and* Presenting Research

First published 2006

SAGE Publications Ltd
1 Oliver's Yard
55 City Road
London EC1Y 1SP

SAGE Publications Inc.
2455 Teller Road
Thousand Oaks, California 91320

SAGE Publications India Pvt Ltd
B-42, Panchsheel Enclave
Post Box 4109
New Delhi 110 017

British Library Cataloguing in Publication data

A catalogue record for this book is available
from the British Library

ISBN-10 1 4129 0292 4   ISBN-13 978 1 4129 0292 2
ISBN-10 1 4129 0293 2   ISBN-13 978 1 4129 0293 9 (pbk)

Library of Congress Control Number: 2005934768

Typeset by C&M Digitals (P) Ltd, Chennai, India
Printed on paper from sustainable resources
Printed and bound in Great Britain by TJ International Ltd, Padstow, Cornwall

Contents

Boxes

Figures

Tables

Hazard Warning

Read in chapter order, this book presents a wide-ranging, introductory guide to the choices to be made in deciding how to communicate research findings in documents and presentations. Once you have familiarized yourself with the contents, the book becomes a valuable reference.

The book is necessary because although pluralism in research methodologies has become accepted, pluralism in the ways in which research can be reported is much less accepted; nor are there many sources of information on the possible varieties of reporting research.

New researchers may find this book destabilizing if they have not previously confronted many choices of how to write up, or present, their research. Experienced researchers may find this book causes arguments about cherished ideas concerning what is, or is not, conventional for reporting research.

If you want to discuss the destabilizing or the arguments with me, do make contact:

Emerita Professor Angela Thody, angelathody450@hotmail.com
International Institute for Educational Leadership, University of Lincoln,
Brayford Campus, Lincoln LN6 7RS, England

Appreciation

Many thanks to

- ☑ generations of my students whose questions drove me to write this book;
- ☑ those who have listened to my presentations, who read my publications and whose comments drove me to envisage this book;
- ☑ my family who were driven to distraction by this book and to Lora and Serena who wrote one of its chapters;
- ☑ my helpful publishers who steered my driving with their experience, particularly Patrick Brindle, Brian Goodale, Vanessa Harwood and Rebecca De Luca Wilson;
- ☑ the driving verve of the many writers and presenters whose examples are included in this book, particularly Professors N.B. Jones and Esther Sui-Chu Ho, The Athena Institute and Beth Bownes Johnson for permissions to use their excellent works, my postgraduate students, Dr. Anat Oster, Hilda Mugglestone, Simon Testa and Gillian Horsley for extracts from their theses in preparation and after completion, and Professors Martin Barstow, Mike Cook, Michael Hough, Olof Johansson, Zoi Papanaoum, Petros Pashiardis and Dr John Baker whose presentations inspired me;
- ☑ Commonwealth Council for Educational Administration and Management for permission to reprint extracts from Ho Sui-Chu, E. (2003), Roberts, V. (2003), Stewart, J.M. and Hodges, D. (2003), and Thody, A.M. and Nkata, J.L. (1997).
- ☑ Professors Mike Cook, Betty Marchant and Mark Brundrett whose helpful reviews drove me to improve the book;
- ☑ my daughters, Amber and Serena, who assiduously hunted references for me when my drive failed and to the author, Steve Coonts, who responded so promptly to my queries;
- ☑ my grandson, Sean, whose early arrival left me time to finish this book.

Part I   Preparation

1 Conventions or Alternatives?

CONTENTS

1.1 Debates to resolve

This book is a guide through the choices to be made when deciding how to report research, principally in social sciences (including health), arts and humanities but also with relevance to, and examples from, natural and applied sciences and law. It covers research written as theses and dissertations, chapters, books, reports and articles in academic, professional or general media such as newspapers. It reviews the options for presenting research orally as lectures, keynotes, conference papers and even TV game shows.

All of these forms of reporting research have well established conventions for their formats. All of them also have growing numbers of alternative possibilities. These have generated debate about what is or is not acceptable. My aim is to make this debate more manageable for those wanting to assess which of the conventional formats (1.3) or alternative possibilities (1.4) on offer is most appropriate for reporting their current research.

This debate, polarizing conventions and alternatives, was encapsulated for me in a conversation with fellow conference delegates following an academic's word-for-word reading aloud of his conventional research paper. The listeners' views on the presenter differed radically. I report this 'mini' research into their opinions as a poem in Box 1.1.

Box 1.1   Differentiating conventional and alternative research writing styles: poetic format

---

Conference Debate

It's like listening to poetry,

He said.

I go to a conference to hear the poetry of the paper;

The paper is like poetry read by the real, actual writer,

Word for word,

Like all papers,

He said.

I learn later from reading the paper,

But not *at* the conference.

There you only go to hear researchers as poets.

You hear them interpreting their own poetry of words,

Their nuances, their cadences, their enthusiasm.

They do not need to explain them to YOU.

It is enough to be close to academic celebrities,

He said.

It should be teaching,

She said.

I go to a conference to learn from the presentation of the paper,

It is research, explained by the originator,

Just the main issues,

Different styles,

She said.

(Continued)

Box 1.1   (Continued)

You should comprehend from hearing a clear summary of the paper

There, *at* the conference.

You see researchers illuminating with PowerPoint,
Duplicated notes, pictures, sound, enthusiasm;
They feel the need to share with US.
So you are close to great teachers,

She said.

Angela Thody, 2005

Did my poem appeal to you, annoy you or intrigue you, as an 'alternative' way of reporting research data? Is it appropriate for the opening of a textbook on research writing and presentation? Did the visual differences in the layout of the two verses add to, or detract from, the message? Should the personal forms of 'I', 'my' and 'you' in this chapter so far have been mixed with the impersonal (it, one)? These exemplify the types of questions which this book explores.

To illustrate the opposite pole in this debate, the poem's information in conventional, 'textbook' form is in Box 1.2. What is your reaction to this?

Box 1.2   Differentiating conventional and alternative research writing styles: textbook format

---

Two styles are suggested to which research reporting should conform:
either
Accepted academic conventions, as summed up by an academic journal editor, 'make life easier for our referees by writing a clear, concise paper; that is, structured in a traditional manner' (Murray, 2004: 1). Natural and social scientists therefore report their research in strictly uniform scientific experiment format; humanities' authors follow chronological, or logical, formats. Both indicate objectivity, neutrality, researcher distance and impersonality.

or

(Continued)

> ## Box 1.2   (Continued)
>
> 'Innovative, user-friendly formats' (Gomm and Davies, 2000: 141) associated with postmodernism and its doubt that there is any one right method. All methods are deemed subjective; they represent particular viewpoints of which the researcher's is one. Research reporting formats embrace widely differing approaches such as poetry, photography or novelistic style. Subjectivity is unavoidable, bias is openly stated, researchers reveal themselves overtly, and personality is more than welcome.
>
> A. Thody, 2005

1.2   Context of the debates

Unusual modes for academic writing are nothing new. Cobbett's 1818 guide to alternatives for the conventions of English grammar, for example, written as letters to his son, was described as 'more entertaining than many novels ... his Grammar is unlike any other' (O'London, 1924: 48). A 2003 example of the same unconventionality in the grammar textbook genre is *Eats Shoots and Leaves* by Lynne Truss (2003) which leavens language rules with humour and idiosyncratic proselytizing.

Nor have the ways which I have termed 'conventional' always been thus. An American 1955 study by Butts of assumptions underlying Australian education, for example, consisted of chatty personal reflections from random encounters. It was regarded as conventional and good research, yet there was no rigorous sample selection, literature review or methodology (Thody, 1994a). Butts was simply a travel writer of his day doing what we might now dismiss as 'educational tourism', but the social sciences had little opportunity to do anything else for some time. As recently as 1979, for example, Parsons and Lyons pleaded that university researchers should be able to get into real schools and risk interviewing real administrators, something we now see as normal and vital. Until then, surveys through questionnaires had dominated subjects such as education management research, for example. Utilizing conventional scientific formats for this type of research fitted the data well and also accorded with the desire of the social sciences to be accepted as being as rigorous as the natural sciences.

This desire to be like the natural sciences can be accounted for by the dominance of positivism for the first half of the twentieth century. Positivism gave credibility to many disciplines and dictated their forms (Hughes, 1990: 36). The scientific formats of writing that emerged from this positivism were adopted by the academic social science writers of the 1960s onwards. In doing so, however, they:

> broke with their own inherited traditions ... They showed little of the nostalgia toward lost practices ... They worked new devices ... to support greater ease of access and better serve the interests of scholarship. (Willinski, 2000: 62)

These are the same objectives that helped to propel a new debate about research writing and presenting from the 1990s, since by then there had been a huge diaspora in research methods, not matched by variety in the academic formats of reporting research. It had also been realized that all research, from any discipline and in any format, has an endemic 'literary dimension ... yet concealed by realist metaphysics' (Scott and Usher, 1999: 19–20). The concealment lies in applying conventional, scientific formats for writing and presenting research without considering their suitability for a particular topic or research method. Any research report should tell a story of discovery from its inception to its conclusion – a story that so captures the reader's imagination that they will act upon the outcomes.

Conventional style is not, however, inherently bad. Arguments for and against conventional and alternative styles are considered next in this chapter, together with an outline of the features of each.

1.3   Conventional formats

1.3.1   Definitions

The conventional (or traditional, or scientific) format begins with a statement of the problem to be solved and the setting of this in its context of previous research on the same topic (including the literature review). This is part of the rationale for the problem which stresses the importance of studying it. Next, the research methodology is recounted. From this the findings emerge, ending with the conclusions drawn from the material presented.

The order will sometimes vary but the elements remain unchanged, whether the research reported is from the natural sciences, the applied sciences of engineering and medicine, or the social sciences. In the humanities and law, the traditional conventions would be either the production of a chronological account in numbered order, or an argument presenting first one and then the other side of the account.

These major formats all have codified conventions for style and language (5.3, 12.2) such as the American Psychological Association (APA, 2001; 2005), the Modern Languages Association (MLA, 2003), the Modern Humanities Research Association (MHRA, 2002) and for American law, *The Bluebook* (Bluebook, 2000).
This style works best where:

- significant amounts of quantitative and/or factual data have to be transformed into easily understandable text (in any discipline);
- the work was following through an experiment (in natural or applied sciences) or a quasi-experiment (in social or health sciences);
- there is a logical chronological or debate sequence (in law and the humanities);
- the research subjects are inanimate (such as literature texts) or dead (as in history);
- results have to be compared, where data are cumulative, and where results have to be replicated.

The aim is to produce an objective, distant report in which the views and activities of the phenomena or respondents are reproduced exactly as they happened. It is assumed that the researcher has not influenced how the natural phenomena or the people have performed, behaved or commented. The researcher speaks only in the conclusions to the report and these conclusions are confined to whatever is obvious from the data. It is assumed that readers do not influence the interpretation; it is important that they interpret it exactly as has the writer. Reader and writer influence on the data is to be, and can be, avoided. The understandings on which this style is based are that the research has produced general, unassailable truths which have been proved from irrefutable evidence and which must be presented to the readers with exactitude.

The current debate about the applicability of alternative formats in place of the traditional must not obscure the value of conventional, scientific reporting. The logical sequencing of writing up research as an experiment possesses an elegant simplicity and the near-certainty of acceptance by peers, policy makers and publishers. It is common for reporting quantitative, qualitative and narrative data. Its advantages are discussed below.

1.3.2 Advantages

1.3.2.1 A training ground

Mastery of conventional formats has become almost an admission ticket to academia with 'tremendous material and symbolic power ... [which will] increase the probability of one's work being accepted into "core" ... journals' (Richardson, 1998: 353). To gain this acceptance, establishment mores must be followed, the establishment being editors, referees, thesis examiners, professorial promotion committees and research funders (Chapter 3). For new researchers, success with conventional formats is a compulsory rite of passage.

Those who argue in its favour point out that it helps students to learn to write and to think like everyone else, in the accepted forms of their disciplines (Zeller and Farmer, 1999: 5). This is much more than just a ritual game, performed for the sake of ritual. It can be seen as marking the end of an apprenticeship. The thesis, or early articles, in conventional formats show that the writer knows the ground rules for the making of the test piece. Once that is perfectly completed, the apprentice can then proceed as a master of the craft and is entitled and enabled to embellish, with the skills of literary and artistic formats, any type of data, quantitative, qualitative or narrative.

1.3.2.2 Simplicity and comparability

The scientific style has seemingly unassailable logic and clarity which demonstrate analytical, synthetic and critical thinking, the hallmarks of a good academic. Alternatives from the postmodernist genre are criticized for their rejection of scientific approaches, rational economics or social justice, and for their incomprehensible language (Stevenson, 2003). The option of alternatives is seen to complicate issues of 'authorship, authority, truth, validity and reliability ... [and] the greater freedom to experiment with textual form ... does not guarantee a better product' (Richardson, 1998: 359).

The challenge with admitting plurality to the options for presentation and writing is that the possible approaches are like the many new methodologies themselves, lacking 'the confident clarity' of positivist approaches (Hughes, 1990: 138). Alternative formats can produce:

sprawling and self-indulgent descriptions that are free of meanings or claims … lazy writing in the sense that authors only reproduce what they have collected and … readers have to work hard to make sense of the reportage and to deduce the claims. (Knight, 2002: 194)

In contrast, conventional formatting does generally avoid such excesses and facilitates comparisons amongst research outputs presented in the same styles, and often in the same places, in reports. Relationships amongst findings can easily be displayed when the data appear in similar ways even in different reporting formats. The presentation of data in tables, graphs and diagrams provides visuals which make assimilation easier.

1.3.2.3 Political, professional and academic acceptance

Conventional formats proclaim the respectability that policy makers need. They have to demonstrate simply, to large and often sceptical audiences, that there is enough evidence for proposed changes. Conventional formatting provides this readily since research findings always appear as unarguable, neutral facts. This provides the necessary persuasiveness to encourage professionals to put research findings into practice (Silva, 1990).

In academia, where careers depend on research recognition, writing theses and articles, and preparing presentations, are much quicker if the most generally accepted format is adopted; alternatives are harder work. Work in conventional formats is more likely to be accepted than alternatives (Chapter 14) since examiners, editors and research assessors work to the standards of conventional formats (3.4.6). The findings of a research project can be sufficiently controversial in themselves without adding contention over an innovative writing style. The 'harsh realities of becoming new members of [the academic] discourse community' (Gosden, 1995: 39) crown convention with success because academic writing is a major means of social communication amongst academic peers (Holliday, 2002: 124; Jakobs and Knorr, 1996). Such successful communication matters, not only to individual careers, but also to university research ratings which determine university research income.

Formal and informal ratings systems are world-wide. The United Kingdom's Research Assessment Exercise (RAE) commenced in 1992. New Zealand adopted a similar system in the early 2000s (Lord, Robb and Shanahan, 1998). The USA's Carnegie ratings, introduced in 1973, operate somewhat similarly though with less force than the RAE (Middaugh, 2001). Japan is investigating the possibility of such a system, and countries such as Israel consider closing colleges that are insufficiently research productive. Hong Kong and Australia also monitor university outputs (Mok and Lee, 2002; Taylor, 2001a; Mok, 2000). This is not a climate in which to take risks.

1.3.2.4 Globalization

The 'market' for research findings is now global; a standardized format helps international acceptance since conventions create meanings readily understood across cultures. Conventions for research writing and presentation are the equivalent of the McDonald's logo, Marriott Hotel bedrooms, shopping malls or aircraft emergency instructions. With all of these, as with the conventional, scientifically oriented format of research reporting, consumers know that they will get the same everywhere; they get what they see and they know the format has been honed to international standards of efficiency and effectiveness. It is unlikely to be exciting but it will be safe.

But is *safety* the context within which academic research should always operate? What are the alternatives?

> **REFLECTIONS**
>
> Section 1.3 above has been written in the impersonal, third person, passive voice. This is the generally accepted style in conventional formatting. In 1.4 below, about alternatives, I employ mainly the personal, first person, active voice since this is more often found in alternative approaches to reporting research (5.3.3.6).

1.4 Alternatives

1.4.1 Gaining acceptance?

I remember my surprise, when first attending North American academic conferences, on noticing that virtually all the papers were identical in their text appearance. Even the font style and size were uniform. Bryman (2001) evinced similar astonishment on discovering how little difference there is between the styles and formats of articles whether the author is presenting qualitative or quantitative data. I soon discovered the reason for the standardization; the American Psychological Association's style manual (APA) has been adopted by other disciplines, particularly in the social sciences. The handbook of the Modern Languages Association (MLA) performs the same standardizing functions for humanities disciplines.

Why, I mused, in the USA and Canada, so often depicted as lands of freedom, is so little discretion allowed to, or taken by, highly intelligent academics on how to present their work? Why have APA guidelines for writing up psychology experiments been adopted so wholeheartedly by other disciplines? These rules are designed for such topics as 'Referential communication by chimpanzees', an experiment which concluded that 'the deployment and gestures and gaze alternation between a banana and an observer were manifested as integrated patterns of nonverbal reference' (Leavens, Hopkins and Thomas, 2004: 55). Can such rules be equally suitable for the behaviours of district superintendents (Griffin and Chance, 1994) or teaching ethics to nurses (Krawczyk, 1997)?

Even where there are no strictures, such as when academics present their research orally, why do many academics still elect to 'read' their papers and to eschew the livelier arts of demonstration and teaching? I have found that these conventions, which result in almost identical written and oral presentations of conference papers, have appertained at many conferences I have attended world wide in the last thirty years and in every set of contributors' instructions for journals. Even the *Review of Religious Research* came up with nothing more than the conventional requirements. 'Oh, for a thousand tongues to sing' a research report as a hymn or a medieval illuminated manuscript! Outside of North America, I have not found quite such tight adherence to APA and MLA, but the requirements of journals, thesis assessments and conference presentations still veer strongly towards the conventional.

I have been relieved to find that I am not alone in questioning APA's domination (Zeller and Farmer, 1999; Vipond, 1996; Bazerman, 1987) or the universal appropriateness of conventional forms:

> We have been encouraged to take on the omniscient voice of science, the view from everywhere … Nurturing our own voices releases the censorious hold of 'science writing' … as well as the arrogance it fosters in our psyche … [and] homogenization through professional socialisation. (Richardson, 1998: 347)

I've also encountered a few brave, alternative presenters, mainly at North American conferences. Their ideas included:

- readers' theatre (where researchers acted their research respondents' views);
- dance interpreting the emotions arising from findings;
- town meetings (researchers reported their findings briefly as political speeches and then invited audience participation, assisted by mobile microphones);
- debates (six researchers had exactly three minutes each to put their cases).

I added myself to these experiments. I assumed the persona and costume of a nineteenth century Tasmanian teacher to deliver a lecture on colonial education with language and props appropriate to the time (though a twentieth century overhead projector had to substitute for a magic lantern). Audio and video recordings made for me of Zimbabwean school pupils in uniform, singing their school song, launched a lecture on girls' education in Africa. I concluded this with leading community singing of the same school song with the audience. When delivering historical lectures, I often wear several changes of clothing or hats, gradually stripping off as we pass through each period. When illustrating the strengths and weaknesses of systems of governance, I pull out members of the audience to represent the stereotypes. A group of us (including two Greeks) ran a Romano-Grecian seminar to report our research on European integration, since the Romans and Greeks had been the first European integrationists. The seating was rearranged into a square, wine and grapes were served throughout, and we all wore matching T-shirts summarizing our main finding. I frequently devise concluding songs that summarize the principal features of research reported in my lectures. While this is meant to be entertaining, it is not gratuitous. Each format is designed to convey the research findings appropriately and better than can words alone, to reinforce learning, and even to transmit ideas that are hard to put into words.

I noticed, however, that mine and others' alternatives tended to come from groups not strongly represented in the academic establishment – women, ethnic minorities and the physically differentially abled. The alternatives thus appear to be 'fringe' events, on the edges of a sea of convention.

As a 'fringe' we could just dismiss them, but we face a conundrum:

> **Successful research is that which proves something new, original, innovative and at the cutting edge of ideas; our most generally acceptable forms of research writing and presentation usually shun all of these.**

What then are the alternatives, and what are the arguments that favour extending the options for writing and presenting research?

1.4.2 Definitions

I cannot encapsulate alternatives so easily as the conventional formats since alternatives can be as varied as word-for-word transcribed interviews (Rice, 2004), photographs with minimal text (Staub, 2002), narrative poetry (Woodley, 2004) (this book's examples are in Chapters 9 and 10) or tabulated quantitative data presented without commentary (Chapter 8). I can, however, formulate their distinguishing characteristics:

- We celebrate and acknowledge the subjectivities of writers, research respondents and readers as positive contributions to enhanced understanding; all will affect research writing and presentation.
- We accept that there are multiple perspectives on any research problem and we must present all of these in order to give as fully rounded a view as possible.
- We can be adventurous, entertaining and emotional, drawing from fiction, poetry, painting, photography, performances, sculpture, posters, music and other creative work.
- We 'expect to be reflexive … to write in the first person … and to write with passion' (Knight, 2002: 194).
- We can question the suitability of any format; we can take this even to the extremes of deconstruction and anarchy where meaning is whatever you and the readers want it to be, and accept that these various meanings may not be the same.
- We will often incorporate most or all of the basic elements of the conventional format (the statement of the problem, its context, literature, methodology, findings and conclusions) but not necessarily in that order, nor will they always be immediately obvious.
- We can apply alternative formats for quantitative, qualitative or narrative data.
- Our aim is to be intentionally focused on language as a persuasive tool (Chapters 3, 4, 5) for who ever is the principal audience for the research. This may be a solitary PhD student who has borrowed your thesis on inter-library loan, a TV game show audience, fellow professionals at a public conference interested in changing practice or experienced, specialist academics examining a thesis (3.4, 3.5, 3.6).

1.4.3 Reasons for emergence of alternatives

1.4.3.1 *Postmodernism*

Postmodernism from the 1970s has led us to understand that research, and its writing and presentation, are always partial and context bound. We can no longer claim that things are exactly right or wrong; our data cannot irrefutably prove anything; we ourselves are irretrievably intertwined in the methodology and the writing. We now accept that our personal judgement, interpretations and subjectivities (and those of other researchers) not only are inextricably involved in all decisions from inception to presentation of a research project, but also have a rightful place that must be publicly acknowledged. Postmodernism also gives us licence to doubt and to suspect; researchers are as much likely to peddle research as propaganda as are politicians. The previously clear lines between subjective and objective or between fact and fiction have become hazy and we should reflect this in how we write and present research. We should flout convention.

1.4.3.2 *Changing attitudes to the natural and social sciences*

As a 1960s' student, the first university lecture I attended discussed how social sciences might, and must, become more like natural sciences. The debate still rages (To, 2000) but there is growing scepticism about the rightness of the natural sciences as scientists contradict each other daily (each contradiction based on irrefutable experimental research) and the natural sciences are themselves finding that their own research reporting is as much open to linguistic questions as is that of the humanities and social sciences. These ferments blur the lines between social and natural sciences and the humanities, particularly in how they reach the public consciousness (Willinsky, 2000: 233). There is a huge debate about whether the conventional formats of 'scientific' writing do or do not aid clarity, and even about the meaning of clarity itself (Zeller and Farmer, 1999: 12–14).

This leads us to question the appropriateness of applying scientific norms to areas which are not sciences. Qualitative and narrative research have had to hide behind structures that depersonalize our outputs (even requiring us, for example, to report participant observation in the third person). We can, however, now begin to quit the paranoia that limits our research writing to the conventional pseudo-scientific style.

1.4.3.3 *New research and technical methodologies*

Qualitative ethnographic and narrative methods have much developed since 1975. We now use focus groups, photography, life history, email interviewing, observation, diaries, critical incidents and more. These do not always fit comfortably with conventional reporting formats. In trying to make them do so, I find that I can lose the excitement, personality and immediacy of the original research. Hence we experiment with alternative ways of writing and presenting research, so widening 'the schism between those who adhere to the scientific model of writing and those who choose to supplement that model with tools from the literary world' (Lewis-Beck, Bryman and Liao, 2004: 1197).

Experiments arising from this methodological pluralism have become more evident and more realizable with developments in computer-based systems for composing documents. From the late 1980s word processors developed, first simply as super-typewriters, getting words down more efficiently and correctly than handwriting. The linear view of writing remained initially unchanged, leaving unrecognized the 'inter-connectedness of and alternation within the writing sub-processes' (Sharples and van der Geest, 1996: 8). By 2006, computer progress had made writing a different experience, one that significantly influences what appears in a research report. We take variations in **font** (typeface) size and colour for granted. We now incorporate them **boldly** to enhance conventional and alternative styles, reporting with, for example, variegated pie charts, graphs and diagrams (though I wait to see a PhD thesis with its title in rainbow hues). Photographs and drawings can be inserted cheaply and quickly. Text blocks can be formatted at the commencement of a project report and remain unchanged without the further intervention of the writer. We can enliven with animated pictures, the thousand and one PowerPoint slides that raise our professionalism in any presentation. Utilizing analysis software, tables of categorized data appear as if by magic. I write theses, books, articles and reports directly on screen, mail and mark, read, annotate and question without ever downloading to paper. Text can be data in itself; it can be moved outside the flat space of a computer screen through hypertext and three dimensions, becoming 'geometrical forms, objects and structures ... [which] may hang on the wall, rotate on hinges or unfold' (Tonfoni and Richardson, 1994: 32).

So far, I think we have been playing with these developments as with a new toy, but they have democratized hitherto restricted print techniques. From the 2000s, we are all now sufficiently computer literate that our computer techniques are not just embellishment but an essential part of reporting that can affect meaning itself. Computers have given us the power to be alternative.

1.5   Resolving the debates?

1.5.1   The middle ground

The conventional versus alternatives debate has the disadvantage of problematizing what is often regarded as non-contentious (Cresswell, 1994: 193). Postmodernism generates this contention since 'there are no universal methods to be applied invariantly' (Scott and Usher, 1999: 10) but it does have the advantage of offering many options and alternatives are increasingly accepted (Holliday, 2002). Fortunately, postmodernism also presents us with a way of resolving the conventional/alternatives debate because it does not automatically reject the conventional but asks instead, 'What is appropriate?'

The conventional and the alternatives are best seen as ideal types at either end of a continuum. In any one piece of writing or presentation, a researcher will lean towards one ideal or the other, but it is possible to incorporate elements of both. Ways of reporting research can combine the rigour and precision of conventional scientific formats, as the spine of a research report, with the flesh of alternative humanity. The latter will reveal all the voices which have contributed to the research (including your own as the researcher). The whole combines the literary, narrative arts of arrangement, accentuation and artistry. The following extracts show combined conventional and alternative styles from refereed journal articles.[1]

Extract 1

Fail, Thompson and Walker's (2004) study, on identity and Third Culture Kids, admirably combines the conventional and the alternative. The first half is an extensive, and traditionally expressed, literature review, all written in the impersonal passive voice and in past tenses (5.3.3.5, 5.3.3.6): 'Reverse culture shock has been well documented in the research on Third Culture Kids ... Downie (1976) drew certain conclusions from his study of TCKs returning to college in the United States' (Fail et al., 2004: 321, 322).[2]

The data are then presented as substantial verbatim extracts from life history interviews, in the first person present tense, without commentary or linking text, such as:

'*Anna*: (My) friends in Geneva are all international ... I see myself as a vagabond, based in nothing. I could die in any country in the world ... I am FREE like a bird.'

After the verbatim data, the article reverts to the original impersonal, passive past as the author summarizes the collective views of the respondents in relation to each of the themes extracted from the literature.

Extract 2

My report, on nineteenth century school management, is an invented account of a nineteenth century headteacher's fictional day, created from original sources, but presented as imaginary non-participant observation by myself as the fantasy researcher (Thody, 1994b). This semi-fictional record shows, for example: 6.45 a.m. Equipment orders: [the principal] selects the order book for equipment. He is listing the number of slate pencils required. He pauses to consult a supplier's catalogue for guidance on the appropriate length of pencils for different ages of children.

This fiction is firmly embedded within conventional elements of an introduction (11.10) with the research questions followed by a rationale for education history, a justification for its disparate sources and a literature review. The fiction is justified in the text, by its conventional origins in real sources, by advice from postmodernist experts requiring readable history, and by its uses of imaginative literature and its portrayal of multiple voices.

You must also be aware that attitudes to 'convention' are changing. Those who developed the 1960s' scientific, traditional modes are now retiring from academic life; thus the tentative questioners of the 1990s could take the opportunity to engage in more trenchant debate in the 2000s towards a new break with tradition. Your careers have ten–fifty years to completion, time to see the alternatives themselves become the 'new conventions' and time to become the new conveyors of alternative styles to those whom you are, or will be, teaching. You can be the generation that rewrites the thesis regulations to offer freedom to candidates.

It is also possible that we may just be witnessing a time lag while academics adjust to, and start to employ, alternative possibilities regularly. It is nothing new for changes in presentation and writing up requirements to lag behind new opportunities for change, as a 1990 author noted:

Since 1984, when the first edition of this Green Guide [to publishing in scholarly journals] was published, dramatic changes have occurred in the technologies for processing text and graphics. There has been considerably less development in the general principles and procedures for publishing. (Sadler, 1990: Foreword)

1.5.2   The guiding principles

To find a way to meet the challenges from this ferment, you have to make choices. Your choices should be determined by:

- your own dialogue with your data generated as you write from the start of your project and as you plan all its stages, including its final written or spoken formats (2.2);
- the precedents for reporting the type of research you have done and whether or not you want to break these (2.3.1);
- your personality and what appeals to you (2.3.2);
- the practicalities of time and money that constrain your formats (2.3.3);
- the people reading, or listening to, your research (Chapter 3);
- the purposes for which you are reporting your research (Chapter 4);
- the arts and craft of writing (Chapter 5).

1.6   Chapter outlines

In the rest of Part One, 'Preparation', I discuss the above guiding principles.

In Part Two, 'Selection and Reduction', I apply these principles. Chapters 6 and 7 consider how to reduce, to manageable quantities, your primary research data and your secondary data for literature and methodology reviews.

Part Three, 'Production', offers quantitative, qualitative and narrative styles for the findings from your research. Each of them is most usually associated with a particular form of data but is found with the other types of data. They are:

1   the conventional (scientific) style, mainly reporting quantitative data, experiments and quasi-experiments (Chapter 8);
2   the alternative of artistic reporting, largely associated with qualitative data (Chapter 9);
3   the alternative of literary styles, often restricted to narrative data (Chapter 10).

It is important to remember that 'most of the ideas [for writing] apply equally well to qualitative and quantitative approaches' (Cresswell, 1994: 193). Just because your data are qualitative does not mean that you should confine your options to the artistic; look also into scientific and literary forms. Likewise, the scientifically inclined can include literary or artistic approaches, and the literati should consider more than just the narrative.

Common to all three styles is the need to make an impact with your reporting, since you want to ensure that someone will be persuaded to take action as a result of your work. The rest of Part Three offers guidance on the beginnings and ends of research writing – those all-important titles, introductions, abstracts and conclusions through which to 'hook' your readers (Chapter 11). Having made an opening impact, you need to ensure this is maintained through the demonstrated rigour of your work. Chapter 12 therefore reviews citation requirements.

Part Four, 'Publication: Reference Guides', concerns the end products of your research – presentations (Chapter 13) and publications (Chapter 14) – and raises awareness of the legal issues associated with writing and presenting, such as copyright and intellectual property (Chapter 15).

Part Five, 'Valediction', farewells you with an Epilogue (Chapter 16) reviewing the literature about writing and presentation; reveals the research methodology for the book and the author's biography in the Appendix (Chapter 17); and lists the references and further reading in a bibliography.

1.7 Review

Deciding how to write and present research needs to be as central to research project planning as are all other elements of methodology. Postmodernism has extended the possibilities for formatting and style options, referred to above as 'alternative'. Modernist structuralism continues to support conventional styling. The dichotomy between the two is not as great as these apparently opposing terms indicate. There is middle ground between them. To help you to negotiate this, the first stage is the guiding principles discussed in Chapters 2–4.

REFLECTIONS

Postmodernists believe that researchers must share power with their readers by making transparent the researcher's own attitudes since these will subconsciously affect what is written. Readers are thus better able to judge the validity of the research. From reading this chapter, what do you think are my underlying assumptions? Turn to the Appendix on research methods (Chapter 17) to find out if you were right about me and assess the extent to which this chapter has been affected by my attitudes.

Notes

1 'Refereed' journals are those for which articles are subjected to review by specialist academic experts before editorial acceptance. They are also known as 'peer reviewed', 'core' or 'academic' journals. They are regarded as more prestigious than 'professional' journals, for which only the editor, or a small editorial panel, decides whether or not to accept articles. Academic careers depend upon your research being published in refereed journals.

2 Sources cited solely within quotations are not included in the bibliography.

2 Principles for Selecting Appropriate Writing and Presentation Styles

CONTENTS

2.1 Framework of principles

Chapter 1 discussed the choices between conventions and alternatives. Chapters 2, 3 and 4 help to you to make those choices by providing guiding principles. A summary of these is outlined in Figure 2.1.

2.2 Dialogue with the data

2.2.1 Write from the start

The conventional archetype is to write when everything from which you will draw your data and conclusions has been done and the whole planned. Writing is viewed as a static, concluding exercise. Dismissive of this model, Piantanida and Garman note that:

> novices seem to believe that it is a waste of time and effort to start writing before they have figured out the meaning of the data/text. In our experience, it is often through the act of writing that researchers find their way out of the conceptual morass. (1999: 172)

DIALOGUE WITH THE DATA	
WRITE FROM THE START	PLAN
WRITING and PRESENTING	
PRECEDENT To follow or not to follow?	PERSONALITY OF THE WRITER/PRESENTER How much should be admitted?
PRACTICALITIES Costs, time, word limits	PEOPLE Valuing and assessing readers and audiences
PURPOSES Overt, covert and ethics	PRODUCTION Arts and craft of writing
AFTER WRITING	
PUBLICATION AND SALES	AFTER-SALES SERVICE

Figure 2.1   Framework of principles to guide your selection of writing and presentation styles

Lewis-Beck et al. (2004: 1197–8) are similarly critical of qualitative researchers who use the conventional 'end-on' model derived from the natural sciences.

The conventional does, however, cohere well with data that have a logical progression. It's good for team projects; ideas develop as the team interacts during the process of the research. These will be recorded for later progression but may very well be discarded before a final version emerges.

The conventional advice to write up only after all data have been collected was the standard before 1990 and the advent of PCs. My advice to thesis students then was to gather notes in sets (usually from items written individually on filing cards, stored in shoe-boxes) ready for each chapter or section. Flashes of inspiration occurring as data were being gathered were to be put into a notebook for later incorporation as each chapter was written by hand. The text was then transcribed by a typist to a first draft to which only minor amendments could be made because of the cost of retyping the whole. The coming of mass computer literacy and PC accessibility made the model obsolete, although Wolcott's (1990) seminal book on writing up qualitative research had already recognized the value of writing from the beginning of one's research.

Researchers can now begin to 'write up' as soon as a project commences and can continue throughout it, altering, adding and amending their PC notes continuously. Writing up becomes a non-linear, constant process of producing and revising with the possibility of ideas emerging at all stages, 'an interative or cyclical activity' (Blaxter, Hughes and Tight, 2001: 228). It's a continuing interrogation between yourself and the data collected, producing a 'working interpretive document' (Denzin, 1998: 317) which helps you to make sense of what you have discovered while regularly seeing your work anew (Griffith, 2002). Writing thus becomes dynamic creativity, a means of discovery and a research method itself, proceeding concurrently with other forms of data collection. It is vital to the sense-making of the research itself.

More prosaically, the process of continuous writing from the start makes more obvious where there are gaps in your thinking since you are trying to communicate with an audience from the start (Chapter 3). Writing from the beginning also gives you a considerable amount of text written before the final draft is formally begun, a great morale booster *en route* to finishing.

2.2.2   Plan

The writing and presentation plan must be made at the beginning of a research project since it will affect all other elements of the research design. Planning is usually deemed to be complete once the research question is settled, the dominant philosophy is selected, sources for literature are identified, the methodology, samples and research instruments are designed and ideas for data analysis are investigated, but the dissemination campaign must also be included in this planning. This dissemination campaign consists of deciding on the primary and secondary formats through which you will spread your research and of setting up a template for the primary one at least (with experience, it is possible to have the templates for secondary formats concurrently in place).

2.2.3   Plan for the primary formats, consider the secondaries

Primary formats are the intended, or required, outcomes of a project and its most substantive, and substantial, output, such as reports to sponsors, theses, teaching materials, books, refereed journal articles or conference keynote speeches and papers. These need planning for in advance of a project since they will influence the writing shell, or template, that you set up (2.4) and the choice of data to present (Chapters 6 and 7). For your chosen primary format, you will be able to find out its precedents (2.3.1), the practicalities that determine timing and costs (2.3.3) and the people and purposes for which you are writing (Chapters 3 and 4). You then write with these in mind. Never write in a vacuum.

You also need to be aware of secondary formats, the 'spin-offs'. These are optional outcomes, such as newspaper items, conference papers or journal articles, TV and radio programmes, books or book chapters, which usually deal with only part of a project or look at it from another angle. A secondary format will usually differ substantially in appearance from the primary format. It should not influence the choices in a research design but you need to allocate adequate time and money to enable you to prepare secondary outputs. These usually reach larger audiences than those for primary formats and can provide additional income, both of which are important to your career.

A dramatic illustration of using research in both primary and secondary formats is from those who are successful academic and fiction writers, such as Kathy Reichs, professor of forensic anthropology, practising forensic scientist and successful crime novelist (2003; 1990; 1989), as Box 2.1 illustrates.

Box 2.1 Example of the same research data in both a primary (journal article) and a secondary (crime novel) format by the same author

---

In Reichs' bestseller novel *Bare Bones*, fictional forensic anthropologist Dr Tempe Brennan is assessing bones from a potential crime scene:

> The rear seat passenger had definitely been male. Not that useful. Larrabee would nail that during his post…
>
> On to age…
>
> I returned to the cranial wreckage.
>
> As with dentistry, skulls come with some assembly required. At birth, the twenty-two bones are in place, but unglued. They meet along squiggly lines called sutures. In adulthood, the squiggles fill in, until the vault forms a rigid sphere…
>
> Generally, the more birthday candles, the smoother the squiggles…
>
> By stripping blackened scalp from the cranial fragments, I was able to view portions of suture from the crown, back and base of the head…
>
> Though the vault closure is notoriously variable, this pattern suggested a young adult…
>
> On to ancestry.
>
> Race is a tough call at any time. With a shattered skull, it's a bitch. (2003: 64–5)

The same material originally appeared in one of Reichs' academic papers on cranial structure eccentricities:

> First the human remains, designated n86–336, were cleaned, sorted and examined …The skull was exceptionally narrow, with a maximum cranial breadth of 116 mm (length 182 mm), and exhibited complete ectocranial and endocranial closure of the sagitall suture (Fig. 4). The cranial index was 63.7, considerably below the threshold of 70 suggested by Brothwell [3] as demarcating scarphcrania. Although of unusual shape, the skull looked male …The low nasal bridge suggested negroid ancestry. A small portion of preserved pubic symphysis showed a smooth, inactive face with some definition of its lower extremity, but lacking distinct rim formation or lipping. This suggested an age of 22–43 years. (1989: 264–5)

Set up an additional file for possible secondary formats at the beginning of your research. In this, store:

- ideas for placements;
- material that seems inappropriate for the primary format;
- material for which you do not have room in the primary format;
- the templates of any other formats into which you can add materials as you are already doing for the primary format shell.

You can then be writing more than one output simultaneously or, at least, you will be ready to prepare the spin-offs as soon as the primary output is finished.

REFLECTIONS

Enjoy a few minutes planning the title of the novel that could emerge from your current research. Devise a few characters to carry the plot. Read a novel by Malcolm Bradbury, Kathy Reichs or Alexander McCall Smith – all academics who have successfully published both fiction and non-fiction.

2.2.4 Setting up templates

Planning for writing and presenting has to be visible from day one of a research project. Prepare a template, the empty shell, of the principal written output of the research, to be gradually filled in as you write throughout the research. Place your data, as they are collected, into their appropriate chapter from the start (though possible locations in other chapters should also be noted). Insert bibliographical references in their correct formats from the very first source you use (12.2 and Bibliography). This writing into the template can be 'proper, joined-up and grammatical' (Knight, 2002: 3) from the start, though I find that notes are preferable, with the polished version emerging at a later stage.

Thus on day one of a sponsored research project for a commercial corporation, immediately after the first team meeting and while arguments still rage about the best ways to collect the data, you set up the template on empty files, with the headings from Box 2.2 (PCs usually have suitable templates).

Box 2.2 Template for the basics of a research report

Title page Title, who it is from and whom it is for, date.

Executive summary or key points summary.

1 *Introduction* 1.1 Outline, 1.2 rationale, 1.3 company needs' context.

2 *Summary of preceding research.*

3 *Collected data demonstrating the findings.*

4 *Recommendations.*

Appendices 1 Methodology, 2 brief bibliography, 3 acknowledgements, 4 researcher's brief biodata; 5 others as appropriate to topic.

Complete the title page immediately. Then add the material from your application for research funding from the company, and from their contract with you. Now start the research.

Similarly, a university thesis outline would be as in Box 2.3.

Box 2.3   Template for the basics of a university thesis

Titling pages   Title page (title, author, degree, date); acknowledgements; abstract; contents; list of tables and figures

Chapter One   Introduction (11.10)

Chapter Two   Literature survey (7.3)

Chapter Three   Methodology (7.4)

Chapter Four   Findings; this may need to be divided into more than one chapter

Chapter Five   Discussion/conclusions/recommendations (11.7); for doctorates, these will usually be separated into three chapters; for other postgraduates, into two chapters; for undergraduates combine all in one chapter

Bibliography

Appendices

Complete the title page immediately. Then add the material from your thesis proposal, dispersed into the appropriate files. After that, you add new material as your research continues.

Books, articles, conference papers, all follow the same routine. For each section of your template, record the minimum and maximum word allocations, such as 4000–5000 words per chapter. Use these initially, as a rough guide only. Do not enlarge or reduce until the final draft.

Template advantages are:

- The morale boost on opening your files to see the title pages; it now looks like a serious and realistic project.
- The niceties of titling and referencing are done during the project; leave them until the end when you're tired and they are less likely to be correct and you will be frustrated at the delays caused by seemingly unimportant details.
- Minimizing the panic that afflicts researchers as the 'writing-up' stage looms; you will already have some material written and there is no longer a cut-off point when data stop and writing starts.
- You can make regular word counts so you will have a rough idea of how much material you have gathered for each section/chapter; stop when you have twice the number of words for each potential chapter (and it is surprisingly easy to collect at least three or four times as much as you need).
- Material that you don't use in the final version is still in 'ready to use' paragraphs for transfer to other publications.

Having a template helps you to recognize more easily when the data collection phase of a research project is nearing its natural end and you are ready to start putting each chapter/section into its final form. This stage is reached when you find yourself:

- repeating information already entered (to test for this, just use the 'Find' command on the PC to discover if you have already covered a topic);
- becoming bored with just taking notes and entering data; when this boredom starts is when you should start creating the full draft of a chapter;
- automatically writing your own comments, ideas, explanations or discussion as well as the primary or secondary data you are entering;
- staring out of the window reflecting on the data for longer periods than you spend entering it;
- with almost double the number of words you can have in the final version.

2.3 Writing and presenting

2.3.1 Precedents – to follow or not to follow?

Being conventional would appear to imply compliance with whatever are the precedents for the form of writing you are attempting, while adopting alternative forms would seem to indicate being experimental with formats not sanctioned by previous experience. Both conventional and alternative research formats, however, have their own precedents, rules and customs which you are expected to follow.

If these are only advisory expectations, then you have the choice whether or not to follow them. For example, if invited to contribute a chapter to an edited book, the editors will usually provide a template so that each chapter will be comparable. For example, Foreman and Gillett, in their book on animals' spatial awareness, reported that 'The contributing authors … have been asked to concentrate specifically on paradigms and test methodologies … There is less emphasis than is usual in scientific publications on the theoretical models that provoked the research' (1998: 2). Any book editor will tell you, however, how difficult it is to ensure that contributors stick to the brief, as will be confirmed when you read edited books.

If there is a *required* format (be that for conventional or alternative styles) for any research writing or presentation, *then you must stick to it unless:*

1 You get agreement in advance that you can make changes.
2 Your career is so well established that you can afford to have the occasional publication/ paper/thesis rejected.
3 Your career is so well established that the publishers/conference organizers cannot afford to reject you.
4 You like taking risks and 'want to give yourself an extra challenge … don't take the risk unless you really have the freedom to know what you are doing' (Blaxter, Hughes and Tight, 2001: 244). Depressing but true.
5 You have been invited to contribute to a book or journal, or to give a keynote at a conference. The editor/conference organizer will be so glad that your work (or you) arrive as planned that there are unlikely to be arguments over formats.
6 You are aiming to stir up controversy and/or your research is already controversial in itself.

7 Your presentation/writing makes a point in itself related to the topic you have researched.

8 You personally know the journal editors, publishers, review committees and they know and accept your different style.

9 You write very good begging letters.

10 Your experience can match that of your advisers. For example, if you are new to TV or radio presenting, then your director and editor will turn you into a puppet and determine when and how you face camera and microphone, the length of your inputs, what you wear, how you move. Only when you reach the dizzy heights of your own series will you feel able to make some slight contribution to determining what will make a good televisual moment. In comparison, by the time you get to making your inaugural professorial lecture, you will have more experience than almost anyone else in the room, and if you don't want a lectern, PowerPoint or costume drama, then you won't have to have them.

11 You can see no other way of doing it and you write a strongly justified rationale for altering the required format.

12 You are entering work for a journal, or a special issue, that expressly encourages variety.

13 Your publication/presentation is *very* different from the norm. I found that when I just altered a few minor points in a presentation (such as leaving the literature review to the end), some well meaning savant would come to tell me how to improve. Stunned congratulations came when I was the first person to sing in my conference paper presentation at the American Educational Research Association Annual Meeting and when I introduced a presentation in Australia on being a risk taker by performing English folk dancing. Moral of the tale: if you are going to break precedent, then break it big. The result will be invitations to speak and publish but it will take longer for academics to accept you as a serious researcher since:

> Something just ahead of its time is called original, but something that breaks entirely new ground and is a long way ahead of its time may be seen as a threat to, or personal attack on leaders in the field … especially when reviewers [of journal articles for publication] perceive their role as gatekeepers for the discipline. (Sadler, 1990: 16–17)

14 Your publication/presentation provides just a small deviation in an aspect that is not central to your research, such as the title page. This may be a small step for academics but it can be a contribution to a later giant leap. For example, compare the two title pages in Figure 2.2. They were for a paper to be presented at a USA conference. The left column follows 2004 APA guidelines; the right braves a slight variation. Which would most encourage you to attend the paper session?

2.3.2 Personality – how much of it to admit?

Your personality will influence how you write since you will choose the style, format and tone with which you feel comfortable and capable so it reflects 'your intention and your point of view' (Tonfoni and Richardson, 1994: 33). This is the ethos of the research and your aim is to produce a persuasive one. A current debate in research writing is how much of yourself should be overtly revealed, and in what ways, in order to be persuasive.

2.3.2.1 *Conventional approaches*

Conventionally, an author description is given either at the beginning or at the end of a document or when introducing a speaker (11.5 and Appendix, Chapter 17). This

Running head: European school leadership

School Principal Preparation in Europe:
multicultural approaches
Angela Thody, Emerita Professor
Educational Leadership
University of Lincoln
Brayford Pool, Lincoln LN6 7TS
England
Angelathody450@hotmail.com

With

Petros Pashiardis, Associate Professor
Educational Administration
(Project Leader)
Faculty of Education
University of Cyprus
Republic of Cyprus
edpetros@ucy.ac.cy

Zoi Papanaoum, Professor
Education, School of Education
Aristotle University of Thessaloniki
Thessaloniki, Greece

Olof Johansson, Professor
Director of Centre for Principalship Studies
University of Umea, Sweden

Roundtable Presentation at the

2006 Annual Conference

USA Educational Administration Society

November 3–6, 2006

Philadelphia, Pennsylvania

Running head: European school leadership

SCHOOL PRINCIPAL

PREPARATION IN EUROPE:

multicultural approaches

Come and discuss with professors from
around Europe at our ROUND TABLE
coffee session. We welcome your views
on principal preparation in other countries, to add to our experiences.

Annual Conference
USA Educational Administration Society

November 3–6, 2006

Philadelphia, Pennsylvania

Angela Thody, Lincoln University, England
Zoi Papanaoum, Aristotle University of
Thessaloniki, Greece
Petros Pashiardis, University of Cyprus,
Cyprus
Olof Johansson, Umea University,
Sweden
Address for correspondence: Emerita Professor A.
Thody, IIEL, Lincoln University, Lincoln LN6 7TS,
England

Figure 2.2   Contrasting formats for the title page of a conference paper

invariably centres on the writer's academic credentials such as degrees, books written or international stature, in order to establish the status of the writer/speaker. This helps to guarantee the integrity of the research being reported and the competence of the researcher. Once past the introduction, the writer/speaker is not evident. This establishes that the research stands or falls on its own merits and those who attack it must do so on substantive grounds, not on those of personality.

This suits well the modernist perspective in which authoritative proof of a single viewpoint is the *sine qua non* of research. It well suits team research in which the authors have melded to produce one viewpoint. It well suits current understanding of the objectivity that is regarded as so important to conventional research writing, that of personal decentring (1.3).

To some extent, however, this overt exclusion of the author is fictional, 'masks that are hidden behind, put on, and taken off as writers write their particular stories and self-versions' (Denzin, 1998: 317). The researcher is dominant whether or not this is shown by the language chosen. The researcher has already selected the direction of the research and the methodology, will have chosen which data to include and which to ignore, what to include in the final reports and what to omit.

2.3.2.2   Alternative attitudes

Postmodernist alternatives need to convey a rounded proof, combining as many different perspectives as possible, all of which are deemed to have partial authority. Amongst these perspectives are your views as the researcher and you have to make these 'evident for the meaning to become clear' (Holliday, 2002: 131). You may report your own views and actions directly in the document, making the researcher just one more of the researched (as in participant observation or action research), but even where you are not also a respondent, your views will influence what is written and how it is written.

You should make yourself obvious in the research because, like it or not, you are intertwined in it since this is 'in the age of inscription [when] writers create their own situated, inscribed versions of the realities they describe' (Denzin, 1998: 323). In making yourself obvious in the research report, you are overtly accepting personal responsibility for what you have produced. You therefore need to decide how much autobiography to reveal and in what ways, as the following examples demonstrate.

An immediate impression of an author and her personal commitment to her research topic emerges in an article by Bergerson (2003) on 'Critical race theory and white racism: is there room for white scholars in fighting racism in education?' (and note how that title combines the conventional and the alternative). The first paragraph begins:

> Today I received an email from an aunt interested in knowing if I had been offered a faculty job for which I recently applied … She asked if I think one of the reasons the university is taking so long to notify me is that … [the university might be] involved in a federal affirmative action court case. (2003: 51)

I don't know if the aunt is fictional or real but she provided a means of introducing the research question, the status of the author, and the researcher's personal involvement in the issue. You know immediately what is the personal polemic of the researcher and can, therefore, filter the data she presents to you, through that sieve. The aunt reappears in the conclusions to the research.

> Today I composed the following message to my aunt:
>
> Dear Tante,
>
> Thanks for your interest in my job news. I just found out this week that another candidate was selected … I think he will be a great addition to the faculty there. He is African-American. Before now, they have had no people of colour on their faculty. I know there is a tendency for us, as white people, to wonder how affirmative action … might have played into their decision, but I urge you not to jump to those conclusions. This professor

should not have to answer for his qualifications because of his race ... I hope you and Uncle are well, and look forward to seeing you this summer. (2003: 61)

It sounds a little stilted to me – I don't write to my aunts like this – but it made the conclusions more lively, gave us major clues to the personality and attitudes of the researcher, added the researcher's perspectives to the data and breathed emotion. All this is essential to demonstrate the required postmodernist reflexivity (the implications for the findings of the researcher's life, education, social class, professional background, prejudices, expectations, values and place in the research) but you still have to establish academic respectability in the same way as in the conventional mode.

This combination can be achieved by including personal information in the researcher's professional biography (11.5 and Appendix, Chapter 17) or by building in personal information in the course of the written or spoken text. Limerick, Burgess-Limerick and Grace choose to do this in their article, largely the outcome of a triangular conversation amongst the article's authors, about power relations in interviewing:

> Treating the researcher's experiences as central to the research makes space for a new kind of knowledge ... A legitimate and important question to ask when appraising interview-based research is 'Who are the interviewers?' ... [because] The meaning of communication is inescapably situated and contextual ... Consequently we begin with an encapsulated history of each interviewer. (1996: 450)

Likewise, Brandon wove her painfully diffident stance into the second page of a 2003 refereed academic journal article on cultural politics in multicultural teaching:

> I am a white, middle class, female teacher educator, and my only experience teaching diverse students occurred in 1970 in rural Georgia. I am culturally disadvantaged, experientially limited, and often linguistically deficient in both preparing and teaching ... children of colour. (2003: 32)

Such personal history becomes even more significant to readers' understanding of a research project, if the researcher belongs to the same group as the researched and if the research has arisen because of who and what you are. Kelly (2001), a Roman Catholic single mother, interviewed others in Ireland in the same category (including her own mother). All were breaking deeply embedded conventions. They were asked how their roles had been influenced by Church, state and society.

> At least one from each mother–daughter group was a personal friend of mine, making for interviews of great emotional and experiential depth ... My experiences are aligned with those of the women I interviewed ... my analysis of the larger social movements in Irish society is paralleled with my personal experiences. (2001: 21)

At its simplest level, you can demonstrate researcher involvement by substituting 'I do' for 'It was done' (5.3.3.6), but you need also to reveal emotions in the written or presented record. Readers should know your feelings at the time of collecting data since this could have affected what you selected to record. For example, this researcher's attitude to convention is only too apparent in his justification for avoiding the 'mincing steps of academic debate [because] I would never get it right … seeking to do so was a futile waste of energy … I should proceed with this "truth" in mind and allow myself to be more playful' (Marshall, 1995: 29).

Playfulness includes admitting personal emotions. Reporting a study of chief executives, for example, for which I used non-participant observation over thirty-six days, each of twelve hours, I introduced my emotional reactions in my methodology record, with the words of an old song. When making presentations on the topic, I either sang it or used a recording:

> *I'll walk beside you through the passing years*
>
> *Through days of rain and sunshine, joy and tears.*
>
> Walking beside CEOs over the passing years to record and report their daily activities, was fascinating, time-consuming, tiring, analytically complex, challenging and emotionally involving. (Thody, 1997a: 197)

Autobiography, emotions, reflexivity, your own opinions – include all these and you 'run the risk of researcher dominance, making commentaries which place you as the researcher in the superior role of one whose analysis of other people's words shows that you understand what took place, while they do not' (Winter, 1989; cited in Coghlan and Brannick, 2001: 115). In one extreme case, this led to 'The research [being] in danger of becoming more about me than about a social phenomenon of which I am part' (Kelly, 2001: 23, 25).

Becoming thus 'part' of the written account adds to the conventional power researchers already have in choosing subject, methods, language, format and conclusions. To mitigate this, Darlington and Scott (2002: 161) recommend keeping the researcher in but not to the extent that other participants' voices become overshadowed. Kelly (2001), for example, achieved this by dedicating one chapter to her voice alone with the other respondents' views in other chapters. Hytten and Warren, in their article on whiteness in racism, found their way out by stating that their 'research began out of shared concerns about engaging our own privilege … As co-authors, we encountered … whiteness at different times and in different ways … Before sharing these discourses, it is important to note that we do not position ourselves as researchers outside of the discourses we describe' (2003: 69).

REFLECTIONS

What information about yourself would you include in the final document from your current research and where will you put this biographical information? (In this book, information about myself is in the Appendix, Chapter 17.)

2.3.3 Practicalities

There are sensible conventions that govern the practicalities of research but sometimes these have to be tempered with reality, as Box 2.4 makes clear.

Box 2.4 Research writing and presentation: dealing with the practicalities

Sensible conventions	Realistic alternatives
Set aside time to write when you know you will be at your best.	There is never an ideal time to write. Just get on with it anytime.
Allocate the time you think you will need for the research and double it.	Due dates, sponsors' demands, staff availability and family needs will halve the time you have allocated. You simply have to remove, or decrease, other elements of your life to fit in the research and writing.
At the halfway point between the inception of the research and the due date for the complete written product, you should have commenced the joining up of the paragraphs you have been storing for each chapter. At the three-quarter point, a whole, fairly polished version should be out for comment from colleagues, supervisors, publishers for return within one month. At the designated end point, the whole will have been handed in and you will be on with the next project.	As the due date for the finished product draws near, you will start to link paragraphs into chapters, send part polished chapters to colleagues for comment, continue collecting and analysing data, write through the night, negotiate a new due date (*but this latter option is not for university theses or for funding sponsors*), write through the night, write through the night, day, weekends, holidays and *finish* triumphantly.
You leave ample time for revisions. This reflection time is vital to being able to express yourself effectively.	Reflection time is never enough. Looking back at her research, three years later, Liz Kelly (1999) said, 'I don't think I was as clear ... when I wrote it, as I am now, and I don't think that it is stated there as strongly as I would now' (cited in Darlington and Scott, 2002: 168).
Ensure you have costed your project realistically. For the writing stages, this must include:	• Labour costs are usually underestimated and most researchers write in their personal and leisure time.

(Continued)

Box 2.4   (Continued)

Sensible conventions	Realistic alternatives
• The cost of the time for writing. It's easy to forget that both principal and assistant researchers need to remain with the project until the writing up is complete. It's easy for an undergraduate to forget to allow for wages forgone from the part-time job that has to be abandoned as the due date looms. • Paper for printing. • Binding for theses. • Technical help with graphical exuberances if you are not fully PC literate. • Payments to journals which charge for publication. • Conference fees if you are making an uninvited presentation. • Costs of making or buying extra copies to send as 'thanks' to respondents, supervisors and mentors.	• Most people beg, borrow or steal paper. • Most people happily spend on binding costs; it's what makes the finished product look so good. • Other costs are unavoidable but it's possible to be creative in finding money from various sources, scholarships, charity funds, commercial sponsors.
There is a set word limit (or a time limit for a presentation). You stick to it.	There is a set word limit (or a time limit for a presentation). You stick to it. You can negotiate a minimal increase if the editor/publisher/ conference organizer desperately *wants* your work. Word allocations for theses are almost immovable.
Arrive in advance of a presentation so you can test the microphone, ensure that the PowerPoint works and see that the room furnishings are arranged for your style.	Your plane is late. There is no microphone, PowerPoint or furniture. You cope brilliantly.

2.4   After writing

2.4.1   Publication and sales

Conventionally, research writing is for personal satisfaction and to add to the world's knowledge. That applies to whatever format of writing you adopt, but the additional alternative perspectives are that publishing is fun (Sadler, 1990: 2) and if you want your work to be read/heard by more than yourself, your family or your students then you have to work at extending dissemination through publication (Part Four).

In order to sell that book, you must make clear to browsers that they need to buy your work. Use devices that attract attention in the opening pages (Chapter 11) and make clear for whom the book is intended in the Preface. For example:

> These volumes will be of interest to new and old students alike; the student new to spatial research can be brought up to speed with a particular range of techniques … For seasoned researchers, these volumes provide a rapid scan of the currently available tools. (Foreman and Gillett, 1998: 2–3)

To help you to reach, and extend beyond, publication, you need to network:

- At conferences, trawl the delegates' list for publishers, editors and the well known in your discipline. Ask their advice, leave your business card and collect theirs.
- Send thanks and copies (or a brief summary) of completed work to everyone who has helped you: respondents, librarians, supervisors, proofreading assistants, mentors, family, editors, colleagues who recommended you for a research grant. Any thanks are rare in academia; yours will be a memorable beacon.
- Offer to edit a journal's special edition. You will please the editor (who can take a rest) and the contributors you ask.

Take every opportunity that is offered. For example:

- Be enthusiastic about your research in your first conference paper even if the audience is one or two (as it was for my first paper, but from those two came an offer of an external examinership and an article placement – and I concluded my conference career twenty years later with the audience queuing to get in).
- If an article or conference paper is turned down but you are offered a colloquium/ symposium mini-slot instead, swallow your pride and take it.
- If an unpretentious professional association newsletter wants a few hundred words from you, write it. You can use the opportunity to practise unorthodox alternatives; other academics and editors will be alerted to your work and it can result in invitations to fee-paying presentations.
- Volunteer as an associate editor for a journal.

2.4.2   After-sales service

Once publication is achieved, the report presented to the sponsors or the thesis completed to the examiners' satisfaction, there is still work to do. Some will come to you: queries from other academics, requests to republish your work as book chapters. For others, you need to be proactive. Suggestions for this can be found in Box 2.5.

> ## Box 2.5   After publication: marketing your research
>
> - Invite the research respondents to a launch party.
> - Ensure that copyright fees come to you for photocopying of your articles or other publications. For example, in the UK, register with the Authors' Licensing and Collecting Society (www.alcs.co.uk).
> - Send copies (or summaries) to colleagues who might cite your work and make sure you cite your own work in subsequent publications (known as product placement in commercial terms, but just as vital in academic cultures where citations are counted to assess the value of your work).
> - Cultivate 'ways of influencing policy ... [make] links with the power groups who decide policy' (Cohen, Manion and Morrison, 2000: 43). Work out at what point in the policy process to intervene with the findings from your research.
> - Find other ways to publish material from the research project that were not used in the original document – web publishing, different journals, professional rather than academic journals, distance learning materials.
> - Visit bookshops to see if they stock your book. If not, ask for it. It will at least alert the bookseller to something that might be stocked. Ask your publisher why it's not at that bookshop.
> - Inform the publisher when you are attending conferences at which your book might be displayed. Do not assume that the conference organizers will do this for you.

All this may sound a little too alternative for you but remember: if you don't want to 'sell' your work, then why should anyone want to read it?

2.5   Review

The principles to apply when deciding which of the conventional or alternative styles to use for writing and presenting research are:

- Begin a dialogue with your data by writing from the start of your project and within its template (2.2).
- Check precedents for reporting your type of research and decide whether or not you want to try alternatives (2.3.1).
- Assess your personality and what appeals to you (2.3.2).
- Consider the practicalities of time and money (2.3.3).
- Adapt to the people reading, or listening to, your research (Chapter 3).
- Adjust for the purposes for which you are reporting your research (Chapter 4).
- Post-publication, networking and further dissemination are important.

3 Adapting to Audience: Adjusting for their Aims

CONTENTS

3.1 The value of an audience

An essential question for participants was 'Who am I writing for?' Certainly, this issue is consistent with what most authors experience ... One participant aptly summed up this concern, 'I couldn't figure out what I wanted to write about until I could picture my audience.' (Ackerman and Maslin-Ostrowski, 1996: 6)

This quotation is from research into the value of trainee leaders writing up their personal experiences. No audience was designated for them but they quickly discovered that knowing the people for whom they were writing was essential – an expected development since research writers show 'growing awareness of audience and writing as social action' (Gosden, 1995: 52).

The aim of this chapter is to help readers grow more aware of what their specific audiences can be expected to know about particular research topics, what styles are most likely to appeal to different audiences, what formats they will be expecting and what are their purposes in reading the research. The chapter begins with a discussion of conventional and alternative attitudes to readers and listeners, and continues with guidance on how to analyse audiences in general. Specific groups of people who are likely to be research users, both inside and outside academia, are then examined.

3.2 Attitudes to audience

3.2.1 Conventional

The extreme conventional view is that you are not writing for an audience at all. You are writing about your research; your interpretations are dominant. The central relationship is between the researcher and the data. Conventionalists view audience as a 'constraint' (Cohen et al., 2000: 89) and the desire to persuade others of our views as unethical manipulation. Such views can be criticized as 'naïve realism … the doctrine that language and the texts created from it directly represent in an unproblematic way the world as it is' (Scott and Usher, 1999: 150).

3.2.2 Alternative

The extreme alternative view is that audience is as integral to your research as you are. Research is as much about the relationship between an audience and the researcher as about that between the researcher and the data, since the audience has the power of interpretation. Postmodernism gives us the opportunity to experiment with different formats for different audiences, arising from the understanding that language is not a simple given but is created by a writer's subjectivities (Richardson, 1998: 349). This is nothing new. Cicero (first century BC) insisted that good style 'be understood as a *relationship* with an audience, rather than a … linguistic or positivistic achievement' (Zeller and Farmer, 1999: 13). Such views can be criticized for allowing anarchy.

3.2.3 Resolving the differences

In practice, the two sides of the debate are not very far apart. Conventional formatting is as it is because the intended audience expects conventionality. This expectation does not have to be acknowledged overtly, as it can be in alternative formats, but it is there nonetheless. The two are 'more similar than you would imagine at times because it's the same stories, just told with a different level in mind' (Darlington and Scott, 2002: 171).

Hence you should adapt your language and style to those most likely to be appreciated by the intended audience. What you write will affect the readers but it cannot dictate a particular reaction from them. Readers will deconstruct and reconstruct your writing (Barone, 1995: 64). I would not go so far as to suggest that the power relations in research have shifted so much that the researcher's adaptations to audience are more important to credibility than the research; but in centring on audience, you hand over some power to them. As a writer, you try to direct that power towards your chosen interpretation. To do this, you begin by assessing the primary audience's characteristics.

3.3   Assessing readers and listeners

All readers of research are potential users of your findings, not readers seeking entertainment only, but it is from the entertainment industry that researchers can acquire lessons about targeting audience (Shroder, Drotner, Kline and Murray, 2003). TV programme makers, for example, have been enjoined to know the values and moral codes of all parts of society so that their messages can be delivered in a way that fits in with prevailing values (Belson, 1967). Without this 'there is a very real risk that people in the audience will reject or distort or select from [a programme] in accordance with what they feel or believe' (1967: 10). This should not mean that you pander to readers and give them only what they might want to hear, but knowing your audience is a guide to good decision making and one of the determinants for the format and language of any report or presentation.

3.3.1   Assessment principles

To help determine the format, language and style of your research writing and presentations, you need to 'guesstimate' the primary readers'/listeners':

- subject knowledge;
- subject interest;
- relationship to you;
- needs;
- wants;
- likely mood when they receive your documents or presentation.

Each of these is discussed in the succeeding paragraphs which relate to all research readers/listeners. These are followed by evaluations of the characteristics of specific audiences (3.4, 3.5, 3.6).

- *Subject knowledge*. At the polar opposites of academic and 'lay' public audiences, the academic can be deemed to be likely to know more about the subject of your research than can the lay audience. However, *any* audience, even of highly specialist academics, is unlikely to have as much knowledge as you do about the particular research you are reporting. If they did, then there would have been no point in doing your research since research is meant to break new ground. Hence, the more specialized and academic your audience, the less you will have to explain of the subject groundwork, but for all audiences you will need to provide significant detail.

- *Subject interest*. It is depressing to realize that 'no more than a fraction of [the] intended audience is interested primarily in the specific program and setting that was the object of the study' (Hammersley, 1993: 203). They want the conclusions only so they can quickly assess how your work relates to theirs or if, and how, your ideas can be put into practice.
- *Relationship to you*. The greater the power of the readers over you, the more carefully you need to adapt your writing to their characteristics. The most powerful audiences are usually small and homogeneous which assists your assessment (thesis examiners, professorial promotion commit- tees, journal editors and reviewers, research assessors).
- *Needs*. Above all, readers/listeners need to be convinced that your research matters to them. Hence the importance of what you write/speak in the first few lines (11.1). Some still need to be educated in alternative ways of writing and presentation; so enjoy doing so if you've selected one of these.
- *Wants*. They want to understand you quickly, 'to learn from you economically … with as little trou- ble as possible' (Griffith, 1994: 236), but they do *want* to learn. Research readers and listeners are, therefore, generally kindly and well disposed towards you. They will forgive most things except excessive length, pomposity or being patronized.
- *Likely mood*. Most academics have to fit in reading other people's research late at night when tired- ness impairs concentration or when they are trying to write their own. Hence comes the impor- tance of clarity and brevity. Policy makers and full-time students can usually fit you in during their daylight hours. You face strong competition, however, from other distractions so your work needs to stand out even if it is only through having a coloured cover that can be easily located on a full desktop.

These assessments should be made of the intended audiences for each different written or spoken product from your research. You then vary what you write for each specific group discussed below. Hence, for example, you would need to respond to your fun- ders first for the report from a sponsored research project. Assuming you had their per- mission to publish the results elsewhere, you might then rewrite part of the report for the academic audience at a subject specific conference. At the conference, the editor of a generalist magazine is interested in your theme so you need to rewrite again with a lay, but interested, audience in mind. Finally, the local newspaper picks up on your suc- cess and you have five lines in which to attract the attention of a disinterested public to your discoveries.

The following two extracts, concerning the same research, demonstrate how adjust- ments are made to suit different audiences.

Extract 1: Wolf Predators

From *National Geographic*, an international circulation science magazine.

- *Audience*. What might be termed 'educated hobby-professionals', wanting to be entertained while gaining knowledge; the magazine's editors want to encourage readers to continue purchasing a journal that is not required reading.
- *Topic*. The effect on the ecosystem of the reintroduction of wolves. The piece is written by one of the senior editors of National Geographic (Holland, 2004).

The article hooked the readers with 75 per cent of its opening double page as a photograph of a snowbound elk skeleton. The titling similarly electrified: 'Where the elk fear predation, an ecosystem returns'. Following this was:

> It seemed obvious. Because wolves prey on elk, and elk feed on plants, the wolves' reintroduction to Yellowstone National Park in 1995 should have led to a decline in elk numbers … That would then explain why some plants elk eat are suddenly thriving.

This opening short sentence made dramatic impact. The conjunction 'because' that starts the second sentence breaches grammatical correctness but draws the readers in by its conversational nature. The rationale for the topic then feeds the curiosity. The literature review comes next:

> But when Robert Beschta and William Ripple of Oregon State University began to study plant recovery in the park, they found a *different twist*. 'What we're actually seeing is that the size of the elk population hasn't changed significantly,' Beschta says … it seems that fear of predation, not elk numbers, is driving floral recovery – by changing the ungulates' behavior. In some areas where wolves now prowl, 'elk no longer hang out … [so] river loving woody plants … once overbrowsed by elk … are *going gangbusters. (my emphases)*

Holland thus managed to cite the work of the researchers while dragging the readers into the mystery story. The colloquialisms (my emphases) make the non-specialist readers feel comfortable (5.3.3.3) while still flattering their scientific knowledge by assuming that the readers understand 'ungulate' as the correct terminology (5.3.3.4).

Extract 2

From *Forest Ecology and Management*, an international refereed academic journal containing the article about the research from which the above originated.

- *Audience*. Likely to be international academic experts, wanting to gain knowledge for either professional or academic developments.
- *Topic*. The effect on the ecosystem of the reintroduction of wolves, written by those who researched it (Ripple and Beschta, 2003).

The format is conventional and without photographs. The article begins at an apparent tangent but respects its specialist audience with its language:

> Deciduous woody species, such as aspen (*Populus tremuloides*) in terrestrial systems … have been unable to successfully regenerate … in various forest and range landscapes … Wolves cause mortality and can influence the distribution and behavior of herbivores. Thus when a top trophic level predator interacts with the next lower level herbivore and this interaction in turn alters or influences vegetation, a 'tropic cascade' occurs.

3.4 Academic audiences

3.4.1 Collective academics

Academics are the prime audience for all of us as researchers. They are 'usually intelligent, literate and serious … They don't mind some levity, some lightheartedness' (Griffith, 1994:

236) but the latter must not dominate. They are 'a community of writers who greatly value scrupulous scholarship and the careful documentation, or recording, of research' (MLA, 2003: xv). Writing and presenting must, therefore, be 'acceptable to the "expert" readers who function as gatekeepers of the academic community' (Gosden, 1995: 53) by providing:

- systematic, transparent and rigorous work to produce evidence which proves your conclusions;
- extensive methodology;
- lengthy and comprehensive literature review that includes accurate citations (Chapter 12);
- contributions to theory and debate.

You then need to adapt for the specific academic subspecies described below.

3.4.2 Thesis examiners

There is a choice about the way to write for thesis examiners:

- *either* conventionally, following all the university's regulations;
- *or* with an exceedingly, extremely, magnificently well argued alternative with which your supervisors are in 100 per cent agreement and only then if you are at doctoral level.

If adopting the more common first option, you can risk alternatives within the chapter(s) reporting your findings, especially if the data are from qualitative or narrative sources, but the overall, conventional format remains sacrosanct. Nor is there choice about the rigour of the language to be adopted in a thesis, be it conventional or alternative. You have to be absolutely correct in vocabulary, punctuation and grammar. Even the typing errors will be noted. This nicety is not because examiners are pedantic traditionalists who actually prefer the 'double spaced drabness' (Knight, 2002: 198) that afflicts theses but because of the importance of theses as training pieces (1.3.2.1).

3.4.3 Conference audiences

See 12.6.3 and 13.3.5.

3.4.4 Journal editors (and their corollaries, conference committees)

These powerful people determine whether or not your articles/papers will be passed on to reviewers. Editors and conference committees tend to be dedicated to their discipline. They need to be since their editorial work (often unremunerated or extremely poorly paid) has to be done in their personal time after all their other administrative, teaching and research commitments. Editors are dominated by deadlines: the date of despatch to readers of the just completed issue, the date the next issue must reach the printers, the date by which all articles for inclusion in the subsequent issue must be returned to the editor by reviewers, the date by which writers must submit articles for inclusion in an issue later in the year or the conference date. In between, editors will be writing tactful letters of rejection, joyful letters of acceptance rephrasing unkind reviewers' comments so they do not destroy the confidence of writers, and correcting the grammar of a generation who never learnt it at school. They sit amidst the whirlpools of easily bruised egos, who will articulately complain of editorial neglect of their talents, and readers who want their specialist needs accommodated and their minds stimulated and entertained in the shortest possible time if they are to continue paying the high costs of journal subscriptions.

I was a journal editor, so obviously my description above is sympathetic. You may feel you agree more with an Australian view that 'a small proportion of editors are possessive of their academic territory, or are given to prejudice and favour and operate as part of an invisible college of scholars in a cosy club atmosphere' (Sadler, 1990: 10).

Whichever perspective you have of editors, there are ways to please them. They are most likely to send your articles to reviewers if your writing passes the test of clarity, your research appears to offer something new and relevant to that journal or conference, your article arrives on time and you followed the contributors' instructions or …

REFLECTIONS

Read this extract to detect *what else attracts* editors. It's an editor's thoughts about an article submitted for the journal she edits.

> The rule utilitarianism article was weighty, but largely unreadable … It appeared to be written in English, but it was a variety of English which Isabel felt occurred only in certain corners of academia where faux weightiness was a virtue … everything sounded so heavy, so utterly earnest. It was tempting to exclude the unintelligible paper on the grounds of grammatical obfuscation, and then to write to the author – in simple terms – and explain to him why this was being done. But she had seen his name, and his institution and the title page of his article, and she knew there would be repercussions if she did this. Harvard! (McCall Smith, 2004: 92)

This extract is from a novel, but one written by a Professor of Medical Law at the University of Edinburgh who will therefore have experience of writing for many different audiences and editors.

3.4.5   Article reviewers

This group of your peers usually receives your articles without any identifying author details, so your name or institution will not affect reviewers' views (unless you are in a very specialized area of your discipline in which everyone knows everyone else and established or new writers are instantly recognizable). You can guess who some of the reviewers might be since many journals list their associate editors who are usually an editor's first choice for reviewers. You could check that you have cited the books and articles written by those in this group who are germane to your research; maybe try to read some of their work to see which style they prefer. However, you cannot be sure to which reviewer(s) your article will be sent, so the value of reading work by the board member lies in being better able to judge the general tenor of what will be accepted or not.

For example, the *Journal of Imperial and Commonwealth History* 1995 advisory board came from the oldest established universities in Australia, Canada, England, India, The Netherlands and the USA. The 2003 editorial board of *Auto/Biography* (from the British Sociological Association) were all from late twentieth century English universities. *International Studies in Educational Administration* (2003) had advisers from fifteen different countries, including a rare sighting of one practitioner from outside the academic world.

Article reviewers mainly incline towards the attitudes of thesis examiners (3.4.2) and established academics (1.3). They will also be reviewing your articles late at night, in their own time, and unpaid. *So* try to avoid annoying them by, for example, ignoring the latest APA guidelines if the journal specifies these, or omitting a methodology report or authorizations from the literature or forgetting to include theoretical significances. Such annoyances are compounded by reviewers struggling with poor bedside lighting and a preference for other distractions at this time.

But many reviewers are partial to, and very accepting of, alternative styles if they are suited to your data and justified. They can remember their own struggles to break into print and mostly write very helpful revision comments. They like their post-midnight slumbers to be prevented by the arrival of new ideas. Well, most do, but at some time all of us will have found ourselves subject to less than kind and tactful reviewers (Chapter 13).

3.4.6 Research assessors

These combine the characteristics of article reviewers and thesis examiners but with the added job of grading your work on a scale that takes in more than just pass or fail (1.3.2.3). To do this, they have to assess all the various outputs you, and everyone else, have available for rating (a minimum of four must be submitted from each person for the UK's RAE for example).

Assessors' judgements in the UK's RAE are rumoured to be influenced by the status of journals which have accepted your publications, as I assume happens in other countries operating similar assessment systems. There are equal claims that decisions are taken only after the reviewers have read articles for themselves since good journals can accept poor articles and vice versa. There are anecdotes that books count for less than articles and chapters in edited books count for even less and editing a book counts even less … and so on. The UK's RAE understandings of what counts as 'good' has expanded since its inception in the early 1990s so more unusual types of publication are now acceptable.

This all sounds reasonable assuming that assessors really could read everything submitted to them, but the UK's RAE assessors do not spend two or three months in total seclusion with only research publications for company. It seems highly unlikely, therefore, that they can read more than a quarter of them fully (just one for each academic). The majority must be skimmed so first impressions will affect decisions greatly. Hence, write your titles carefully (always include the word 'research' in the title) and polish your abstracts and conclusions so the reflections of your method, emergent theories and findings immediately shine forth (11.1, 11.2).

3.4.7   Supporters' clubs

Those who guided your writing are the most easily overlooked, and kindest, of audiences. If you've published an article, or a book, thesis or report, from work with which they helped you, send them a copy, if you can afford it. In all cases, at least send a thank you letter. Old fashioned courtesy, academic networking or showing off? All of these, but necessary in case you need help again, to keep yourself in your supporters' minds as potential research collaborator or conference speaker, and to give your supporters the satisfaction of knowing that good teaching is effective and valued.

3.5   Audiences outside academia

This heterogeneous group divides into those whom you want to:

- arouse to action as a result of your research, such as professionals in your discipline, corporate, party political and government funders and policy makers;
- entertain so much that they will want to publish, read, listen to or watch more of your work, such as professional and house journal editors and readers, general circulation magazine editors, staff writers and readers, newspaper and broadcast media reporters and programme makers (editors will decide if they want to publish your work, staff writers and reporters will decide if they want to extract from it, rewrite it or summarize it).

Assume all of these to be widely educated readers but with less specialist knowledge than academics. A less charitable view, from the health services, is that they:

> lack the time and the skill to sift out the relevant and useful information from the rest ... do not have the skills to critically appraise the papers they read – i.e. to assess their quality and relevance to practice ... are threatened by the challenges to their practice, particularly by researchers ... [especially as] Research findings may conflict with long-held beliefs ... Researchers and practitioners inhabit 'different worlds' and speak different languages. (Gomm and Davies, 2000: 135, 136)

Whichever view you adopt, the interests of this group lie in your 'core story' only (Coghlan and Brannick, 2001: 117) and they require unequivocal conclusions.

3.5.1   Appropriate style for less specialist readers and listeners

Box 3.1 outlines the elements of style most generally appropriate for less specialist audiences. The way you write the whole document, or make a presentation, should direct the readers to where you want them to go, be that policy making, relaxing entertainment or making changes in their professional practices. These purposes may entail making some changes in the general style. Adopt more formal language to influence policy, a more informal tone with illustrations if entertainment is intended.

Box 3.1   Writing appropriately for less specialist audiences

Writing appropriately for less specialist audiences requires:

- ◀ᵗ⁾ Non-esoteric language without pompous verbosity and jargon (5.3.1, 5.3.2).
- ◀ᵗ⁾ Specialized academic language, since it compliments readers' abilities, but with overt or covert explanation (5.3.3.1).
- ◀ᵗ⁾ The particular language of the group for whom you are writing to show that you have related to their world (5.3.3.2, 5.3.3.4).
- ◀ᵗ⁾ Chatty colloquialisms (5.3.3.3).
- ◀ᵗ⁾ Eschewing slanging matches with other academics.
- ◀ᵗ⁾ Few in-text references and only a short bibliography just to add a little authority (Knight, 2002: 198) rather than to prove your points *ad nauseam*.
- ◀ᵗ⁾ Literature reviews, methodology and theorizing to be absent or minimal (Figure 7.1).
- ◀ᵗ⁾ Plentiful visual aids whether you are writing or presenting. Tables, graphs, arrows, flow charts, colours, pictures, graphics – and remember, these are what will be the most reproduced part of your work. Margin width, paragraph spacing and length, white space around and within your work can all help to promote the story line.
- ◀ᵗ⁾ Putting the conclusions in the introduction; that way, readers don't need to peruse the whole document (11.7.1). This is not recommended for spoken presentations; it adds to the audience's reasons to leave early.
- ◀ᵗ⁾ Emphasizing what is new about your research.
- ◀ᵗ⁾ Comprehensible and extensive statistics. The better they are, the better will your research be rated, since policy makers prefer figures which are easy to remember, have straightforward meanings and are not subject to frequent revision (Hammersley, 1993: 160).
- ◀ᵗ⁾ Note that practitioner conference audiences will need the same treatment as the academics but they are likely to be less sceptical; they will take notes copiously, ask fewer questions and, above all, will want to come away with something they can implement.

REFLECTIONS

Professional and house journal editors are the ones who have to search hardest for material for their publications because they lack the academic ratings of research journals and the finance of the general circulation magazines. They can, however, provide valuable publicity for research, influence professional practice quickly and get researchers launched onto the professional, and paid, conference circuit. They also need shorter articles than do other outlets.

3.6   Academic and less specialist audiences combined

3.6.1   Book purchasers

In order to get published commercially (Chapter 14), research books need a wider audience than just the academic community from which you emanate. Catching the interest of disparate groups leads to variations in language within the same publication, well illustrated in this extract from Dubin's (1999) book on controversies in museum studies. Note how he writes the first two questions in 'academic style' while the remaining questions are much more aimed at the hearts and minds of more generalist audiences:

> questions that generally surface in discussions around contemporary museums ... [are] '*Should* the community be involved in exhibitions?' '*Do* people have a right to offer input or to exercise oversight, especially when the subject relates to them?' 'Why do exhibits rouse such passion?' 'Why do groups feel that so much is at stake in what is depicted in museums?' (1999: 11)

3.6.2   Research funding agencies: government and charitable

Both types of agencies will need an executive summary or key findings (11.2) at the commencement of your report and this is its most important element. This will circulate to potential direct users of the outcomes of your research and it is certainly the part that will be read most often (since most readers are too busy for the whole document). Each brief paragraph of this summary concludes with a list of the numbered paragraphs in the main report in which can be found the data that give all the details on that element. Figure 2.1 is an example of a diagrammatic executive summary but text is more usual, as in the following exemplar. This is from the executive summary of the report to Industry in Education (a charitable research funding agency in the UK) on the ways in which business people operate as school governors.[1]

KEY FINDINGS OF THE SURVEY

- A relatively small number of employees from the business community are school governors ... (1.1).
- Most school governors are male, middle/senior managers (2.1, 2.2).
- Half the sample of school governors have only served for two years or less (3.3). (Thody and Punter, 1994: 1)

Governmental grant awarding agencies are staffed by academics and send your grant requests and project reports to academics for assessment. They must, therefore, have the full academic treatment in terms of the content, sections and language of a document but in the format of a formal report rather than that of the more 'essay' like academic article or thesis. The scaffolding of such reports is their many subheadings and every paragraph with its number, as signposts for busy readers who need to know quickly how each bone of the skeleton connects to the next. The conclusions need to show awareness of policy and political implications. Full literature and methodology reviews are required but may be relegated to appendices. Often, the agencies will specify the form of the report to be made and, if so, you follow this determinedly.

Charitable agencies (often endowment funds from present or past corporate sponsors) will likewise want the full academic information in report form though you can afford to employ rather less specialized language in some cases. They are less likely to specify the final format. Photographs are welcome additions; charities need to continue to attract funds, and transferring academic research to the public mindset to encourage donations is infinitely easier with photographs.

3.6.3 Research respondents

In the human sciences, respondents and/or subjects are a possible audience from qualitative or narrative research or from very small surveys. It may have been a condition of your research access that they are allowed to see the raw data collating their views and/or your finished writing or presentation. You may have placed a moral obligation on yourself to let them see what you have developed from their contributions. You may want to check if they have anything they want to add. Additionally you will have decided whether or not to allow them to alter what they see in advance of publication because much trust resides in you to report their views accurately and sensitively.

If you are presenting raw data, then you only show respondents their own. This must be clearly transcribed, put into a cover so it shows the respondents that you value their work sufficiently to protect it, and prominently labelled with their name and yours and instructions on how to annotate it and return it (and of course, the cost of postage).

If it is a finished draft of the whole work you are sending, then again, make clear what you expect respondents to do with it (and remember they have a right to refuse to read it, as did one respondent in one of my research projects; he said it reminded him that he had failed in his career). I discovered an unexpected benefit of requesting views when I sent the draft of my book on chief executives to the nine whom I had researched. The comments were so extensive and interesting that I was able to add a complete chapter (Chapter 11 in Thody, 1997a).

> ## REFLECTIONS
>
> *Never* send the same written document to different audiences. Even documents intended for similar audiences will need variations. If, for example, one journal rejects your article you will need to alter it before sending it to another. Journals have differing expectations of how headings, bibliographies and footnotes are presented and can have different audience perspectives which will require you to recast the focus of the article. I even encountered one that eschewed capital letters so all my proper nouns had to be recast in lower case.

3.6.4 International audiences

I have assumed so far in this chapter that all the readers and listeners discussed were either native speakers of your language or very competent as second language users and knowledgeable about the country settings of your research. Most journals will have their majority readers in their country of origin but increasingly journals have global circulation; conference audiences are invariably polyglot, international funding agencies make grants for transnational research and commercial corporate sponsors are multinational companies. For all such audiences, language may need some explanation, grammar and punctuation must be absolutely correct (Lindle, 2004: 2) (5.3.2), context will need elaborating, and formatting is much more likely to be acceptable in largely conventional modes (though alternatives for data presentation can be tolerated within these). Other adaptations are suggested below.

3.6.4.1 International readers

The following extract demonstrates good contextual explanation for an international audience. It is from a journal with markets in at least twenty countries and is expressly aimed at a mixed readership of professionals from all parts of the education system (primary, secondary and tertiary) and academics from universities. Very few of these can be expected to know much about the countries which are the focus of the article. The extract also provides a good example of how to incorporate the research question and an outline of the article in its introduction (11.10).

Extract 1

From 'Overcoming barriers to access and success in tertiary education in the Commonwealth Caribbean' (Roberts, 2003: 2).

> ENROLMENT IN TERTIARY education in the Commonwealth Caribbean has remained comparatively and consistently low over the years. Not surprisingly, the actual numbers of tertiary education graduates have also been well below the optimal level. On the other hand, indications are that there is a increasing demand by potential students and private sector employers as well as by governments for tertiary education graduates. Additionally, educational leaders and policy makers continually express a need for, and a desire, to expand tertiary education opportunities to a wider range and greater number of its citizens in an attempt to promote national and regional development.
>
> In spite of concerted effort by many stakeholders, the goal of increased access to tertiary education has been elusive to date. It seems reasonable to infer therefore that there are resistant barriers to the expansion of tertiary education access and that these may be related to persistent challenges which also place limits on the success of learners in the tertiary education system.
>
> This paper attempts to identify some of those barriers to access and success and to highlight some of the initiatives which have been taken in an attempt to overcome these barriers. Before proceeding to a discussion of the barriers themselves, it may be useful to define the terms tertiary education, access and success and to examine also what constitutes the Commonwealth Caribbean tertiary education context and to locate within this context some inherent barriers to access and success.

Extract 2

To demonstrate how this might change if written for a specific audience in its country of origin, I have invented a *Caribbean Secondary School Principals' Bulletin* in which the above would become:

Helping your students to access and success in our tertiary institutions

The CSSP Annual Conference reminded us that we're becoming increasingly successful at persuading students to progress to our colleges and universities. This is beginning to alter the low enrolment rates they've had until now and that fits with the government's drive to increase post-16 enrolments. So what has been holding them back and what can we in schools do to encourage staying on to higher education?

3.6.4.2   International listeners

- *Yes*, you do need to speak more slowly and with greater articulation for international audiences than when in conversation with speakers of your own language (and *no*, you don't need to shout, spell words or speak in slow motion).

- *Yes*, you have to reduce the length of your presentation if there is no simultaneous translation and you are reliant on translations following each of your sentences. With simultaneous translation, you usually need occasional pauses to allow the translator to catch up with you should your own language be more linguistically sparse than the one into which you are being converted. Try to talk with the translator before your session to discuss how best you can help each other.

- *Yes*, always expect to have your allocated time foreshortened by opening ceremonies and introductions: the longest introduction I received lasted the whole two hours scheduled for my presentation as Maoris spoke and sang a welcome, but I was happily given another two hours to speak and sing back.

- *Yes*, utilize as many and as varied visual aids as possible (and *yes*, expect there will be no, or the wrong or broken, facilities for technological pyrotechnics, so have back-ups; this applies in your home country too).

- *Yes*, have your visual aids, and at least a summary of your lecture, translated in advance if possible – though, as I discovered when mine were translated into Greek, I had the amusing challenge of working out where each slide fitted into my presentation as I could not understand them. I had to follow the clues of pictures that were on the originals (and *yes*, it's very popular if you can manage hello and goodbye in the language of your hosts; I've had the fun of learning a range including sign language).

- *Yes*, if you are presenting in a language other than your native one, then read your paper unless you are supremely confident of your linguistic abilities (and *yes*, still use visual aids as well).

- *Yes*, unless you have a protocol adviser, you are likely to transgress some cultural norms (so *yes*, apologize at the beginning for the likelihood of this, explain that you are operating within the meaning of 'polite' in your own culture, and ask for your contraventions to be pointed out to you at the end of the presentation so you can learn).

3.7   Acknowledging the power of readers and listeners

Since audience matters so much it's worthwhile making clear, in the documents and speeches you produce, who you anticipate should be reading your research.

   For articles in any type of publication, theses or broadcasts, the location of the item is usually enough to provide clues to its intended audience. A research report will have those to whom it is addressed named at its commencement. Books have potentially much wider audiences than these so their authors usually describe their target audience, and the audience's likely purposes, in their prefaces or opening chapters.

Delineating the audience ensures damage limitation; anyone not in the designated groups of readers can hardly criticize if the book does not meet their needs.

For example, a book on girls' education in Africa offers itself to 'those principals, teachers, school councillors, inspectors and local, regional and national government administrators who view themselves as reflective practitioners and who, therefore, require information on which they can base their own theory and justify their actions' (Thody and Kaabwe, 2000: 3). Similarly, a book on the broadcast media extensively defines its audience:

> For students and teachers of mass communication ... [to] provide information about the efficiency and impact of television ... for program directors and producers whose difficult task it is to provide broadcasting services which are entertaining and interesting and ... social and government administrators, interested in the efficiency and standards of broadcasting services, educationalists who want to teach the many and be understood by them, teachers who want to know what television is doing to people. (Belson, 1967: vi)

3.7.1 Flattering the readers and listeners

In the above extracts is another useful device to encourage audience acceptance: flattery. Thody and Kaabwe (2000) refer to their readers as 'reflective practitioners'; Belson (1967) directs his work at readers concerned with the 'welfare' of the viewers. Another such device flatters readers by assuming they are as well read as the researcher, as in 'Central to [Headrick's] ... *well-known The Tools of Empire* ... is the assertion that European imperialism resulted from ... new technological means' (Bossenbroek, 1995: 27, my emphasis).

Such linguistic strategies acknowledge the power and capabilities of the audience and aim at integrating the audience into the sense-making of the research. A charming example of this comes from a philosophy article. After the abstract and before the introduction is inserted:

Health Warning

> Reading this may damage your epistemological health. Kant said that we have no knowledge of things as they are in themselves. Perhaps he was wrong. Perhaps you, gentle reader, do have knowledge, right now, of things as they are in themselves. But look out. In the half hour it takes you to read this, you may lose it. Proceed at your own risk. (Langton, 2004: 129)

This example compliments readers by acknowledging how busy academics usually are by slipping in the information that only thirty minutes are needed to read the article, thus also adding a challenge that is hard to resist.

3.8 Review

Audiences' aims matter. Adjust accordingly. But take account also of your own purposes and how these can ethically balance with those of the people reading your research (Chapter 4).

Note

1 Each school in England has an advisory body of elected and appointed volunteers, the school governors.

4 Adapting to Audience: Adjusting for your Purposes

CONTENTS

4.1   Contrasting purposes

The following three extracts describe exactly the same elements of the lives of chief executives but each researcher had different purposes. The language in each is clear and direct but differs according to readers' needs (Chapter 3). These needs have had to be balanced with those of the researchers, the subject of this chapter.

Extract 1

From an English novel using research from the author's personal experiences as a local government administrator.

- *Researcher's purposes.* Entertaining readers; encouraging sales of this and future books by the same author.

  Aspirate-dropping politicians, educational psychologists, parents hot under the collar, lunatic school teachers, had all added to the tally of ludicrous error but then so had he. His whole career was shot through with misjudgement, mismanagement, support of wrong causes, failure to assist decent men and women, yet he was still praised as one of the most successful directors of education in the whole country since the war. He could not see why he had made such a name, except that the favourable publicity or circumstances had helped him and his pleasant but utterly serious committed manner and approach had led people, political masters or paid subordinates alike to act more sensibly. (Middleton, 1986: 70–1)

Extract 2

From a USA refereed journal using research from surveys and interviews.

- *Researchers' purposes.* Enhancing readers' knowledge; gaining acceptance and progress in academia; building on to past research; providing guidance to superintendents.

> The superintendent moves between the nomothetic and idiographic dimensions to trans-actionally and transformationally interact with board members, principals, parents … to persuade these individuals to accept the goals of the organization as defined and visualized by the superintendent. The superintendent acts to persuade these individuals to participate in the formulation of goals additional to his own. (Griffin and Chance, 1994: 81)

Extract 3

From an English academic book using research from non-participant observation.

- *Researcher's purposes.* Entertaining readers; encouraging sales of this and future books by the same author; enhancing readers' knowledge; gaining acceptance and progress in academia; building on to past research; possibly providing guidance to chief executives.

> [Chief executives are] hubs of wheels endlessly transmitting and receiving information along different spokes … linking joint initiatives from different points in the system … CEOs are both the effective centre, as the organizers, and the affective centre since their symbolic role in representing the unity of the service must be acknowledged. (Thody, 1997a: 182)

4.2   Defining your purposes

An overarching purpose of all these examples is the same – to enhance readers' knowledge and so persuade them to 'do something' (Raimond, 1993: 167). What a researcher then wants readers to do specifically will differ for each of the different products of any research. These rationales divide into *overt* (conscious or deliberate) and *covert* (conscious or subconscious), and are discussed below in 4.3–4.5. Each of the rationales should be decided at the beginning of the research planning process (Cohen et al., 2000: 89) and a balance struck between the aims of the researcher, the researched and the readers/listeners (Hammersley, 2002: 126). The resulting ethical dilemmas are discussed in 4.6.

4.3   Overt purpose: enhancing knowledge

A researcher's overt, overall purpose of any research is to make a difference to understanding so that policy, practice, theoretical or conceptual problems will be solved. It is therefore most important to state how your research has enhanced the knowledge in ways that justify new solutions to problems.

This is almost always stated in the introduction to all research documents (11.10). For example, here is the first paragraph of a legal academic journal paper:

> Surprisingly little attention has been given to the public domain in the statutes establishing and regulating intellectual property, in the case law interpreting these statutes or concerning the common law of intellectual property, or in the scholarly literature … In this article, the concept of the public domain will be addressed as generally as possible … The modifications to the basic model necessitated by the introduction of an intellectual property system will be addressed. (Oddi, 2002: 1–5, 8, 10)

A book on Hollywood film settings defines its purpose negatively in its opening line, an arresting mechanism: 'This is not a "how to" book as if reading films were a mechanical process that could be achieved by following a set of preconceived rules' (Thomas, 2001: 1). Sadly, the writer then undermines this clarity with the half-hearted aspiration of the next sentence: 'In this book *I hope* to suggest a number of useful questions we can ask' (2001: 2, my emphasis). Warning: never be half-hearted about what you have contributed to knowledge. There are usually enough detractors without becoming one yourself.

An alternative is to state the purposes in the conclusions when researchers inform readers what has been discovered and/or what the readers are expected to do next (11.7.1). The Epilogue to this book is an example of this (Chapter 16). The example below is from a local newspaper. This reported research into the different types of supporters of Leicester Tigers rugby team and Leicester City soccer team. The research was done in order to find out if the two teams could share one ground. The newspaper article ended with:

> An older, more affluent, more county focussed, but lower-spending rugby crowd for Tigers, and a younger, more diverse, and rather higher-spending football crowd at City … Old certainties are being carved up in the debate over a common ground. Right now, what really matters is not the colour of your shirt, but where you will be wearing it this season. (Wakerlin, 2004: 10)

REFLECTIONS

In between the opening and closing points of a document, the purposes become the theme of the document or speech, reiterated as each part of the reported research adds to one of the purposes. The overt purposes thus structure the entire document or presentation. For example, Chapter 4 of a book on Hollywood films states that the 'aim of this book so far has been to provide a few ideas about some of the ways Hollywood films create and present significant spaces...it is now necessary to say a bit more about certain potential ambiguities in our understanding of offscreen space' (Thomas, 2001: 95).

4.4   Covert purposes: careers and finance

These two are additional to the production and utilization of the knowledge that the research was overtly designed to find. They will not usually be stated in the public documents arising from the research but they will influence their framing.

Research writing and presenting matter to researchers' careers, so much so that a journal editor felt driven to note that, 'the only one message that seems to emanate from some manuscripts is that the author is desperate to publish something' (Lindle, 2004: 1). Getting published marks your professional identification (your signature), showing that you work in a particular field and how you work in that field. It establishes and enhances your reputation and that of your employer, department or university. Becoming an effective presenter can help your career financially. Keynote speakers receive a minimum of conference fees and expenses and usually fees as well. The career purposes behind writing may make you veer to the conventional if you need rapid acceptance from the establishment, or towards alternatives if standing out from the crowd is the right thing at this stage of your career. Whichever it is, your overriding aim must be to achieve publication (14.7).

Researchers producing books, and their publishers, obviously have sales in mind. Publishers are aware of markets much more than are researchers; hence publishers' advice on titles, formats and language is to be followed. Any research report or article is a plea for further research for which money is needed. Hence researchers need to demonstrate the value of what has been achieved so far in order to strengthen the plea, especially as research funding is not easy to obtain.

4.5 The overt and covert combined: influencing policy

Research aims to influence action (3.5). This may be micro, encouraging others to undertake further research to test your results; it may be macro, encouraging policy developments by governments, commercial enterprises and agencies. It can be overtly stated because policy making is the concern of the funders, or it may be a covert purpose of the researcher if one accepts that all research is to some degree 'political' in its relation to concerns about what is needed in one's discipline (Mason, 1996: 160).

Achieving the purpose of influencing policy is not easy and 'immediate and direct linkages between study results and policy decisions are relatively rare' (Bradley and Schaefer, 1998; Tooley with Darby, 1998; Weiss, 1983: 219). Policy makers and practitioners appear to expect too much of research, which needs to show unequivocal findings to be of value to them, while researchers appear to be overly optimistic in expecting immediate and direct implementation of their every conclusion (Hammersley, 2002: 148).

From all three of the following extracts, the writers intended to influence policy. All three extracts arise from research by Professors Macbeath and Galton, *A Life in Secondary Teaching* (2004). The first two are reports on the research by other people, and this not only illustrates contrasting purposes but also shows how little influence researchers can have over how their own conclusions are used for others' purposes.

Extract 1

From a national, right of centre, British newspaper, front page headlined story.

Ministers and unruly pupils 'causing collapse of schools'

> After questioning a nationally representative sample of teachers…[it was] concluded that behaviour was their main concern. They had a constant battle to be allowed to teach, a struggle compounded by confrontational parents … Less experienced teachers welcomed the prescriptiveness of the Government's Key Stage 3 strategy, which dictates how English, maths and science are to be taught to pupils aged 12–14 … they used it as a comfort blanket. (Clare, 2004a: 1)

Extract 2

From the website of the teachers' professional association which commissioned the research.

Secondary education – the battle to teach

Teachers are fighting a constant battle to be allowed to teach as a result of deteriorating pupil behaviour, says an independent study for the National Union of Teachers published today, Thursday 27 May, 2004. The problem is compounded by lack of support from parents, says the report by Professors John MacBeath and Maurice Galton of Cambridge University.

Extract 3

The following are my comments based on comparison of the newspaper story and the website text with the report itself. (Macbeath and Galton, 2004)

1   The newspaper stated that the report used a 'nationally representative sample of teachers'. The actual sample in the research was 1.89 per cent of Britain's schools and 0.11 per cent of Britain's teachers. The tables in the report which describe the sample do not give this cumulative figure, though they do show that the sample did indeed represent a cross-section of the UK's types of schools and types of teachers according to the variable of years of experience. So representative? Yes, of some variables. National? Not in the sense a general readership would assume such a word implied.

2   Both the newspaper and the teachers' website cited bad behaviour by pupils and lack of parental support as major factors inhibiting good teaching. Data extracted from a table in the report itself, shown here as Table 4.1, does confirm the primacy of poor pupil behaviour, but the researchers found seven other factors more important than parental influence. A wary reader must also ask what the outcome would have been if a national union of school students had commissioned the research. Would inadequate teachers be cited as a factor inhibiting good teaching? It's also noteworthy that most of the factors amongst which teachers had to choose are critiques of government policy. Would government funded research have presented the same factors?

It would be reassuring to be able to report that improved writing and presenting would greatly improve the chances of public and private action arising from research. I have to report honestly though that the consensus is that effective writing and presenting *do* matter in this arena but the effect may be less than hoped for. A small part of the reason for this failure of influence is deemed to be that when 'research findings reach and are read by practitioners they are not sufficiently accessible to be understood and valued' (Gomm and Davies, 2000: 135). This quotation is from a report on research in the health services but it appears to be appropriate elsewhere. Willinsky (2000), for example, questions how we ensure that research, other than from natural or applied sciences, has credibility. The answer lies, it seems, in being more persuasive, to 'engage the public [by] rethinking every phase of a research project from how a study is conceived … and into the writing-up and publication of the results' (2000: 5).

Disseminating findings in as many different forms as possible also helps. The most common forms of publication (journal articles, academic books, research reports)

Table 4.1   **Extract from a research report: tabulated data from which varying priorities were selected by different users**

Teachers' ranking of obstacles to teaching	
	Rank
Poor pupil behaviour	1
Lack of time for discussion and reflection	2
Large class sizes	3
Too many national initiatives	4
Overloaded curriculum content in own subject	5
Pressure to meet assessment targets	5
Poor resources, materials and equipment	7
Inclusion	8
Lack of parental support	9
Inadequate pay	10
Preparation for appraisal/inspection	11
Poorly maintained buildings	12
Prescribed methods of teaching	13
Limited professional opportunities	14
Insufficient pastoral support	15

were rated as only 'passive dissemination' in a 2000 study and the least effective for influencing practice. This same research also classified conference presentations as passive dissemination unless in 'innovative, user-friendly formats'. Turning research findings into direct teaching fared a little better as a means by which research can influence practice. Studies reported in the 1990s showed that health practitioners' behaviour was modified, and patient outcomes improved, after doctors attended educational conferences but 'the effects are small'. The greatest impact on practice (and this was still small) was informing practitioners of research outcomes in meetings at individual health practices, through peer meetings at performance management sessions and through mass media campaigns (Gomm and Davies, 2000: 141).

This may sound depressing but remember that your research is at least one of many factors influencing policy makers who must respond to parties, elections, stakeholder groups, economics and social pressures. The policy makers who do read your research still have to convince other groups of its worth and over these you have no influence. What you must aim to do is build up relationships with policy makers over time as you do more research, network and present your ideas publicly. Write your research appropriately for policy makers (3.5). Your research will then at least be kept on file; you could be called in for other research and your work can be seen as one step along a long road.

There are some signs of hope. Natural and applied sciences research does not appear to face the same credibility gap in gaining public and political influence as do the social sciences and humanities, but the growth of transdisciplinary research is pulling social scientists into the same arena. Social scientists are involved in natural science research teams as increasingly government policy needs input on the social impact of possible policies (Gibbons, Limoges, Nowotny, Schwartzman, Scott and Trow, 1994: 147).

4.6 Ethics

The two opposing views on the ethical dilemmas posed by conflicts that may arise between the purposes of the researcher and those of the readers are ably displayed in the following quotations:

> The fact that all manner of motives may underlie … research … does not in itself mean that the accounts of research findings are distorted … [but] both writers and readers … need to pay attention to the effects of authorship and sponsorship, of intended and anticipated audiences and of the different purposes. (Hammersley, 2002: 133)

> Inconvenient findings [from clinical trials] were often not disclosed to the public. In several cases, the stated purpose of the trial was altered … so that acceptable findings, rather than inconvenient results, could be published … almost 90 per cent of the research teams denied that they had failed to report everything, despite evidence to the contrary … [it was] claimed that it was because of pressure from journals … to publish positive findings and to keep the length of papers down which can lead to negative results being omitted. (Matthews, 2004: 6)

For those in the social sciences, literature and humanities, it is easy to dismiss this debate over purposes as one that afflicts mainly the natural and applied sciences in which potentially large amounts of money and commercial sensitivities are involved. The debate is, however, just as prominent for all subjects, whether the intended outcomes will impact social justice or scholarly argument. The publication of statistics relating to racial issues, for example, 'has not been a neutral exercise in pursuit of knowledge … These statistics became part of the "numbers game" used to justify racist immigration laws … More recently arguments about the use of statistics in favour of black populations … have been put forward' (Ahmad and Sheldon, 1993: 124).

To enable readers to assess research fairly, researchers should ideally admit to both their overt and their covert purposes. The latter seems unlikely since researchers themselves may not even be aware of their subconscious aims or, if they are, may be determined to mask them. Kinsey, for example, who produced the first major research on human sexuality in 1948 (*Sexual Behaviour of the Human Male*), promoted the image of himself as a white coated, neutral, detached, scientific observer. Would his findings on the extent of sexual practices outside of the then norms have been greeted with such acclaim and belief had current assessments of his purposes as a very sexually active deviant been known at the time (Sutherland, 2004)?

Readers usually have to infer from author descriptions, from comments in the text or from acknowledgements to the funders, how any covert purposes of the writer(s) might have affected the findings. You have to decide how much of yourself to reveal in order to assist these inferences (2.3.2, 11.5); this book's Appendix on research methodology (Chapter 17) shows how much I chose to reveal to help you assess my purposes.

Your caution as an academic may well conflict with those who want to use your research to justify policy changes. They will want unequivocal conclusions from your research but this presents you with an ethical dilemma. Your education as a researcher will make you want to explain the limitations to everything you have discovered, but if you insist on doing this you will find that others who make use of your research will remove the restrictions you have so carefully delineated. Consumers of your research need unequivocal findings – newspaper and magazine editors or staff writers who are summarizing your research, politicians who need one clear route along which to persuade their followers to go, corporate sponsors who will have to justify decisions to shareholders. So your choices are to leave it to them to decide what to extract from your research, or to decide yourself to what you most want to direct their attention. You can make your directions obvious by only offering one conclusion or recommendation. More subtly and effectively, offer a selection of recommendations, any one of which you would be happy to see in place, or offer evidence that mainly leads to option A while offering the readers a choice also of B. Intelligent readers, you will thereby imply, will choose A.

A further ethical issue arises when the researcher has to decide whether to write up, or present, what he/she feels that the funders *want* to hear since the 'impact of research on policy-making depends on its degree of consonance with the political agendas of governments [or of any funders] … and policy-makers anxious for their own political survival' (Cohen et al., 2000: 44). Such financial purposes can pose ethical dilemmas. It is tempting to exaggerate the implications of your research findings and to minimize methodological or access problems. On the other hand, such congratulatory writing can be seen simply as good marketing. In either case, you have to decide whether to do it or not.

Hopefully, and usually, your research findings will not set you on a course diametrically opposed to that of your sponsors. If they do, then the sponsors will select what appears in the public report and you will have to decide on how far your disagreements should be made public. You can:

- State your views but also make clear that you accept that policy makers have to take many views into account in order to survive in a democracy, or to keep their firms in profit or their charitable foundations solvent. Yours is just one of many views with no greater claim to priority than those of others.
- Give priority space to areas where you do agree with the funders; make the other areas less obvious visually but still include them.
- Obfuscate your findings by hiding behind all the specialized and abstruse language you can muster.
- Present your findings in as neutral a language and a format as possible (this is where the conventional is vital). The discoveries will be there but you will appear distant from the values. Leave the readers to make their own deductions from the conclusions. They have the power of decision anyway so don't fight them.

All the above dilemmas concern potential conflicts of interest between researchers and the users of research but there is a further purpose to consider, that of those used by the research. Viewing respondents (subjects) as audience can lead to ethical dilemmas for researchers. You may feel you have to include data from all of your respondents even if what emerged from their views is not precisely what you wanted. You may feel obligated to include lots of quotations so respondents will feel valued, can enjoy seeing themselves in print and can compare their views with those of others. You may feel you must exclude publishing data that will be painful for your subjects to read. I advise against any of these, but you should at least try to express yourself diplomatically and follow the suggestions in Box 4.1 for tactful and ethical ways to report to respondents.

Box 4.1   Ways of reporting to research respondents

☺ Produce an expanded version of your report/article specifically for the respondents so you can include more of their actual words.

☺ Send a thank you letter, stating the degree or publication you achieved, and attaching transcripts of original data in full.

☺ Invite them to a presentation you are making on the research and publicly thank them.

☺ Refer to their contributions in the written acknowledgements (and give their names if they have not requested, or been promised, anonymity) (11.3).

4.7   Review

All research aims to influence its audiences. These intentions can be overt or covert. Overt purposes will be used as a frame for the whole research document and will usually be stated in the introduction. Covert intentions can sometimes be inferred from a document or presentation. Writers and presenters should adapt their research reports to satisfy their purposes but, in doing this, ethical issues have to be resolved.

REFLECTIONS

Adapting for precedents, practicalities, your personality, the people for whom you are writing and your purposes, all sound very time consuming. You'll be pleased to know that they only take a few minutes of mental activity for 'guesstimates'. Then confirm and compare these by reading similar documents to the one you have to produce such as back issues of journals, research reports and previous conference papers (usually web accessible), books by authors in the same field and with the same publisher, and theses from your own university library.

5 The Arts and Craft of Writing

CONTENTS

Note

To illustrate different styles, 5.1 and 5.2 are designed for a generalist magazine, 5.3 and 5.4 for a textbook. Paragraph numbering and academic referencing have been retained throughout for the book's consistency.

5.1 How easy is writing?

'Suddenly I was just writing ... my writing took off ... the words were flowing ... it was wonderful' ... 'There was a moment when I knew I had it ... the story was just coming ... bubbling up ... I was writing away.' (Ackerman and Maslin-Ostrowski, 1996: 8–9)

And that's how we all want to feel – just like these USA school principals whose feelings when writing up stories about their personal experiences were recorded in the above quotations. But reaching this stage is enormously difficult (Darlington and Scott, 2002: 167). It's even harder if you're beginning research writing, this 'new, strange discourse' (Holliday, 2002: 1).

Even experienced writers can't always make the grade. The editor of *Educational Administration Quarterly* reported that after 'slogging through 812 manuscripts that range the gamut from the pretty intriguing to the pretty awful, I have substantial evidence that writing does not come easily to most authors' (Lindle, 2004: 1).

Fortunately, most agree that writing is enormously exhilarating and exciting. Each day's writing brings nearer the day when your discoveries are unleashed on the world.

5.2   The writing process

5.2.1   Telling the story

'Telling a story' is what writing research is all about. You should produce a 'vital text [which] invites readers to engage the author's subject matter' (Denzin, 1998: 321). Follow the detective novel formula, outlined below, and you can't go wrong.

- The mystery your research is to solve is your purpose (Chapter 4), *your research question, hypothesis or debate*.
- How others tried to solve the same mystery is your *literature review*.
- How you tried to solve it is your *methodology report*.
- What you discovered from your investigations are your *findings*.
- Your solution to the mystery is the *conclusions*.
- How this improves on previous investigations and what mysteries it leaves to be solved is your final *discussion*.
- The '*research participants and sources* may be seen as the characters in this story, and will need to be introduced and developed as they would in a novel' (Blaxter et al., 2001: 242, my italics).

The 'story line' must sing clearly throughout every chapter or section, with each part uncovering some of the solution but not revealing the whole until the last chapter.

5.2.2   Getting started

The question most frequently asked by novice researchers is 'How do I get started?' on writing up the final version. Now you will have eased the challenge of this by following my advice in Chapter 2 and you'll have been writing from the beginning of your research, following a template. But now, the final draft looms. You have to leave the cosy world of shouting 'Eureka!' in your shower and go out, feeling naked, putting your writing into the world of public debate with critical academic equals, examiners, publishers or buyers.

Experienced writers know there's no magic formula and no choices about starting to write. Don't wait for inspiration, or for an ideal time to write. Neither is frequent.

Your options are:

1 If panic prevents even the simplest sentences emerging, do other writing tasks as 'warming up exercises'. Rigorously check the bibliography, design the title, do a spell check on a section or set up the format templates for sub-headings and footnotes.

2 Take the first topic that emerges in your notes, whether or not you are sure that it will eventually be the first topic in a chapter. Use your PC's 'Find' command to locate material that deals with the same topic. Once grouped, turn that material into paragraphs. Repeat the process as you come to the next topic in your notes. When all is in paragraphs, put them into the order you want and finally produce the links between the paragraphs and sections.

3 Read through all the notes you have for a chapter or section, plan the outline, then go back and gather all the material to match that outline. When you have it all in its intended order, then commence writing the joined up paragraphs.

4 Don't expect that what you write initially will remain unchanged. When you read it later, you may want to revise or even abandon it so don't waste time agonizing over creating unchangeable perfection. Expect to relinquish anything up to two-thirds of a first draft. My most challenging reduction was to create a 5000 word article from a 14,000 word research report, all of which seemed vital to me. I did the deed, however, and reading that article now I see that it is not missing anything (Thody, 1989).

Figure 5.1   Starting writing

Reading just one more book, arranging for just one more interview, checking the statistical analysis just one more time, won't help you to write. Writing is work, just like any other, and the only way to get started on writing up or preparing a presentation is to write anything, from somewhere in the intended document, not necessarily at the beginning. Go look at Figure 5.1 to help you get started.

5.2.3   Maintaining momentum

Sure – you have other activities in your life besides writing and presenting research. You've got to fit in work, study, leisure, family and home. Tick the best option on the following list. Should you write:

☐ Something every day, however little?

☐ A set number of words or paragraphs each day? That way ensures a satisfying growth rate from which you will not be distracted and you will have an agreed end to each day's work.

☐ Daily at predetermined times? That way, you can claim an undisturbed period as your writing time.

☐ Daily at every possible time, however short? It's amazing how much your document grows from writing in the five minutes between phone calls, the twenty minutes while waiting to pick up your child from swimming lessons, the massive thirty minutes in between putting loads into the washing machine, or even a whole hour on the train *en route* to your mountaineering weekend. To use these interstices of time, it helps to have a laptop PC but it's not vital. Substitute real paper and pen.

☐ Several projects at once? Avoid boredom by simultaneously planning one book, writing two journal articles, collecting new research data.

☐ In binges? Spend days doing nothing but writing, followed by about the same number of days on other activities. This way you remember the flow of your 'story' and you enjoy seeing large swaths of print emerge.

☐ In vacations? Write only in the week-or-longer breaks from other work; it ruins your vacation but can mean completing the whole at one time.

☐ On sabbatical study breaks? A luxury for only a few but one that has its own disciplines. If you're not used to writing without distractions, it can be a mental and physical challenge to do a full day's writing.

☐ In combinations of any of the above? Variety lends enchantment to the process.

Score yourself ten for whichever you selected. All of these work; I know, I've tried them all and seen colleagues adopt them all effectively. Your choice depends on those guiding principles in Chapters 2–4. For example: the practicalities of the completion deadline may enforce vacation performance; your PhD thesis will benefit from a binge approach; while the satirical column in a professional magazine can be done in a one-off set time. Your personality may dictate that you work best in uninterrupted blocks or that you find working in the little breaks dictated by other activities is the way to go for you; precedents in your organization dictate whether study leave is likely or not.

Whichever way you choose to write, however, most people seem to find ways of delaying the actual starting moment, as Figure 5.2 demonstrates. Used any of these yourself? Yes – just a few types of procrastination symptoms common to experienced and neophyte writers alike, all 'extremely reluctant or fearful of committing their ideas to paper' (Blaxter et al., 2001: 227). Overcome your fear, confront it and *write*.

Procrastination reduces your writing time and dissipates your creative energy. Waste time on planning your next expedition, commenting on students' assignments, writing the annual family letter or completing the intricacies of a patchwork quilt, and you'll have significantly diminished mental powers for writing the research. Other activities, in small doses, can be valuable mental relaxation – but that's all. So, if procrastination activities aren't the way to get you over your writer's block, what is? All is revealed in Box 5.1.

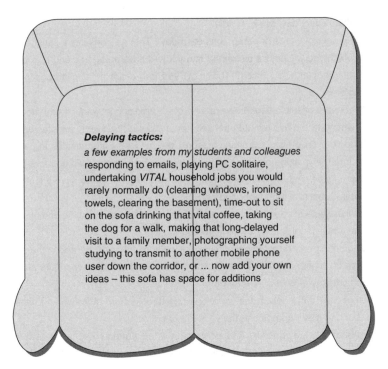

Delaying tactics:
a few examples from my students and colleagues
responding to emails, playing PC solitaire,
undertaking *VITAL* household jobs you would
rarely normally do (cleaning windows, ironing
towels, clearing the basement), time-out to sit
on the sofa drinking that vital coffee, taking
the dog for a walk, making that long-delayed
visit to a family member, photographing yourself
studying to transmit to another mobile phone
user down the corridor, or ... now add your own
ideas – this sofa has space for additions

Figure 5.2   How to procrastinate

Box 5.1   How to stop writers' block

1   Don't panic more than once weekly.
2   Reward yourself for completing your daily writing goals. Just small rewards will do. True, they mainly involve non-PC drink, chocolate or rubbish TV viewing but remember – you're burning calories even as you write.
3   Change to another of your writing projects if one is proving intractable.
4   Set a time limit for relaxation activities, just as you do for writing.
5   Don't expect perfection – give in occasionally.
6   Reflect on your writing while taking breaks.
7   When you stop writing, make notes of your plans for the next sentences; recommencing is then less daunting.

TAKE-A-BREAK

The work is writing.
Writing is work
(and it takes precedence over other activities).

So should you keep printing out your work as you progress?

YES, when you feel you have a reasonable first draft of the whole (or at least a whole chapter) but **NO** before then. It's just a time and paper waster. Learn to write, read and revise direct to screen. Save yourself some leisure time and save the world a few forests

YES, if the finished document is to appear in hard copy but **NO** if it's intended for electronic use only (websites, CDs, electronic journals)

YES, if it's your first lengthy piece of research writing but **NO** once you are in the postgraduate years

Figure 5.3   Do you need print versions of work-in-progress?

5.2.3.1   PC assistance

Those of you born after the universal application of PCs will never have had the luxury of simply sending off a handwritten text, held together with sticky tape and string, for someone else to type, knowing that even having to write a second version was unlikely. With PCs, we all have to do our own typing and clever formatting, expect to run through several drafts before completion, and happily insert the final tweaking of a little underlining on the night before the thesis is due in.

Such easy revision is both an advantage and a disadvantage of the PC age. It certainly adds to our personal workload but the screen view, which looks so perfect, is a definite morale booster for maintaining writing momentum, and even the simplest graphical touches can help immensely in explaining your ideas. A document map (6.3.6) shows you how your work is growing and helps you keep track of what you have written.

The screen view, however, can be overly seductive. Bet you don't want to delete that impressive flow chart that took hours to devise, even though it doesn't help to prove your hypothesis. That PC screen is also only a limited view; you can't see how your whole page will appear in hard copy. So should you keep printing out your work at intervals as you progress? Let Figure 5.3 help you to make up your mind.

Regular printing out does mean that you are never without the security of a paper copy should your PC files somehow become deleted or mangled. To protect your work-in-progress, always keep two copies of your files on removable media in addition to the

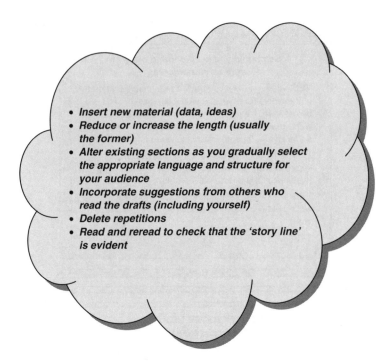

- *Insert new material (data, ideas)*
- *Reduce or increase the length (usually the former)*
- *Alter existing sections as you gradually select the appropriate language and structure for your audience*
- *Incorporate suggestions from others who read the drafts (including yourself)*
- *Delete repetitions*
- *Read and reread to check that the 'story line' is evident*

Figure 5.4   Techniques for drafting and redrafting

ones on the hard drive. If you are using a networked PC, don't assume server reliability or continuous availability, especially during university vacations.

5.2.4   Reaching the end

Revise and polish, revise and polish, revise and polish, revise and polish, revise … But what is meant by revision, what needs polishing, and at what point should you stop doing either and decide that the work's finished?

5.2.4.1   Revisions

Here's a great summary of what revision means from a study of modifications made to the introductions to scientific papers, though it's just as applicable in other disciplines. Revision is:

(a) the *deletion* of particular statements, either obvious arguments which essentially reinforced a certain point or assertions considered 'weak' or 'dangerous',
(b) the *reshuffling* of original statements … and
(c) changes in the *modality* of certain assertions, from the necessary to the possible and generally from the strongly asserted to the more weakly asserted. (Knorr-Cetina, 1981; cited in Gosden, 1995: 42)

You need to make alterations like these throughout your finished document. Such redrafting is not a sign of your failure to write well, it's simply part of the incremental process that constitutes writing. Figure 5.4 explains more about the redrafting process.

Keep making revisions like these until you feel strong enough to unleash a full first draft on colleagues or supervisors. You can let them have part, or the whole, of the intended document – but whatever it is, it should be a complete text, all in paragraphs, properly linked and with any intended tables, diagrams and appearance details. Once you have comments back, then you commence rewriting. Whether or not you submit it to friendly fire again will depend usually on how much time you have left to completion and, more importantly, the willingness of friends to critique your work.

5.2.4.2 Proofreading

Polishing is done after you've completed all your redrafting and you're into your substantive final draft. Now polish it so your brilliance shines, by rigorous, and time consuming, proofreading. For this you need to check the items listed in Box 5.2.

Box 5.2 Proofreading
Check, check and check again

- Text references are fully cited in either the text, the footnotes or the bibliography according to the precedents for the type of document you are producing (Chapter 12).
- Spelling is consistent and correct.
- Grammar and language are appropriate to the audience and purposes of the document (Chapters 3 and 4).
- Requirements for format have been obeyed (2.3.1; 14.2.2).
- The visual appearance of the text enhances the likelihood of readers' understanding.
- Sentences, paragraphs and chapters flow out of their predecessors and lead into their successors.
- Figures, tables, graphs and appendices are referred to in the text and it is clear where they should be placed.
- Any subheadings used in the text match those in the contents listings.
- Headings and subheadings are in the same style throughout the document.
- Ethical considerations have been met: your subjects are anonymized, if this has been requested; their locations are not easily recognizable; your references to them are tactful.

By the time you reach the polishing stage, you are likely to be tired and bored. If you can set the work aside for a few days between final revisions and polishing, you're more likely to be alert to errors. Additionally, and ideally, find a colleague to review it and always adopt their suggestions for changes. If they can't understand it, then no-one else will.

Polishing applies even to those publishing books who will have editorial assistants to check their final texts. They will discover corrections needed that you have not spotted despite your own meticulous scrutiny. Nonetheless, you are responsible for the understanding that the book is meant to convey, so don't just rely on the publisher's corrections. I found this out when the proofs of a book were returned to me with all our planned visual arrangements removed and all paragraphs lengthened to accord with 'correct' syntax. The original's short paragraphs and specific visuals were designed to meet the needs of the expected readership. Much repolishing was needed yet again to reinstate all our formatting (Thody, Bowden and Grey, 2004).

5.2.4.3   Deciding when to finish

Closure to all this is usually dictated by practicalities (2.3.3) decided by others such as the submission date for conference papers, the closing date for article receipt by journals, publishers' completion times or thesis oral examinations – the viva voce.[1] You would go on forever making revisions in the hopes of perfection but external forces thankfully provide the deadlines when all the adjustments have to stop. If your final deadline cannot be met, then be sure to negotiate an alternative well in advance so your recipients are inconvenienced as little as possible. Publishers will have reserved time slots for printers and editors, examiners will have arranged vivas, conference organizers will want to get proceedings printed or to find alternative speakers.

Note

Chapter 5 now changes from populist magazine style to textbook style.

5.3   Style and tone

Style is the way writers/speakers put words together in units of thought (sentences) and then blend them together in the larger units of paragraphs. *Tone* is a writer's attitude toward the material and the readers. You convey tone through style.

5.3.1   Conventional and alternative views

An extreme conventionalist's view could be that the style and tone of academic writing and presenting require not creativity but discipline, organization and conformity to scientific precedents (Berry, 1994: 2–3). This is viewed as the antithesis of creative writing and has such rules as avoiding chatty anecdotes, pomposity and blandness (Blaxter et al., 2001: 228). The style is used for both qualitative and quantitative research in order to reinforce research findings as authoritative, objective reality. It is the language of management control.

The extreme alternativist might look only for the creativity such as might be found in an article composed entirely of photographs, with minimal text, in which the reader is left almost alone to form her/his own impressions of the data (Soth with Weiland, 2005; Staub, 2002). This emerges from the idea of research as an internal voyage of discovery that is a continuum across the researched, the researcher and the readers. Its language is 'vibrant, suggestive, engaged and passionate' (Harper, 1998: 144). It is the language of emotional control.

5.3.2 Default elements for both conventional and alternative styles

Whether you view yourself as conventional or alternative, there are some common requirements:

- Keep sentences as short and simple as possible.
- 'Discipline yourself to write less than you want' (Literati website, 2003).
- Whatever style you adopt, apply it throughout your document otherwise readers can be confused.
- Err on the side of semantic and grammatical correctness and rigorous punctuation. This is particular advice for the natives of England who are apparently less punctilious about correct usage than are other nations, especially Americans (Truss, 2003: 33, 189). US advice is that the 'mechanics of writing for a diverse audience make choice of words, correct grammar, well placed punctuation, and accurate citations far from trivial matters' (Lindle, 2004: 2). Thus there's no substitute for having good dictionary, grammar and punctuation reference books by your side. *Use* them *and* the tools on your PC.
- Select non-prejudicial language which does not discriminate for, or against, any category of people.
- Check abbreviations. They do not usually have full points; hence USA not U.S.A. (the points are assumed to be there). On first applying an abbreviation, explain it in full with its abbreviation in brackets afterwards; thereafter, the abbreviation alone appears.
- In academic text that rarely needs numbers, spell out numbers that can be written in one or two words and thereafter use numerals. In more quantitative subjects, employ numerals, and always when they precede a unit of measurement. In more populist media, use numerals. Where your numeric needs fall between these two extremes, numbers up to ninety-nine are usually written as text and numbers over 100 as numerals but this is only one convention. Sage prefers numerals from 10 onwards. Never start a sentence with a numeral.
- Always state precise dates rather than 'currently', 'recently', 'in the last fifteen years' or 'two decades ago'. Your book/article/thesis could be read *many* years from *now*, but who then will know when 'now' is, and who wants to have to riffle through the title pages to find a date? So in this book, for example, 'currently' becomes 'in the 2000s'; 'recently' becomes 'from 2000 to 2005'; 'in the last fifteen years' becomes 1990–2005; two decades ago becomes '1985'.
- People's names appear in their fullest forms at their first entry. This usually means including both first and second names and sometimes a prefix too, such as Reverend, Dame, Professor, Doctor. After that, revert to surnames only and always without the prefixes. If you decide to shorten a prefix, then use punctuation to show an abbreviation, for example, Prof. (for Professor). Contractions do not need punctuation; hence Mr (for Mister), Ms (for Mrs or Miss), Dr (for Doctor).

5.3.3 Style choices

5.3.3.1 Cautious language

One of the hallmarks of the academic is deemed to be caution. Our lexicon includes the verbs *suggest, appear, indicate, intimate, imply, hint*. Prudent phrases are used, such as: 'It could be said that … '; 'The data indicate the possibility that …'; 'On the one hand there is majority agreement that … but on the other hand there is a strong minority view that …'; 'One might think that … but it is necessary to be aware of a probable alternative'; 'Of the 1300 sample of those using product X, 1000 contracted virus Y, which strongly indicates a causal connection. Further research is needed to see if this finding can be replicated in larger populations.'

Such phrases symbolize academic humility. Sources, data collection and conclusions can never be 100 per cent complete. Limitations to research must be openly admitted and generalizations without qualifications must be avoided. Such caution is appropriately termed 'hedging' (Holliday, 2002: 179) and it is particularly necessary in all qualitative and literary research which relies on interpretations. I think it is similarly vital in scientific researches; in medical research, for example, findings often have to be based on small samples. The mass media may jump to the conclusion that dietary studies on forty people can be generalized to whole populations but you, the academic researcher, will not do so.

An excellent example of hedging is in Middleton's (1995) article on feminist educational theory in the refereed journal *Gender and Education*. She sets out the article in two columns with the conventional format on the left and an alternative format on the right. The researcher includes a justification for thus breaking the mould. The conventional left column formally introduces the topic and discusses the argument in the impersonal and often passive tone. The right column contains a description of the researcher's office written in the first person active, so making the reader aware of the character of the researcher. She introduces the debates on feminist theory in a personal way by writing about her 'daughter's generation's attitudes' in contrast to 'post modernists [who] have rejected the monolithic categories upon which previous feminist research has rested' (1995: 89; cited in Blaxter et al., 2001: 241).

Caution must be abandoned for audiences from outside academia (3.5) when, for example, being interviewed by radio, TV or newspaper reporters, advising on broadcasts or writing in professional and general magazines. Such audiences want answers, not endless qualified responses. When tackling these, therefore, researchers need to select what can be stated unequivocally but truthfully. If the findings need qualifying, then the reservations must be clearly stated and repeated assertively.

The example below demonstrates how definition gives way to caution. It's from a newspaper article about research on the respective characteristics of fans of Leicester Tigers rugby and of Leicester City football (mentioned earlier, p. 51). Professor John Williams of Leicester University was reported in the *Leicester Mercury* as having found that:

> Tigers' season ticket holders are noticeably older – 55 per cent of them are over 50, compared to 24 per cent at City … 'Perhaps,' he suggests, 'older male City fans attend matches to escape from home, while Tigers couples retire together to the rugby.' (Wakerlin, 2004: 10)

5.3.3.2 Appropriate language

Writing style should be direct, clear, organized, cohesive, strong and convincing. Oh how simple it sounds! All one has to do is consider how each of the elements of that homily can be achieved:

- Directness is achieved by avoiding jargon, pomposity and verbosity, 'Latinate words … orotund phrases' (Knight, 2002: 199).
- Clarity comes from a clear, interesting and readable style which avoids complex sentences but varies sentence length and structure (Griffith, 1994: 236). It comes from a time when writing for research was assumed to be for information, not for enticement or entertainment (Charles, 1988), and therefore needed plain language. By the 1990s, the meaning of 'plain' was generating debate and many were the ways suggested of writing in plain English (Zeller and Farmer, 1999). Some equated it with neutral language and held that such was impossible in the human sciences (1999: 15). In natural and applied science writing, plain language is still the required norm, its meaning being to get to the point unemotionally and simply. Emotional language is however almost a *sine qua non* of qualitative and narrative research. Brevity is valued for all disciplines and by science researchers trying to place articles in journals that charge for publication. An analogous style is suggested by Knight (2002: 199) who proposes English broadsheet newspaper language as the most fitting for academic writing since these newspapers are in the business of communicating with those who are most likely to read academic publications.[2]
- Organization and coherence arise from planning (2.2).
- Strength and conviction emerge from using language which your primary audience is most likely to understand and which accomplishes the purposes of the research (Chapters 2–4).

Within these parameters, add to the interest of your style with differing sentence and paragraph lengths, and varying vocabulary. The latter can be easily achieved with the help of your PC's thesaurus tool or, even better, an old fashioned book thesaurus which carries an even wider range of word options.

5.3.3.3 *Colloquialisms*

These informal or conversational idioms are generally considered insufficiently precise for written academic language. It is even advisable to avoid them in spoken presentations unless you can be sure that all the audience has the same linguistic understandings as your own. Where used in academic publications, they are often put in inverted commas. Even here, however, they can be useful as chatty 'hooks' in an introduction, as in this example. This helps to make readers feel comfortable and inclined to read on: 'As a nineteenth-century colonial power, the Netherlands *put up quite a performance*' (Bossenbroek, 1995: 26, my emphasis).

REFLECTIONS

Decide what you think is meant by the following quotation which uses two colloquialisms:

Nearly eighty per cent of heads of independent schools in the central states are fired. Board chairs are voluntary, thus perhaps firing them is a moot point. (ISACS, 2003)

'Fired' is a colloquialism that has gained general acceptance as a replacement for dismissal from a job. It could be used in academic English unless the document is intended for an international audience.

A 'moot point' suggests a doubtful or an unsettled question, but did the author mean 'It is doubtful if the concept of dismissal can be applied to voluntary jobs' or 'The numbers of chairs who are dismissed is an unsettled question'?

On the other hand, at the end of the day, it's a nice touch to make your audience feel at home through your colloquialisms. In presentations, the body language accompanying colloquialisms usually gets the message across even if you're in foreign parts. Colloquialisms make a break in written academic language and can get you the prize of your articles accepted in generalist magazines. *But* a little goes a long way and your stream of explanation has got to run crystal clear. Now count the colloquialisms used in this paragraph. Enough is enough!

5.3.3.4   Jargon

With 100 million words of English at a writer's disposal, the specialized terminology for a particular subject is 'a natural and proper way of engaging in complex and sophisticated debates' (Knight, 2002: 199). The precision of correct words enables thinking to be expressed more succinctly than it could be in layperson's English even if the words are complex and technical. Such language is, however, sometimes referred to derogatorily as jargon. To be avoided is the pretentious gibberish of words such as 'non-foundational epistemology', 'pantisocratic', 'halation', 'heterarchy', 'limitarian', 'rigid designator'.[3] The Literati website (2003) on publishing advises: 'When you use a word of three syllables or more, check yourself. Is there really a good reason to use that longer word?'

The answer to that question depends on the intended audience for a research document or presentation and its purpose. Neither the simple nor the long and abstruse word is invariably right or wrong. Box 5.3 outlines the varying options for employing jargon.

Box 5.3   Using jargon

1   The default position is adopting the simplest word possible from everyday English. This applies to all research writing and especially if, for example, you are writing an article for a popular magazine such as *Reader's Digest* or for a newspaper.

2   Popular journals such as *National Geographic* will err on the side of simplicity but will also include the required vocabulary, sometimes with a glossary.

Box 5.3   (Continued)

3 Academic journals and books will mainly apply the exact wording associated with their disciplines. One assumes that the audience for these will either know the correct terminology or want to learn it. A glossary can be provided for frequently used technical terms in the text. Replacing precise language with lay English also has the disadvantage of adding to already restrictive word counts.

4 Theses should have only the precise words required by the discipline.

5 Particular types of methodology will lend themselves to particular vocabularies. Participant research can present very localized jargon, emerging from the actual situations studied. Its reproduction may be important to the understanding of the respondents' views. Non-participant research establishes distance by applying abstract words.

Jargon can be used to great advantage. Conference papers, for example, desperately need intriguing titles to attract audiences. Hence 'Towards a prolegomenon for understanding what radical educational reform means for school principals' was presented by an English professor at an Australian conference (Ribbins, 1993). Who could miss the opportunity to solve the mystery of a prolegomenon? Would the paper have attracted so many had it appeared in the conference programme as 'Towards a preliminary discussion or a formal critical introduction for understanding what radical educational reform means for school principals'? The translation loses the impact of the original. The choice of the word 'prolegomenon' also flatters the audience (3.7.1) who will either know, or can pretend to know, what it means.

Learning is encouraged by correct, if esoteric, jargon and learning is a central aim of the academic community. On first encounter with a new word, one needs to look it up. Thereafter, it is yours for life. Hence 'Looking two ways: identity, research and praxis in the Caribbean Community' (Henry, 1997) as a chapter title offers one such word. 'Praxis' would be well known to educational experts from the seminal writer on adult education, Freire. The chapter would therefore call to the 'in crowd' and maybe attract others by its mystery. If the author had tried to attempt simpler terms, the title would have had to be about 'Identity, research and practical wisdom from particular examples of actions from which general guidance to others might be produced since where the ends of one's actions can be anticipated from previous evidence then you can gain moral guidance on what you yourself should do'. Much easier to just write 'praxis' and make us all extend our vocabulary (and if you do, then graduate to Gadotti's *Pedagogy of Praxis*, 1996, for some fascinating discoveries).

The middle way for jargon lies in having the correct, technical terminology but melding explanations for it into the text. This can be direct (where the writer or presenter informs the audience that a definition is being given) or indirect (where the definition is woven into the text).

Examples of the direct:

> An example or two before we launch ourselves into the discussion proper may be useful to clarify some of the things I mean by 'meaning'. For instance ... two cases of mounted butterflies ... on the wall ... in the background ... enhance the homeliness of the setting. (Thomas, 2001: 3 – from a book about Hollywood film settings)

> The term 'reinforcement' was adopted to describe the likely outcome of the ... mentoring [of one school principal by another] ... [reinforcement is] the rapid learning of effective established practices or of the repetition of possibly outdated systems and ideas. (Thody and Crystal, 1996: 178 – from a chapter in an edited book on education)

Indirect definition is demonstrated in the next two examples. Compare the two extracts, both concerning the same technical word. Do the extracts contain enough to make its meaning clear?

> The researcher as a writer is a bricoleur. He or she fashions meaning and interpretation out of ongoing experience. As a bricoleur, the researcher uses any tool or method that is readily to hand. (Denzin, 1998: 315 – from a chapter in his own book on interpretive research)

> The bricoleur [in an industrial society] could aspire to gathering ... a number of small but relatively heavy steel tools ... about him. (Dent, 2001: 18 – from an article on the biography of a toolbox)

Jargon can be used to impress an audience, though it may not always be effective. A 2003–4 lively web dispute amongst scholars highlighted this. Falco (2004) criticized Stork's attacks (on Falco's and Hockney's theories about how the Old Masters achieved such accuracy in their paintings) as 'filled with technical-sounding language that provides ... a veneer of scholarly credibility [words such as] (*lichtkroon ... sfumato ... Poggendorff illusion*)'. Stork's (2004) rejoinder illustrates the establishment's preference for the conventional (1.3.2.3) as he responded that the theory had been refuted by 'slow, careful analysis of experts who follow the accepted protocol of expert peer journal articles rather than the broad popular presentations in the popular media'.

REFLECTIONS

This extract appears in a journal article intended for those researching biographical data:

> The polysemousness of these accounts draws upon ambiguity in their provenance. (Skultans, 2001: 5)

The average concise dictionary (*c.* 215,000 words) does not yield 'polysemousness'. Would it have been better to replace 'polysemousness [of]' with, 'many meanings that might emerge [from]', thus utilizing five words instead of one?

Could the following be written more effectively?

The deontological perspective of IT ethics can equip students with the knowledge and skills to apply professional codes … in solving ethical problems. (from an article about teaching business ethics by Taylor, Moynihan, McWilliam and Gresty, 2004: 52–3)

This would need to become: 'Teaching students that they are required to perform certain IT duties because there is rational cause for them, or because the requirements are expected, or listed, in the rules of conduct for a group, can equip students with the knowledge …'. The second version is simpler but it requires more than double the original word count.

In what circumstances would you deliberately use jargon to obfuscate your findings? (Clues in 4.6)

5.3.3.5   Tenses

The vanguards of the conventional and alternative armies meet on the battleground of verb tenses. The big guns fire off passively and abstractly, the snipers nip about actively and concretely. The computer grammar checkers, which now control the weaponry, will refuse to allow the passive voice. Hence, 'the charge was led by Thody' will be put in the firing line and be reborn as 'Thody led the charge'. Heat-seeking missiles will target all but the present tense. The rules of engagement will show that:

1   The past tense is required because the research happened in the past; the passive voice and abstract verbs lend distance from the personal and seriousness to the account.

2   The present tense is required because the research is being reported now and its outcomes will, hopefully, be applied in the future; it lends currency, immediacy and involvement to the account.

By this point in this book, you will know that the choice you make will depend on those guiding principles of:

- *Precedent*. I have yet to read a PhD thesis written in the present tense.
- *Audience*. Those from outside academia would expect the past tense for the research that justifies your recommendations but they will want present or future tenses for guidance on which actions to take.
- *Purpose*. This book, for example, has to combine textbook style guidance with more abstract discussion of the reasons for the guidance, and tenses can vary accordingly.
- *Your personality*. With which tenses are you most comfortable?
- *Practicalities*. The present, active tense uses fewer words than the past, passive. If quoting interview or focus group data verbatim, use the tenses of the original speakers but report speeches in past tenses (Darlington and Scott, 2002: 163).

REFLECTIONS

A noteworthy example of the 'tense' dilemma came in a series of articles that filled a special edition of the *International Journal of Qualitative Studies in Education* (2002, vol. 15, no. 1). The articles were written by university students after a term's full participative, reflexive, ethnographic research with inhabitants of the US/Mexico borders, an intensely emotional experience for the students. They wrote the articles at the poignant time of leaving the worlds in which they had spent the term, to return home. They received no instructions on what tense to utilize; all chose to write in the present tense. The editor – the students' professor – reflected that perhaps 'this choice was each student's response to the urge within that the experience … not be relegated to the past, but carried forth always. Perhaps it was each student's insistence and vow that learning continue' (Swanger, 2002: 9). Nonetheless, the professor-editor 'made the decision to change most of their language into the past tense; after all, they were describing a specific moment in time, one that had definitely passed' (2002: 9).

Was the editor's decision right?

5.3.3.6 *Personal or impersonal?*

If tenses are one of the battlegrounds, the real heat of war focuses on that issue of whether one should or should not employ the personal, first person voice (I, we, you, mine, our, yours) or the impersonal third person voice (it, one).

We, the troops who want you to adopt the impersonal conventions, advise that you will thereby avoid the impression that you are 'subjective and egotistical' (Griffith, 1994: 237). If you are an ethnographer, you will be aware that researchers introduced the impersonal to distinguish your rigorous studies from those of merely observant missionaries and travellers (Richardson, 1998: 353), a distinction you will be happy to continue. You will not want readers to think that any evidence presented is just from your solo, and invalid, personal experiences. In the personal formats, our writing can sound like an elementary school textbook. The impersonal voice was given us by the non-human sciences; transferring it in other disciplines will give our findings strength and certainty.

The alternative army insist that the personal is vital where individual judgement is being expressed or where personal participation in any research is being described, discussed or reported. The revelation of self within the data recognizes that the researcher makes data as well as collecting and selecting them and that the views and experiences of the researcher are as important as the views collected from others. Hence 'the use of the first person has for some time been acceptable and is becoming more so' (Holliday, 2002: 129). The inclusive 'we', 'you' and 'our' acknowledges that the readers' perceptions are an integral part of the sense-making from research outcomes and makes them complicit and supportive of the conclusions.

To negotiate your own peace between the two camps, reflect on the two preceding paragraphs. Did you prefer the one advocating the impersonal (but written in the personal) or the one supporting the personal (but written in the impersonal)?

If you are still uncertain, then combine both – the impersonal for generally agreed facts and the personal where you are expressing opinions. In the 2000s it is sensibly accepted that the two can even appear in the same paragraph, as these two extracts demonstrate:

> Thus, the research proposal is a document which is a product – the end result of a process of planning and designing. As I will stress throughout this book, it is also an argument which needs to have a coherent line of reasoning and internal consistency. (Punch, 2000: 11)

> Museums are important venues in which a society can define itself and present itself publicly. Museums *solidify* culture … The stories I will be telling are stories about power … I will not attempt to force these examples into a single theoretical box. (Dubin, 1999: 3, 4)

Another way to solve the dilemma is to relate voice to research methodology. In action research, for example,

> There is no consensus … A useful guideline in our experience is that if the report contains extensive reflection on the personal learning of the author researcher as agent of the action in the story … then the first-person narrative adds a considerable strength to the published report. Third-person narrative gives a sense of objectivity. (Coghlan and Brannick, 2001: 115)

REFLECTIONS

Compare the two following examples, both from academic journals. Do they support Coghlan and Brannick's views above? Are the voices appropriate for the type of research reported?

The impersonal

> Genetic tools are available for only a few organisms. Double-stranded RNA could conceivably mediate interference more generally in other nematodes … several studies have suggested that inverted repeat structures … are involved in dependent co-suppression in plants. (Fire, Xu, Montgomery, Kostas, Driver and Mello, 1998: 810)

The personal

> At the conference of the Auto/Biography Study Group … Andrew Sparkes presented a paper … Whilst I was thoroughly persuaded by Andrew's argument that autoethnography … is … legitimate … and important … [it] set me thinking … as I was in the early stages of trying to formulate … criteria for assessing autobiographically based creative writing. (Hunt, 2001: 89)

The choice between the first and third person in the above examples was dependent upon the discipline, politics, purpose and audience for the articles. Of these I rate the audience as the most significant since, 'if yours will be academics who think not wearing a skirt or tie a lesser sin than using "I", then act accordingly' (Knight, 2002: 194). If there is a political audience, then an 'I' would prevent any policy influence hopes the researcher might have. If the audience is for a two minute report on local radio, then 'I' is appropriate.

Even this advice is inconclusive since there is always scope to break with precedent. In the highly respected, refereed, academic *Australian Journal of Philosophy* (in which one might expect the conventional, impersonal, third person voice) one article goes way beyond just the personal of the pronouns and subsumes the tone of the language too. A research article on the elusive knowledge of things uses 'we' to refer both to the author and to the expert about whom he is writing and, in some places, to the author and the readers as well, so they will identify with him. Then, at various points, conversationally personal phrases are used such as:

> Hold on, though. If it is our predicament, then you, gentle reader, have no knowledge of things in themselves ... This might just help save your knowledge ... The good news for my reader is ... The ungracious reader may complain that ... Perhaps you had knowledge of things in themselves at the outset. Lucky you. (Langton, 2004: 130, 131, 135)

I personally found myself, a disinterested outsider to philosophy, carried along by these devices and feeling very lucky indeed by the end of the article to have had such an apparently sympathetic guide.

5.4   Review

Writing up research is hard but enjoyable work. Regard it as story telling and don't delay getting started. Maintain momentum by writing something every day, however little. Polish repeatedly as you near the end. Select your conventional or alternative styles and tone in language, tenses and voices according to the precedents, practicalities, people and purposes for whom you are writing, your personality and your research methodology.

Notes

1 Doctoral regulations in the United Kingdom require a candidate first to present a written thesis which will be assessed by two examiners, and secondly to defend this thesis in an oral test, known as a viva (colloquial for Latin *viva voce*). In the viva, the candidate has to defend his/her thesis against stringent questioning from the two examiners. One of the examiners will be an academic from another university who is a specialist in the candidate's field and one will be from the candidate's own university, but neither will have been part of a candidate's supervising team. A senior academic will chair the viva but will not take part in the questioning. The candidate's thesis supervisor can be present at the viva but is not allowed to speak. The viva is an extremely demanding final test. Doctoral vivas are also used in other countries where some universities have followed UK systems, such as Australia, New Zealand and India. In USA-based systems, the oral discussion of an almost finalized thesis between the candidate and the supervisory team is developmental rather than an assessment. Oral 'examinations' are common everywhere in the early stages of doctoral work, where a candidate is called on to defend her/his proposed thesis.

2 UK broadsheets are *The Times*, *The Daily Telegraph*, *The Independent* and *The Guardian*. Although *The Times* and *The Independent* became tabloid in 2004 and *The Guardian* moved to Berliner size in 2005, their style remains unchanged. Equivalents include *The New York Times* and *The Washington Post* (USA), *The Globe and Mail* (Canada), *The Age* (Australia) and *The Times of India*. See *The Guardian Style Book* for further guidance (Marsh and Marshall, 2004).

3 Admit it – for how many of these did you have to consult a dictionary?

Part II Selection and Reduction

6 Primary Data

CONTENTS

6.1   Selection and reduction

Part I covered preparation for research writing. In between Parts I and II lies the research itself – setting up the research instruments, collecting the primary data and analysing it, seeking the literature, and entering the notes on all this into the template established during preparation (2.2.4). From this inevitably large epic, Part II reviews how to select what's appropriate to proving your hypotheses without overwhelming your readers/listeners, exceeding required word limits or compromising the validity of your research. To do this, 6.3 discusses how to use the guiding principles established in Chapter 2, and 6.4 debates categorization. First, however, 6.2 presents a brief digression into the commercialized reduction of research findings.

6.2   How little do you need?

It's challenging to realize that what seems wildly exciting and important to you as the discoverer is not always seen in the same way by your intended audience, nor do they need as much detail as researchers think is vital. Your ability, and willingness, to degrade, summarize or simplify data is therefore an important prerequisite to successful presentation of research.

The advertisement in Figure 6.1 shows how far it is possible to reduce data while still transmitting the principal findings in a way that establishes their validity. All the elements of a conventional research paper are incorporated in this advert – the researcher's credentials, the findings of the research, data from interviews with respondents, how to use the product, the briefest of literature reviews and even the limitations of the research.

Photo of the lead researcher, Winnifred B. Cutler PhD *Photo of hands pouring liquid through a funnel into a vial*	DR. WINNIFRED B. CUTLER • President of Athena Institute • Ph.D., U. Penn. in Biology; Postdoctoral at Stanford • Author of 6 books and 35+ scientific articles • Co-discovered human pheromones in 1986 (*Time* 12/1/86; *Newsweek* 1/12/87)
PHEROMONE DISCOVERER'S FORMULA INCREASES ROMANCE IN YOUR LIFE	
ATHENA PHEROMONE 10X **Unscented aftershave additive for MEN** Text then gives supporting testimony from men who have used the product *Photo of a different bottle and box*	**Add to your aftershave or perfume.** These odourless additives contain synthesized human pheromones. Vials of 1/6 oz, added to 2–4 oz of your fragrance, **should be a 4–6 months' supply.** Increases your attractiveness *Photo of bottle and box*
	ATHENA PHEROMoNE 💟 10 💟 13
	Unscented fragrance additive for women Text then gives supporting testimony for women who have used the product
ATHENA PHEROM💟**ONES:** **The Gold Standard since 1993**	
Products not guaranteed to work for *everybody* (body chemistries differ); will work for *most*. These cosmetics increase attractiveness, not aphrodisiacs. Patents pending. Visit our website Reprinted with permission, Athena Institute, copyright 2004	

Figure 6.1   Illustration of data reduction: extracts from an advertisement for a commercial product developed from research (From NorthWestAirlines World Traveler Magazine, June 2004: 68)

This is not to suggest that all research should be written or presented like advertisements but it demonstrates that a great deal can be conveyed in very few words (and it serves as a reminder that all research is an advert – for you and for your findings – so the ways in which it is written or presented are important). Contrast Figure 6.1 with an extract from the website reporting the research from which the commercial product developed. This gives some indication of the extent to which the data had to be reduced, and also how they have been adapted for different audiences and purposes (Chapters 3 and 4).

> The development of both a men's and a women's formula began with careful planning of research protocols, assembling a team to conduct the first rigorous double blind placebo study in Philadelphia and subsequently two more teams to independently test the women's formula on reproductive aged and postmenopausal women. Importantly, all 3 studies achieved peer-review acceptance and were published in 3 different prestigious scientific journals. The first study on men testing the male pheromone formula (Winnifred B. Cutler, Ph.D., Erika Friedmann, Ph.D., Norma L. McCoy, Ph.D. *Archives of Sexual Behavior* Vol. 27, No. 1, 1998) was followed by two consecutive experiments testing the female formula.
>
> In the first women's study, Dr. Norma McCoy, a distinguished professor of Psychology at San Francisco State University and her graduate student Lisa Pitino investigated 19 to 47 year olds. Dr. McCoy reported that pheromone users got significantly and substantially more sexual attention than placebo users: more sexual intercourse, more hugging/petting/kissing, more sleeping next to a romantic partner, and more formal dates. (Pheromonal Influences on Sociosexual Behavior in Young Women. *Physiology and Behavior* 75 (March 2002) 367–375 Norma L. McCoy, Lisa Pitino). In January 2005, the positive results of the postmenopausal women's experiment were published. (Vol. 41: 372–380, No. 4, November 2004. *The Journal of Sex Research* Pheromonal Influences on Sociosexual Behavior in Postmenopausal Women. Rako, Friebely). (Cutler, 2005)

Dr Cutler's research is also reported in several books and numerous articles. Lest you have ethical concerns (4.6, 8.9, 9.8, 10.5) about my inclusion of a commercial product in this book, I am not receiving commission or samples for using this advertisement.

6.3 Using the guiding principles to select and reduce data

It's unlikely that you will have to reduce your data to quite the extent of the advertisement in 6.2 but you will find that you always produce more than permitted word limits. Jettisoning your precious material can be made a little less painful by following Chapter 2's guiding principles applied below.

6.3.1 Planning

Your template will direct your data to their homebase for answering each element of your research question or hypothesis (2.2.4). You should normally allocate about one-third of the word allowance for the 'findings' but this can vary considerably. Quantitative data normally need far fewer words than do qualitative or narrative data.

For example, in a conference paper of almost 3000 words on the influence of gender on choice of literature in college, all that appeared under the heading of 'Findings' was:

> At an alpha level of .05, an analysis of variance procedure (ANOVA) revealed two inter-action effects. More specifically:
>
> (a) Females rated readings written by other females higher ($M = 18.79$) than those read-ings written by males ($M = 16.58$). Males rated readings written by males higher ($M = 16.61$) as opposed to readings written by female authors ($M = 14.88$).
>
> (b) Expository readings written by female authors ($M = 18.05$) were rated higher than expository readings written by males ($M = 15.88$). In contrast, narrative readings written by males ($M = 17.32$) were rated higher than narratives written by females ($M = 15.01$). (Johnson and Newton, 2003: 7)

The subsequent discussion and conclusion merited around 900 words; the introduction, literature and methodology filled the remainder. In contrast, in a paper of 6000 words, almost 5000 words contained findings, each with discussion built around it. The topic was very wide ranging and needed findings from many sources to validate the title: 'Assessing gender and race in leadership preparation: a retrospective journey along my faultlines' (Rusch, 2003). It was a journey through the many research projects in which this author had been involved.

6.3.2 Precedents

Quantitative data scream for reduction; qualitative and narrative data whisper 'leave everything in' since ethnographers must provide rich pictures. Quantitative, qualitative and narrative data are all, however, subject to the same word limits and various solutions for reduction are possible (Chapters 8, 9 and 10).

6.3.3 Personality

Any researcher wants to include everything that has been found, everything that proves the hypothesis and as little as possible of what does not. You will have to resist all these yearnings in favour of producing a balanced report.

6.3.4 Practicalities

The word 'allowance' is the major determining factor of how much you have to confine data. Write the first draft paying little attention to the word count. After finishing it, then reduce it to the word limit following the techniques proposed in Box 6.1.

Box 6.1   Reducing drafts

➤ Remove subordinate clauses and qualifying words.

➤ Cut sentence length by half.

➤ Reduce paragraphs to one sentence and regroup into new paragraphs.

➤ Eliminate quotations and references that are not absolutely essential.

➤ Eradicate whole paragraphs or sections that are descriptive rather than essential to the progress of the research 'story'.

➤ Convert text to charts, diagrams or tables.

➤ Alter passive to active verbs or vice versa (5.3.3.5), whichever uses fewer words.

➤ Change personal to impersonal or vice versa (5.3.3.6), whichever uses fewer words.

➤ Use appropriate technical terminology (5.3.3.2, 5.3.3.4).

➤ Use a thesaurus to find alternative words; computer ones are adequate but hardcover versions often offer more sophisticated substitutes.

➤ Repeat all these summarizing activities several times as each redraft removes a few more words.

Do not reduce font size (it won't fool anyone) or move material to appendices (11.4).

6.3.5   People

All likely research readers have to restrict reading time (except thesis examiners) and listeners give your presentation close attention for only about twenty minutes. What they most want is summarized findings with enough evidence to give them confidence that your discoveries are justified, ethical, reliable, valid and credible. Audiences from outside academia will want less proof but more discussion of generalizability and transferability (Chapter 3).

6.3.6   Purposes

Answering the research questions (or proving the hypotheses) is the prime purpose for any study and forms the spine in each chapter or section (Chapter 4). To keep this spine in the forefront of your mental processes, put the research questions at the beginning of each chapter. They will then appear in the document map of your chapter which can be displayed concurrently with your text to the left of your PC screen (for Word users, call up the document map from the 'View' menu). As you select and summarize elements of your work, look across to the research questions and ask yourself if what you have selected really does answer the questions. As you write each paragraph, make clear how its contents relate to the research questions. Once the chapter or section is complete, just delete the research questions from the beginning of your text. For those confined to handwriting, or without document mapping, put the research questions on a separate sheet of paper and keep referring to this as you write each section.

REFLECTIONS

Overall, you must show that there is more evidence to prove your answers than there is to disprove them but:

- In academic publications, you must not ignore contradictory elements completely. Academics do not trust tidy proofs; there must be some qualifications (3.4, 5.3.3.1).
- In other publications, readers will be less concerned if you limit data only to those which prove your views (3.5).

6.4 Using categorization to select and reduce data

Selecting from your data requires categorization – deciding which principles/ideas/themes are common amongst your data and then collating your information into these categories. You are looking for recurrent 'general patterns' (Taylor, 2001b: 37). Various possibilities for patterns will surface gradually from the start of your project, as you dialogue with your data (2.2) in 'anticipatory interpretive writing' (Denzin, 1998: 319). Sorting your data thus helps readers make their own analyses and assimilate the data more readily.

For example, researchers grouping data from a study on pedagogy found themselves:

> identifying relevant types across all our data; progressing from primary types (which applied to one case) to secondary (which had more general application); securing a tight fit between typology and data; and resolving contradictory cases ... [maintaining] coherence and connectedness of the categories. (Woods, Jeffrey, Troman, Boyle and Cocklin, 1998: 575)

They could have chosen styles of teaching, types of students, teachers or schools. They eventually categorized by types of teachers according to their differing attitudes to pedagogy.

Categorization can help reduce your data. Aggregating all related data enables you to avoid repetition since only one explanation is needed for each category and only the most effective examples need to be retained. Kelly, for example, in her 2001 study of Roman Catholic mothers in Ireland, avoided quoting long interviews verbatim by classifying data into 'role', 'guilt' and 'opposite sexualities' and then taking relevant extracts from the recorded speeches. She explained that these themes 'were not prede-termined, I decided to separate the data this way having completed the interviews as I was analysing my feelings' (2001: 31). For narrative data, Barnett and Storey's (1999) collection of stories showing how innovation is regarded used dominant meta-narratives as categories. Each was a theme that had emerged from several stories. For these they devised appropriately 'story' type titles such as 'When I came back from Japan' and 'Opportunity stories – Aladdin's lamp'.

Collated data increase the explanatory force of your arguments; you can indicate the most important issues by placing their categories earliest in the findings and by pre-senting the greatest amount of information about these. For example, US research investigating which factors most impacted on states' policy making selected these cate-gories in the following order: 'economic forces' (*c.* 1000 words); 'state constitutional constraints' (*c.* 800); 'an emerging elite ideological consensus' (*c.* 600); 'gubernatorial politics-driving towards the conservative middle' (*c.* 800) (Fusarelli, 2002).

Reduction by categorization can be further enhanced by adopting tabular layouts as shown by the extract in Box 6.2.

Box 6.2   Data categories in tabular form

Extract showing schools' classification in relation to the effectiveness of their governance (Lomotey and Swanson, 1990: 74, part of Table 5.1).

Characteristic	Typical Urban Schools	Effective Urban Schools	Rural Schools
School and District Size	Very large and unwieldy; typically over 1,000	Same as typical urban schools	Small: most high schools less than 400; frequently K-12 configuration
Nature of Pupil Population Cultural diversity of pupils	Highly heterogeneous and increasing	Poor and minority	Tend to be ethnically homogeneous

---

6.4.1   Selecting categories

Box 6.3 offers advice on how to select your categorization.

Box 6.3   Selecting categories for your data

Categories should:

1   Include, and build on to, those used by others in order to help validate your research. Woods et al., for example, used others' 'models and typologies ... as interactive devices to aid the initial analysis' (1998: 575) but used their own classifications for the eventual report. The same use of categories developed by others is similarly acknowledged in Taylor's study on women's views on their places of residence, which divided the findings into two categories 'following Edwards (1997)' (2001b: 37). University theses at any level should particularly follow this advice since humble, neophyte researchers need all the credibility they can muster.

2   Illuminate what you are researching; they must make 'analytical sense' (Mason, 1996: 115). The categories should thus be created around what you want to prove and why the research is worth doing (Punch, 2000: 66). You can, for example, classify by *types of data* (such as questionnaires, interviews), by *types of respondents* (for example Buddhists, Jains, Christians), by *chronological periods* (the order in which the data were collected, or the periods of time to which they relate), by *interpretations from the data* (attitudes of Olympic medal holders to the inclusion of ballroom dancing as an Olympic sport might be anger, disbelief, acceptance, excitement) or by *your reactions to the data* (such as guilt, pleasure, empathy, sympathy).

3   Be as few as possible; brevity lends impact.

4   Be able to absorb virtually all of your data. *But* if a finding does not readily fit any category, you need to decide whether it is atypical and can be abandoned or is sufficiently significant and holistic to be a category on its own. Quantitative researchers are used to ignoring outlying data but qualitative and narrative researchers can use a 'lone voice' legitimately.

5   Be changed or abandoned as your writing reveals what works and what doesn't.

The following example illustrates the advice in Box 6.3 and also shows how different methods of categorization can be used at different stages of a research report. Writing about 'Belonging, identity and third culture kids (TCKs): life histories of former international school students', Fail et al. (2004) grouped the literature around categories established by other researchers: 'sense of belonging'; 'reverse culture shock'; 'identity in TCKs'; 'marginality and identity'. These classified data were followed by substantial extracts from individual life histories without any commentary or linking text. These extracts were organized into categories which reflected the locations of the interviewees but also showed what the researchers felt could be the major influences on interviewees' reactions: 'those living in their passport country'; 'those currently living outside of their passport country'. The final section, which compared literature and primary data, used inferential categories, developed by the researchers, to link the initial and the later data categories: 'encapsulated marginality'; 'constructed marginality'; 'reverse culture shock'.

6.4.2 How do categories emerge?

Simply, you read through your data at any stage – don't wait until they're all in (2.2.1) – and, as recurrent items become evident, you devise, and insert possible titles for any repeated, related material (a 'tag' or 'code'). Use the tags to collate the data. This is neatly termed mining or 'slicing the data' (Mason, 1996: 112). The most basic procedure is just to cut up your pages of notes and shuffle these into packs for each tag. If your computer literacy is basic, then use the 'Find' command ('Edit' menu) to chase up all the material to which you have allocated the same tag and move the text blocks together.

Beyond this, early twenty-first century computer programs are already powerful enough not only to speedily organize your data into your categories but also to suggest categories for you. The list of such computer-assisted qualitative data analysis software is extensive, including NUD*IST (the 2005 version of this is No. 6) NVivo (Gibbs, 2002), Ethnograph, MacSHAPA and many others. Some can cope with multimedia data, some deal with very specific types such as observational data or open-ended survey questions, and some operate for particular disciplines. Each performs a range of text mining and sorting tasks, from simple word sorting counts to annotations, codings, analyses, concept mapping, data visualization, and producing indices and dictionaries. It can't be long before they sing and dance too! Consult the web, and your university's services, for the latest provision. Useful websites I located in 2005 included:

- www.caqdas.soc.surrey.ac.uk
- www.lboro.ac.uk/research/mmethods/research/software
- http://academic.csuohio.edu/kneuendorf/content/cpuca/qtap.htm
- www.qualisresearch.com/main.htm

Such computerization will undoubtedly assist in gaining political acceptance for qualitative data. Before rushing to replace yourself with a robot, however, remember that you have to accept or reject the suggested categorizations.

To do this, I have found it best to start with categories suggested by the literature. Then I keep reading through my data as I collect them, trying initially to fit them into the classifications established from the literature. New categories then emerge as data won't fit and you can see what your research is contributing that is new. You then formulate further categories, some survive, some don't, but you get to know your data well before you make your final selections. Alternatively, Mason (1996: 120) recommends categorizing after all data collection is complete. You then read through it all and take a break before even trying possible data sets.

> **REFLECTIONS**
>
> When writing up each category, ideally put scene setting data first, then the most complex data, and then end with data that give the clearest responses to the hypothesis or question. Finally, discuss the implications of the data unless all discussion is being retained for the conclusions (11.7).

6.5   Review

Only you will cry over what you have had to leave out of your final document or presentation. Your readers and listeners will be delighted that you have met their needs and won't realize that you've deleted material. Years later, when you chance upon your work again, you will agree with the Victorian novelist, Anthony Trollope, that:

> It is indeed a matter of thankfulness that neither the historian nor the novelist hears all that is said by their heroes or heroines, or how would three volumes or twenty suffice! In the present case so little of this sort have I overheard, that I live in hope of finishing my work within 300 pages. (1855: 87–8)

7 Literature and Methodology

7.1 Literature reviews and methodology surveys: definitions

The word 'literature' includes all secondary sources for your research, such as printed texts, film, audio tape, presentations and lectures, paintings, handwritten diaries, archival sources, legislation, websites, artefacts, CDs, DVDs and theses. Such sources provide information related to your research but have not been produced specifically for your current topic. The review is the written summary of these sources. Don't confuse it with the literature survey. This is the seeking out, and listing, of as many sources as possible on which you will need to report in the review. The survey is done as part of the initial proposal for your research project.

The methodology review in reported research provides both:

1 primary data, that is, the record of your own methodology;
2 secondary data from other sources about methodology, which justify what you did and enable comparison with the methodologies of other projects.

The location and extent of your literature and methodology reviews are considered jointly in 7.2. Thereafter, the style for each is separately discussed in 7.3 and 7.4.

7.2 Literature reviews and methodology surveys: locations and extent

Literature and methodology reviews are both vital demonstrations of the validity of your research as justified by secondary data. How much you report of these secondary data will differ according to the purposes and audiences (Chapters 2 and 3) for your document or presentation (Figure 7.1) and because of the varying precedents for particular subjects (2.3.1).

The location of the literature and methodology reviews can vary for different disciplines, as summarized below.

- For empirical social sciences research, and also for some humanities topics, the literature and methodology reviews will appear as sections or chapters early in the finished document.
- Research on literature itself, or humanities topics reliant on literate data sources or theories, or evaluations in any discipline, may have a defined literature review section but may also have the other literature threaded throughout the whole text as it becomes relevant to a particular critique.
- For law, natural and applied sciences, the 'review' is more likely to be found as footnoted references (12.6).
- The review of your methodology is always regarded as very important in the social sciences, almost more so than in the natural sciences from whence experimental methods originated (1.2). I assume this is because social sciences have more varied methods than do other disciplines so it is not possible to take for granted the way in which social science research will be conducted.
- In other disciplines, the extent of the methodology report appears to vary in length according to how far your methodology differs from the expected norm or deals with a specific aspect of it. For example, it would be assumed that law research would study past law and its interpretations in the courts. Hence, this needs only brief comment such as, 'I analyzed this issue by collecting a database of all claims construction appeals to the Federal Circuit from 1996–2000' (Moore, 2001: 4). This author also used a footnote for the methodology which added that 'In 1999, I conducted a survey at the annual conference of the Association of Corporate Patent Counsels' (2001: 4).
- Likewise for history and for canonical literature, the methods of research are relatively obvious. However, you need to specify which particular documents and texts have been consulted. Historians will note from whence they obtained these and their degree of difficulty in doing so. Non-canonical literature may need to add more to the methodology since the reading and methodology will have had to include sources from outside the immediate discipline.

Generalist magazines or newspapers: almost invariably, none

Presentations: usually none or just *passing* references; for an academic audience, methodology and literature should be briefly mentioned and notes on each provided (unless covered in an accompanying conference paper)

Book chapters: a paragraph on methodology and on literature

Books: chapters on both literature and methodology *or* threaded through each chapter as appropriate *or* in appendices

Professional journal articles: a few literature references threaded through the article and occasional references to methodology *or* a separate paragraph at the end of the article (italicized or as an appendix)

Refereed journal articles: a section on both literature and methodology or several substantial paragraphs, normally preceding the findings

Undergraduate theses: short chapters on both literature and methodology, usually preceding the findings

Research reports: both literature and methodology are usually in appendices; if they are in the text, length will vary considerably according to readership

Postgraduate theses: substantial chapters on both literature and methodology, preceding the findings

Figure 7.1   Literature and methodology reviews for different audiences and purposes

7.3   Literature reviews

7.3.1   Purposes

These are defined in Box 7.1.

Box 7.1   Purposes of literature reviews

➤ To justify your research by showing that others have not already researched your topic or researched it in the same way.

➤ To pay homage to those who have gone before you and whose work has influenced your thinking (so include seminal research for academia, bestsellers for publications outside academia, relevant work by your supervisors, friends or thesis examiners for theses and books, and your own previous research in the same field for all documents).

(Continued)

Box 7.1   (Continued)

➤   To demonstrate your analytical and critical skills; the literature review sets the tone for whatever is to come.

➤   To establish the credentials for your research; it's important because others have investigated the same general area.

➤   To reveal current understanding of your topic so you can more easily prove what you have added to this later in your document. Your work will be judged in comparison with that of others, hence the significance of the literature.

➤   To explain the emergence of your research topic and data gathering methods.

➤   To show how you generated your conceptual framework.

➤   To provide a general overview of the area of your research (therefore use as many sources as possible; don't rely on just a few).

7.3.2   When to start writing the literature review

The conventional approach is not to design the research instruments, finalize the research questions or start collecting the data until after a first draft of the literature review is written. An alternative approach is similar, in that you will be writing from the start (2.2.1) and most of your early writing will be about the literature. You will, however, pursue an interactive process, letting ideas develop as you relate to the literature. My approach has had to be a practical combination of the two: I start my writing with notes on whatever sources I have, adding to this as I access new sources. During this time, the methodology emerges and data gathering commences but I also keep reading and writing. Often, the final source may be added the day before a document is completed. Much depends simply on how quickly I can obtain sources through the web, library and inter-library loans.

7.3.3   Style for literature reviews

Examples of appropriate style can be found every day in newspaper arts pages which carry reviews of films, books and other media. *The New York Times* book review section, for example, carried Stephen Burt's review of recently published poetry (2004). His audience would be expert poets and less specialized readers. He reviewed eight books, providing a neat synopsis and an in-built, tactful commentary, as this extract demonstrates:

> Laura Kesischke's poems probe the lives of supposedly ordinary women … Brian Blanchfield's [poems] appear at first to depict nothing at all. Then they come into focus and portray a life … Jean Valentine's … preoccupations include religious mysticism… imprisonment, mourning, maternal care and erotic experience … If Bang's weaker poems

fly apart into unrelated quips, the stronger ones speed from odd sights into pithy hypotheses ... Mark Nowak's terse reactions sometimes sound shrill ... The best segments though, make ... elegant stanzas. (2004: 6)

This style is restrained, calm, justified, appropriate to its audience and a good guide for the style you are trying to attain. You can be much more trenchant than this in more populist media (5.3.3.4, *vide* Falco) and when you have your tenure and professorship (2.3.1).

7.3.4   Organizing the literature review

The process is:

Record ➲ *Summarize* ➲ *Integrate* ➲ *Analyse* ➲ *Criticize*

Each of these is discussed below.

7.3.4.1   *Record*
Immediately you start making notes from any source:

> Put all the information about that source into your bibliography file, and insert the same details in your notes, including precise page references.

(For visual media, such as films, you have to provide a detailed description of the scene since there are no numbers to guide the readers.)

Should you fail to do this, you will find, when you finalize your academic script, that the most wonderful quotation that you wanted to use has no page reference. You must therefore abandon it, paraphrase it, or spend hours searching through the source cited to find the quotation again. You will remember that it is on a left-hand page, about halfway through, at the top, next to a table – but it will mysteriously have disappeared. If you risk quoting it without the page reference, it will be spotted by those eagle-eyed reviewers of 3.4. They will also spot if you have failed to provide all the necessary details of your source in the bibliography (12.3) and you will return to the web or your helpful university librarian to, once again, seek out the absent information – time consuming activities. You will also need all your references for later research so always keep full details.

7.3.4.2   *Summarize*
You want to capture the essence of the findings of the sources you have selected and their relationships to your research.

First, make only minimal notes on each of the sources you read/watch/listen to. When making notes on any single source, you should aim to make no more than:

- one paragraph if the material is for a thesis (*c*. 150 words);
- one sentence if you are writing or presenting in any other format (20–30 words).

This applies whether your source is a book of 1000 pages or a page of 1000 words. Why?

A doctoral candidate reading 100+ books plus articles and other sources, and taking even the minimal notes recommended above, could quickly gather 15,000 words for the literature review chapter alone – and that is before you have started analysing the books and adding your own critique (for other postgraduates about 50+ sources; undergraduates about 25+ sources). For a doctoral thesis you should allow about 7000 words for the chapter on literature (progressively fewer for masters and undergraduate dissertations), so even with the shortest notes there is still almost double what will be needed. For academic book chapters, research reports and articles you will have 5000–7000 words for the whole finished piece; all other formats average about 2500 words. The number of these words that you can allocate to the literature review is therefore few.

Secondly, when making the notes:

- *either* write them in your own words (that way you avoid plagiarism and you commence your own interaction with the information, which is a precursor to successful analysis and critique);
- *or* if copying the original verbatim, put it in your notes in quotation marks (that way you remember that you have to paraphrase it into your own words when you write your final version or, if you are retaining it verbatim, that you need to cite the source).

Thirdly, when building the final literature review from your notes, you can expect to be able to reduce it by a maximum of two-thirds of its length by summarizing (Box 6.1).

Summarizing on its own is the simplest, but most boring, form of literature review. It's effectively a listing of who said what, one source after another, with some comparisons implied. It's acceptable for undergraduate dissertations and is useful in articles in which you can devote only a few hundred words to the literature review. The following example from an academic journal illustrates the summary style:

> A fundamental question regarding teaching professional ethics is can ethics actually be taught? Peppas and Diskin (2001) in a study of the attitudes of university students regarding professional and business ethics concluded that ethics teaching appeared not to promote significant differences in ethical values compared with students who had not been taught ethics. However, Clarkeburn (2002) and Haydon (2000) argued that ethics should be taught because ... Waldman (2000) stated that because all mature professions have a well-developed code of ethics, this should ... In terms of how to include ethics teaching within the curricula, Krawczyk (1997) described three approaches ... [and] concluded that formal lecturing did not appear to stimulate the development of moral judgement ... Wright (1995) identified a number of factors that may have an impact on the effectiveness of ... (Taylor et al., 2004: 44)

> **REFLECTIONS**
>
> Don't allow the literature review to overwhelm your document or presentation just because you've kept so many notes that you can't bear to jettison them. You need all the space you can get to write/talk about *your* research rather than other people's.

7.3.4.3   Integrate

Summary needs the added sophistication of integration to gain good marks at under-graduate level. For postgraduate work, integration is a requirement, though it is only the first building block for doctoral theses, books and research reports. In more populist writing, integration is vital; the brief literature references will be collated, often without attribution, and prefaced by a phrase such as, 'Many writers agree that ... '.

Integration requires that each source cited should be collated into categories with other related literature (6.4). In articles, it is better to keep the integrated categories as individual paragraphs without subheads. Subheads disturb the flow for readers and can also give the impression that you don't believe your readers are capable of following the main issues without major signposts.

For example, in the article on teaching business ethics quoted in 7.3.4.2 (Taylor et al., 2004), the summary was followed by other literature organized into the categories of:

- Ethical problems faced by IT practitioners in IT practice.
- Range of individuals/organizations potentially affected by the actions of an IT practitioner.
- IT practitioners' responsibilities to employers, professional bodies and law enforcement bodies.
- Societal and cultural perspectives on ethical behaviour related to IT.
- Perspectives on IT attitudes.

Each of these subheads announced only single paragraphs averaging eleven lines. Each heading was in bold font at least two sizes greater than the text. The result was an erudite article with less than erudite visuals which disconnected the flow of thought.

In theses or dissertations, which have ample space for literature reviews, categories can usefully be first presented in lists which can be discussed fully later in the chapter. The extract below, which illustrates this, is a list from a masters degree thesis:

Creating teams

(i)   Team members to have a clear sense of self ... (Katzenbach and Smith, 1993: 12).

(ii)   Team members must understand what the rest of the team can contribute... (Katzenbach and Smith, 1993: 45).

(iii) A team must recognise where skills are lacking (Katzenbach and Smith, 1993: 139).

(iv)   ...

Conflict in teams

(i) Teams must use conflict as a learning tool (Sessa, 1996; McDaniel et al., 1998).

(ii) Conflict must be handled [constructively] ... (Rayeski and Bryant, 1994).

(iii) Conflict well handled can generate new ideas ... (Bowditch and Buono, 1997).

(iv) Conflict can be an indicator of team growth (Drinka, 1985).

(v) ...

(Horsley, 2003: 29, 30)

REFLECTIONS

In the first of the above two lists, the researcher has made the mistake of relying too much on one pair of authors. The second list asserts authority for each category by citing several authors and the sources are books, refereed journal articles and conference papers. Such variety would impress a thesis examiner (3.4.2).

7.3.4.4 Analyse

Analysis is the division of information into its constituent parts so that the relationships amongst the parts are evident (categorization, 6.4). Within each category, the sources you cite are then discussed around various themes such as:

- *Context*. This example, from a PhD submission, shows how the researcher used literature to link his study to its time period:

  The central contention is that ... the creation and application of ... standards presented a series of 'opportunities and dilemmas' (Bolam, 1997: 278) [during] the latter part of the twentieth century [which] launched a still continuing revolution in education in England (Thody, 2000). (Brundrett, 2003: 10, 14)

- *Generalized terminology and/or theories*. For example, from a refereed journal article:

  We need to focus upon the ideology of male sexual needs (Mary McIntosh, 1978) ... We need to explore masculinities ... [including] an analysis of the masculinist state tied to the capital accumulation process on the one hand and the myth of democratic legitimation on the other (see O'Neill, 1994). (O'Neill, 1996: 9)

- *Specific results from previous research*. What was investigated and how? What were the outcomes? What samples were used? Were the results supported by the evidence? Were any inadequacies acknowledged? For example, in a refereed journal article on intellectual property law we learn from the text and its accompanying footnotes that:

> Surprisingly little attention has been given to the public domain ... in the scholarly literature (3), at least until recently (4).
>
> ──────────
>
> (3) In an 1981 essay by Professor Lange, he argued that the growth of intellectual property ... has been uncontrolled ... Almost a decade earlier ... Jessica Litman, *The Public Domain*, 39 EMORY L.J. 965 [1990] provocatively [noted that] copyright law is based on ... the notion that authors create something from nothing...
>
> (4) See papers presented at the Conference on the Public Domain, Nov. 9–12, 2001, Duke University School of Law, http://james-boyle.com/papers.pdf.
>
> (Oddi, 2002: 1–4)

- *Relationships amongst previous studies.* How do they compare or contrast with each other? Did they use similar concepts, terminology, methods? Which were seminal? For example, in a refereed journal article we find that:

> It is a virtue of intrinsic properties that things affect other things. This is a widely held view in contemporary metaphysics [Jackson et al., 1982; Armstrong, 1983; van Cleave, 1995] and it is shared by Lewis himself. (Langton, 2004: 130)

- *Relationship to your research.* How do they differ? This might be in methods, philosophical base, sample, focus or results. For example, in an academic monograph:

> One ... important point of difference between our study and that of Buckler and Zien is worth noting ... they follow the path of students of symbols, myths and challenge change ... Our approach is different in that we focussed on story-telling. (Barnett and Storey, 1999: 7)

The following two examples are categorized, analytical reviews demonstrating various of the organizing themes from the above list.

Extract 1

From a chapter about animals' spatial recognition (discussing an experiment with rats) in a book about spatial research paradigms in psychology.

> The task, invented by Richard Morris [the Morris maze] (Morris, 1981), was a perfectly timed answer to the methodological needs generated by the publication of a theory (O'Keefe and Nadel, 1978) that, after Tolman (1948), claimed that ... At that time, most of the research about place learning was conducted in complex mazes ... (see Olton, 1977) ... Theoretically, ... subjects ... can memorise a direction relative to a major landmark ... (Poucet, 1985). The 'Morris maze' has been widely used ... More than 350 references with this single key phrase can be found for the last five years! ... It would be pointless to try to review all these experiments ... A purely methodological description can be found in Morris (1984), Sutherland and Dyck (1984), Stewart and Morris (1993) or Hodges (1996). The basic features ... [are] in an exhaustive review by Brandels, Brandys and Yehuda (1989). (Schenk, 1998: 146)

Extract 2

From a book about the settings of Hollywood films.

> Victor Perkins' work (1972; 1990) is helpful in setting out clearly the terms of the debate and its relevance to the analysis and understanding of films. For a contrasting view see Bordwell (1989), with whom Perkins takes issue. (Thomas, 2001: 7)

7.3.4.5 Criticize

Criticism is at the heart of academic writing since you are evaluating other people's ideas and your own. Box 7.2 defines criticism.

Box 7.2   Criticism in literature reviews

- Asks 'what lies underneath appearances … whose interests are served and in what ways by policies, practices, customs or discourses' (Knight, 2002: 12).
- Involves giving credence to other arguments and showing how much support there is for views other than your own.
- Is usually tactful, not destructive, with criticisms well supported by evidence. Criticism is confined to substance not the researcher's personality. You can only stop being tactful when you are well established and relish the headlines that come from an academic 'slanging match'.
- Is 'about joining in a wider research debate with others whom you may never meet' (Blaxter et al., 2001: 230) but who comprise your virtual research community.
- Is positive and appreciative as well as negative and disapproving.
- Is sceptical in attitude, based on reasoned doubt about your findings and those of others.

The normative words I have emphasized in the following example show a way to incorporate tactful, positive and comparative criticism as Box 7.2 suggests. The extract is from a refereed journal article on Dutch colonial expansion in the nineteenth century:

> So far, not much attention has been paid to the ideas of Daniel R. Headrick … Central to his *well-known The Tools of Empire: Technology and European Imperialism in the Nineteenth Century* is the *assertion* that European imperialism resulted from a combination of appropriate motives and adequate means … coupled with new technological means … Headrick's technological dimension is a *welcome* addition to the imperialism debate, especially since the motives for expansion have been … *given undue attention* [in other works] … Stressing the equal importance of the means of expansion *seems to be particularly relevant* to the Dutch case. (Bossenbroek, 1995: 27, my emphases)

7.4 Methodology surveys

Methodology surveys always give the impression that the research design followed a calm, linear and orderly development from your initial idea, its determining philosophy, choice of methods, design of research instruments, data collection, data analysis, through to its final resting place in a document or presentation. This tidiness is dictated by 'the conventions of academic writing which in all fields tend to obscure the muddled and makeshift nature of what really happens' (Hammersley, 1993: 146). The conventions that bring such order out of chaos entail writing to meet the purposes in appropriate style (7.4.1, 7.4.2, 7.4.3) and organizing the contents, length and location (7.4.4).

7.4.1 Purposes of methodology surveys

Methodology surveys should demonstrate your methods:

- *Validity*. Show their foundation in 'truth' (or received wisdom) through their justification in other literature and similar research projects.
- *Applicability*. Indicate how far the methodology is generalizable.
- *Reliability*. Demonstrate that you 'have not invented or misrepresented your data, or been careless or slipshod in your recording or analysis … [you] must therefore include an explanation of why it is that the audience should believe it to be … accurate' (Mason, 1996: 146).
- *Credibility*. Prove this by showing that other researchers have used similar methods to yours *or* that you have built on other researchers' methods *or* that you have a reasoned defence for not replicating previously successful methods.
- *Replicability*. Include enough detail to enable other researchers to check your findings by repeating the method.
- *Attraction*. Give readers a feel for what it was like to be the researcher (particularly important in alternative styles).
- *Limitations*. Humbly admit to a few difficulties but don't undermine your research by overwhelming self-criticism.

7.4.2 Template for methodology surveys

Box 7.3 Template for methodology reviews

RESEARCH OVERVIEW

The summary of your whole research process

⇓ Then discuss each element of the overview, normally in the following order. ⇓

(Continued)

Box 7.3 (Continued)

PARADIGM(S)

This is the dominant attitude(s) (value, belief, philosophy, overarching conception, epistemology or ontology) which has influenced the way in which your research has been undertaken (see also 2.3.2), such as:

PERIODS: *modernism (structuralism, positivism); postmodernism (poststructuralism, postpositivism).*

POLITICAL: *democratic, socialist, communist, anarchist.*

RELIGIOUS: *Judaism, Christianity, Sikhism, atheism.*

SOCIAL: *feminism, hierarchical, class analyses.*

ECONOMICS: *postcolonial, managerialist, socialist, capitalist.*

ORGANIZATIONAL: *behaviouralist, power analyses.*

VOCATIONAL: *grounded or craft theory.*

EPISTEMOLOGICAL *(concerning the nature and forms of knowledge)*
    either (1) objective, hard, tangible, known
    or (2) subjective, soft, intangible, experienced.

ONTOLOGICAL *(concerning the nature of being)*
    either (1) social reality as external to an individual (positivism)
    or (2) social reality as the product of individual consciousness (phenomenology)

⇓ ⇓ ⇓ **Paradigms influence your choices of** ⇓ ⇓ ⇓
⇓

METHODOLOGY(IES)

This is the approach(es) you have chosen for data collection, such as:

INDIVIDUAL: *narrative or biographical, or single person, incident, law, book or visual media.*

SMALL SCALE: *case study, action research, problem solving, limited experiments or quasi-experiment, grouped-historical incidents, legal precedents, works within a canon of literature, evaluative review.*

LARGE SCALE: *survey, experiments or quasi-experiments, long time spans.*

Within the above choices of research project size, you will need to describe:

1 *the population (universe) from which (or whom) you have selected your sample:*
2 *how and why the sample was selected and accessed;*
3 *where the research was located and why;*
4 *whether or not the research is ethnographic, historical, descriptive, correlational, evaluative, longitudinal (at timed intervals), snapshot (at one time only), post facto (looking back at an already completed event) or ab initio (researching a project from its real-time inception);*
5 *how you have dealt with issues of ethics, bias, objectivity, triangulation.*

Box 7.3   (Continued)

⇓ ⇓ ⇓ Methodologies influence your choices of ⇓ ⇓ ⇓

TECHNIQUES/INSTRUMENTS

These are some of the techniques you may have chosen for data collection, such as:

READING and reviewing literature and other secondary sources.

ASKING through questionnaires, focus groups, personal interviews, diaries.
OBSERVING as either participant, semi-participant or non-participant.
EXPERIMENTING or quasi-experimenting.

⇓ ⇓ ⇓ Techniques/instruments are assisted by ⇓ ⇓ ⇓

TOOLS

Such as software for setting up research methods (like designing questionnaires), for analysis of qualitative data (6.4.2) or quantitative data (such as MATLAB, SPSS and many more; An excellent survey of these can be found at http://members.aol.com/johnp71/javastat.html, accessed 2005).

Box 7.3 provides a template for a methodology review. Set it up as you commence your research and fill it in as you progress. Your methodology plans, and the literature that justifies them, will be the first inserted. You then show how they worked in practice once you've used the methodology to collect your data. For thesis writers, this should mean that your methodology chapter can be submitted for review by your supervisors while you are writing up the findings from the data.

7.4.3   Style for methodology surveys

Exciting, fascinating or elegant are not words I can use for the style of written methodology surveys. They tend inexorably to the pedantic and dull but this seems to be the price of rigour and comprehensiveness. The two extracts below meet all the requirements for the comprehensive overview which should commence any methodology review (Box 7.3). Writing them gives the satisfaction of completing a 10,000 piece jigsaw; it's a lovely picture at the end, but aren't you glad it's finished?

> The study population consisted of all students enrolled in English 101 courses ... The sampling procedure included dividing the state [country] into four regions ... The sample size for this study was determined by performing a power analysis according to procedures recommended by Cohen ... The parameters for the power analysis were (a) specified level for power (power = .80), (b) defined level of significance (alpha = .05), and (c) a desired small-to-medium effect (d = .25) ... The results of the power analysis indicated that a minimum sample of 136 was needed. (Johnson and Newton, 2003: 6)

Underlying this study ... is the premise that the story-form is the dominant sense-making tool for school administrators ... We have examined how school leaders learn to think together ... how story-forms shape meanings for groups of people ... Case studies have their roots in a perspective well articulated by John Dewey ... A theoretical and practical framework for our study draws ... on the work of C. Roland Christensen of the Harvard Business School ... In addition we have been aided by the work of [name] on dialogue, of [name] on problem-based learning...[and] of [name] on critical conversation. (Ackerman and Maslin-Ostrowski, 1996: 1–2)

7.4.4   Organizing the methodology survey

7.4.4.1   Contents
In a thesis or a book which permits a lengthy survey, you ideally include all the relevant elements from Box 7.3. For other formats with a shorter methodology survey (Figure 7.1) you summarize and select items as appropriate to the intended audience, your purposes and the practicalities and precedents for your research topic (Chapters 2–4).

For each element of Box 7.3:

- describe what you planned to do;
- justify these plans from research methodology literature and from methodologies used in other research projects in the same area as yours; for doctoral theses, explain also why you have rejected other possibilities.
- describe what happened when you collected your data (how far did they accord with your plans?);
- discuss the advantages and disadvantages of what happened, and how you might amend the research methodology if you were to repeat the project.

If your research included a pilot, then you deal with each element as above for the pilot, ending with decisions on what amendments you made for the full study. You then repeat the process for the methodology of the full project.

7.4.4.2   Length
As Figure 7.1 summarized, the further removed you are from an academic audience, the more likely is the method to be dealt with briefly. In a thesis or book of about 80,000 words for a specialized academic audience, you should anticipate devoting 5000–10,000 words to the methodology review. You will need much more detail than you could ever have imagined possible in order to make the methodology clear to readers unacquainted with your research.

For example, the following two extracts show how the brevity of a first PhD draft had to be extended:

All of the research projects selected for review [in this chapter] ... are claimed to be in naturalistic or natural settings ... some restriction may have occurred in placing children in specifically requested groups as described by Miell and MacDonald (2000) but data collection took place in as near to natural settings as was humanly possible. (Mugglestone, 2004: 14)

The extended version was:

> All of the research projects selected for review [in this chapter] ... are claimed to be in naturalistic or natural settings though none was entirely in normal timetabled lessons which form the natural setting for this research. Miell and MacDonald admit that some restriction may have occurred in placing children in specifically requested groups but they felt that data collection took place in as near to natural settings as was humanly possible. Their methodology and results therefore form an important comparison with this research but it is important to bear in mind that no alterations in the normal classroom settings, anticipated groups or timetable were made for the children studied for this project (2004: un-numbered)

For documents other than theses or academic texts, the length of the methodology survey will vary wildly but generally seems to attract less attention than the literature, findings or conclusions (unless the document is specifically related to methodology).

For example, in a paper discussing the practical value of leadership academies, the methodology review occupied 600 of the 3500 words – two sides (Lawler, Martin and Agnew, 2003). Under the banner of 'Research Design and Methodology', the authors subheaded 'Participants' (300 words) and 'Data Collection, Instrumentation and Data Analysis' (300 words) (2003: 10–12). The literature review absorbed about 2000 words while the preliminary findings had only 300 words (since the work was at an early stage of development and not all data were gathered). Compare that with this extract from another paper in which the much shorter research methodology review flowed without subheads.

> The sample consisted of 80 graduate students enrolled in ... masters and doctoral programs across three universities. Students were dispersed across five classes ... We chose a qualitative approach because ... With permission, many groups of students ... were audio-taped and/or observed. We also assembled a portfolio ... Given the importance of using multiple data sources, we additionally asked participants to complete a simple questionnaire that asked open-ended questions ... In order to triangulate data further, semi-structured interviews were conducted ... [All of these] were analyzed and coded looking for patterns and inconsistencies across respondents ... This study does not permit generalizations ... but rather provides rich details. (Ackerman and Maslin-Ostrowski, 1996: 2)

Even more of a contrast appears in an article of almost 8000 words (a historical study of the outcomes for policy making of gubernatorial changes in US states). The research methodology occupies approximately five lines and a footnote (Fusarelli, 2002: 141–2, 157). Such brevity can be accounted for in academic articles since authors often 'twin track' the data to produce more publications by writing one devoted to methodology only (14.1, item 12).

REFLECTIONS

Lewis-Beck et al. (2004: 461) noticed that qualitative researchers generally describe their methodology in less detail than do quantitative researchers. I have noticed the reverse, but equal attention should be given to the methodology whatever the form of data collection. Variations in length should be to accord with audience needs and the purposes of your document.

7.4.4.3 Location

The more you write, or present for, audiences outside academia, the more likely is your research methodology to be cited inconspicuously. Even for academic audiences, it may not be prominent unless their interest is likely to be focused on methodology.

For example, Dubin's (1999) book on controversies in American museum history has the methodology inserted after the conclusions and before the notes. The methodology consists of the list of the interviews from which he gathered his data with only the following minimal information:

> All the interviews were conducted by the author. Over two-thirds of them were face-to-face; the remainder were by telephone. They ranged in length from approximately three-quarters to over three hours. All were tape recorded and transcribed, except for two. Any unattributed quotes in the text derive from these interviews. Briefer telephone conversations were held with other individuals, and are duly noted. Identifying information reflects each interviewee's status or position at the time they spoke with the author.
>
> Benny Andrews, artist and community activist, May 8, 1997
> Anonymous member of Ad Hoc Committee of Concerned Irish-American New Yorkers, October 23, 1997
> Stephen P. Aubin, Director of Communications, Air Force Association, April 2, 1998 ...
>
> (Dubin 1999: 247)

I have used the ends of books similarly. My 1997 book on leadership in education has the research methodology as a 6000 word appendix, and this book likewise has a methodology Appendix of 1000 words (Chapter 17). While a journal editor, I asked contributors to put a brief summary of their methodology in italics in a separated paragraph at the ends of articles because the mainly professional readership would regard methodology as much less important and interesting than the findings but would need proof that an author's views were justified. Even in refereed journal articles, I like to reverse the conventional order and leave the methodology until the end. I will, however, warn readers that this is what I am doing. Hence, on the first page of my article on nineteenth century history, I noted that: 'The sources used are discussed in the methodology section at the end of the article' (Thody, 1994b: 355). Without this warning, reviewers could reject an article without even reading the whole (3.4.4, 3.4.5).

The methodology can otherwise be tucked away at the beginning of a book. For example, in a history of swearing there is just a short section amongst the opening materials:

> Sources and Abbreviations – This study is, of necessity, heavily dependent on the master-work on semantic change in English, *The Oxford English Dictionary (OED)*. For economy of reference, a raised 'O' is used to refer to the main dictionary (1884–1928) ... This acknowledgement of logophiliac dependence is in no way intended to implicate any Oxford lexicographer in the inferences and conclusions which follow. (Hughes, 1998: un-numbered)

Likewise, in a university monograph aimed at US school principals and discussing suitable ways to develop education leaders in practice, the authors described the methodology on a separate page before the main text started. Thus it could safely be igored by practising school principals but could be seen by other university academics while also being available should the principals be interested (Leading for Learning, 2003: 4).

The most conventional placement is to collate all the research methodology in one section before the findings are presented but it can equally successfully be threaded throughout a document.

For example, in a paper whose title mixes media 'savvy' with academic respectability, 'Prostitution, feminism and critical praxis: profession prostitute?' (O'Neill, 1996), the methodology appears in brief, disaggregated sections during the article without the usual signpost of 'Research methodology' heading a single segment. Hence, on p. 1, paragraph one we find out the method and the instruments:

> 'Making out' in prostitution will be explored through excerpts from life history narratives conducted with female prostitutes between 1990 and 1994. These narratives focus on …

Two paragraphs later, we learn the research philosophy: 'This essay … is rooted in feminist participatory action research' which is then explained in that and a subsequent paragraph. Page 4 reveals that some of the data came from attending the 1991 1st European Whores Congress in Frankfurt am Main, Germany, and we catch up on the 1993 'Soliciting for Change' conference in Nottingham, England on p. 5. Page 6 includes a brief evaluation of ethnography. Suddenly, amidst the data on p. 8, we discover that, in addition to the life history narratives, other data came from hand transcribed quotations gathered at a discussion in the spring months of 1993. That is the entire methodology. Did you want more? Only if you are researching the same area and, if so, you can contact the author.

Another 'threading' device involved a brief outline in the first paragraph of an article with pointers to later expansion of items where they became relevant:

> Ethnography is a research methodology originally developed in anthropology which involves participation in and observation of particular cultural groupings (see below). Science and Technology Studies comprise a field of sociological research particularly focussed on relations between people and technology (see The analysis of strategy below). (Neyland and Surridge, 2003: 9)

Such 'threading' devices should be more common in alternative styles than in the conventional. In the former, the researcher is meant to be part of the research. Academic audiences, however, still expect a clearly delineated methodology section and its omission would limit your chances of publication (Chapter 14).

7.5   Review

Adopting the techniques of 7.3, assess the appropriateness of the following mythical literature reviews on this book:

1 A postgraduate thesis

Thody's (2006) early twentieth century proposals for widening the choices of writing formats for research have been criticized as 'unwieldy' for low ability students tested in 2010 (Boring et al., 2011; 21), though they found a welcoming audience amongst students of all abilities in the natural sciences research conducted by Tedious (2009). One needs to consider, however, that Thody's views at least accord with those of Rigorous (2014) and her opportunity sample of her colleagues and students showed an ideal way to test ideas.

2 A practitioner, polemical journal

Thody's (2006) unwieldy proposals for widening the choices of writing formats for research were clearly an attempt to pander to the low abilities of students entering our universities in the early twentieth century.

3 A generalist magazine

The early twentieth century produced a well-justified clamour for better research writing.

4 A newspaper

Right about Writing.

To put into practice the proposals I made in 7.4, the research methodology for this book is in the Appendix (Chapter 17). Does it meet the purposes suggested in 7.4.1?

Part III Production

8 Quantified Data

8.1 Quantified data presentation: purposes

Table 8.1 Purposes of quantified data writing and presentation (version 1)

Overt	%	Covert	%
Facilitates comparisons	33	Lends numerical weight to findings	14.4
Increases chances of the research having policy impact	10.2	Projects an aura of scientific respectability	23
Visually demonstrates the generalizability of phenomena	11	Minimizes apparent researcher impact	0.2

Survey evidence: $N = 13$, postgraduate management research students,1999, Lincoln University, England; opinions collected from open-ended discussion during the author's class on presenting quantitative data as part of a second semester programme on research methodology; the discussion was tape recorded for later analysis; the class was on a Wednesday afternoon on a chilly day; the author determined the categories that emerged from the data; the results were not further discussed with the students.

Did you read the explanatory small print under Table 8.1?

If not, it alerts you to one of the challenges in the presentation of quantitative data: few readers are interested in the small print. You therefore have to decide how much such notation you will include in explanations directly attached to tables and which of the information you will transfer to the main text.

Once you have read the information under Table 8.1, you'll be aware of the other questions it raises:

- Did the notes alter your opinion of the validity of the Table 8.1 data?
- Was there sufficient, too little or too much explanation for the sources of data and their method of collection?
- Should the explanation be above or below the table and should it be in a larger font and the same style as the table?
- Do you need to know if the discussion took place before, during or after the class on presenting quantitative data?
- Which is more memorable – the table or the notes?

The table itself poses yet more dilemmas:

- Should the table have been a bar chart?
- Should the 0.2 per cent category have been omitted as too insignificant?
- Should the figures have been rounded down?
- Are each of the purposes self-explanatory or should there be more explanation for each category?

REFLECTIONS

What would have been the impact of the data in Table 8.1 if they had been conveyed only as extracts from the conversation they quantified?

8.2 Quantified data presentation: the challenges

Table 8.1 and its subsequent questions introduce challenges for quantitative formatting which are each discussed in this chapter:

- Quantified formatting is often assumed to be confined to quantitative data but qualitative and narrative data can also be presented figuratively (8.3).
- Quantification obviously reduces data but you need to avoid both too much reduction and too little (8.4).
- The extent to which you influence readers' inferences from your data will be affected by how you choose to display it and by the text that accompanies the quantified formats (8.5).
- The quantified data may need supporting proof from raw data, mathematical workings and statistical techniques to demonstrate how you gathered and reduced your data, found correlations and established the robustness of your findings (8.6).
- Language and style in quantitative presentations require as much attention as in qualitative or narrative presentations (8.7).

- Ethics need consideration because research proved numerically appears to have unassailable realism and certainty. Most readers are only too ready to believe figures even if they are poorly presented or inaccurate (deliberately or accidentally) (8.8).
- The appearance and placement of quantified data affect readers' interest and comprehension of your data (8.9 and commentaries throughout this chapter).

8.3 Qualitative and narrative data quantified

Categorizing of qualitative data works on the quantitative principle that the more data there are for a particular category, the stronger is the proof of that category (6.4). Some qualitative researchers would regard this inference as inappropriate (Mason, 1996: 118) and some quantitative researchers would see the small scale surveys and case studies of the social sciences as too statistically insignificant to make quantification worthwhile (Table 8.1 could be criticized for this). However it is viewed, once categorization is done, then the decision needs to be taken on how far the data in each category can be displayed quantitatively.

Journals such as *Historical Methods: A Journal of Quantitative and Interdisciplinary History* demonstrate that quantification is valid as methodology for subjects not normally associated with sciences or mathematics. Its topics are selected because quantification is deemed to be the best method for data collection as well as presentation. Volume 37, no. 1, 2004, for example, has articles on 'Multilevel modelling for historical data: an example from the 1901 Canadian Census', 'The size of horses during the Industrial Revolution' and 'Integration of specificity variation in cause-of-death analysis'.

Such types of data reduction can be especially helpful in conveying great sweeps of history. Table 8.2 is an extract from a figure covering the period from before 1200 to the present with simple, descriptive statistics. The data categorized colloquial terminology for women, showing when each term was dominant. Through the 800 years, 117 terms were followed, of which just five are reproduced here.

Other forms of data collected qualitatively can also be considered for quantitative treatment. For example, 'standardized, structured interviews may yield numerical data that may be reported succinctly in tables and graphs' (Cohen et al., 2000: 286). Data from qualitative observations can be reported in simple quantified forms which can greatly speed readers' assimilation of data and reduce the potential boredom of long, qualitative passages. For example, from a nine year longitudinal observation study of nine chief education officers (CEOs) which I conducted, I produced copious notes detailing their every activity every minute of their day for thirty-six days.[1] Quantifying and tabulating some of these data in simple, descriptive statistics made changes over time, and comparisons amongst the CEOs, much more apparent than they would have been in text, as Table 8.3 demonstrates.

8.4 Reduction

When there are figures to report, it is easy to assume that the best way to reduce them is to use tables, figures or graphs. These formats for presenting quantitative data are,

Table 8.2   Extract to illustrate quantified reduction of historical and literary data: the incidence of terminological categorizations of women (Figure 10.3 in Hughes, 1998: 213–15)

	1200	1300	1400	1500	1600	1700	1800	1900
Witch								
... Wench								
... Gossip								
... Darling								
... Maiden								

Key: a solid bar indicates the historical extent of the present dominant meaning; a slashed bar indicates the period when the term in question was not exclusively feminine in application ... a dotted bar indicates a neutral or favourable sense of the word over the period demarcated.

My commentary
Table 8.2 is a good example of how to translate the qualitative to the quantitative, though its actual presentation raised some problems. The original figure stretched across three pages but the key could only be viewed on the first of these three. It needed to be at the bottom of each page to facilitate assimilation. The author stated that the choice of italics for some words (as for '*witch*' above) could be found earlier in the text. This assumes that all readers will have followed the book in the same linear fashion and would remember on which page the explanation occurred.

however, 'non-discursive and spatial' representations and should not be used for data that cannot be quickly and economically presented (Sharples and van der Geest, 1996: 35) or which can be more quickly and economically presented as text. For example, in a paper concerning the influence of gender on choice of literature in college, the text summary we saw earlier in 6.3.1 was used instead of a tabular representation.

It is easy to assume that the figures themselves are enough reduction but readers can be overwhelmed with too many figures, especially from large scale surveys. These offer so many possibilities for different data presentations, from simple frequency additions to calculations of relations or correlations amongst data sets and sources, that it's tempting to use them all. In a thesis this is acceptable, provided that you select what proves your hypotheses, but in other formats a much restricted selection must generally be made.

Unless you are reporting on the internet. Electronic publishing offers the option of not reducing at all and thus opens quantitative research to much greater 'alternative' interpretations. All the data collected can now be available in electronic storage, however extensive they are. Readers can consult as much or as little as they wish and thus are better placed to make their own judgements. Look up, for example, the research reported in The Cochrane Library, an internet and CD database of systematic reviews enabling comparisons to be made amongst many studies in the same fields. It specializes in health research but the methodology reviews are valuable in any research. For

Table 8.3 Extract to illustrate quantified reduction of observational data: time spent alone by CEOs (Table 4.7 Solo time (desk work, lunch, travel) in Thody, 1997a: 52)

	1 County Tory margin 1986	2 County hung 1986	3 County Tory 1987	4 City Labour margin 1987	5 City Labour 1987–88	6 County Labour margin 1994	7 County hung 1995	8 Town Labour margin 1995	9 City Labour 1995	All 1986–88	All 1994–95
% of time spent solo	25.87	20.75	16.86	27.18	44.50	21.60	11.09	34.01	30.81	25.67	24.60
% of solo time spent at desk	54.91	69.79	49.06	47.18	71.18	29.37	50.98	63.03	63.54	61.75	54.5
% of total time spent at desk	14.21	14.49	8.27	12.83	31.90	0.34	5.65	21.43	19.57	15.85	13.42

My commentary

This table was one of several to help to ascertain the extent to which CEOs consulted others in the process of their policy making and the extent to which each CEO viewed her/his role as principally an oral connections hub or as a director of written communications. Each CEO was categorized according to her/his geographical location and the party-political control in that locality in case these should turn out to be influencing variables. The political terminology for each column was explained earlier in the book and applied to several of the tables (Tory and Labour are the two major British political parties; 'margin' means the main party had only a slight majority; 'hung' means no one party had control).

Note that I forgot to include the explanation that the time was in decimal hours and that readers would have to check back to other tables to see what the total time had been for each CEO – not ideal arrangements. The table had to be presented landscape, so needing a separate page for which the reader had to turn the book around – again, not ideal. The columns are not meant to add up to 100 per cent since each figure relates to a different total, but as soon as readers see percentages there is a mental assumption that they will produce the magic 100 per cent. The table entries were separated by horizontal rules only; is this sufficient differentiation? Would it have appeared too distractingly 'busy' to have the vertical lines in too?

example, 'Methods to influence response to postal questionnaires' runs to 168 pages, showing the detailed comparisons amongst over 300 studies on the topic. It has a masterly abstract of only one page for readers who prefer predigested outcomes (Edwards, P., Roberts, I., Clarke, M., DiGuiseppi, C., Pratap, S., Wentz, R., Kwan, I. and Cooper, R. www.update-software.com/Abstracts/am000008.htm as at August 2005).

8.5 Influencing readers

'Tables should be comprehensible without reference to the text' is the sound advice from the instructions to contributors in the *British Journal of Psychology*. Readers should therefore be able to understand your findings just by looking at figures and tables. In theory, the tables will be left as unadorned as possible so readers can make up their own minds about what the data infer, and this is also what alternative approaches would favour. In practice, you can influence readers even in your choice of titles for your tables (8.5.1) and you can direct readers' attention to particular findings and how you see correlates and variables even in the ways in which quantitative data results are formatted (8.5.2).

8.5.1 Titling your tables, figures and graphs

To make sets of quantified data comprehensible, title lengths may need to be extensive but they can then sound pedantic. Shorter titles sound 'snappy' but may not contain enough detail to explain the contents of a table. To test if a title contains sufficient detail, ask yourself if it would still be possible to know what it is about if it existed independently of your document. This usually becomes apparent when you have to list the tables and figures in the title pages of your work. In this list, there can be no explanatory text for each table, so will readers know what the tables contain simply by their titles? If so, then the titles are acceptable. If not, they have to be altered.

Question the following examples of titles for quantitative data presentations. Do you need more or less explanation? Does the title prejudice the readers' expectations from the data?

Ride 'em Cowboy

(This headed a map showing the varying numerical concentrations of work-to-home bicycle riders in the different USA states: Russell, C., 1995, 'Overworked? Overwhelmed?', *American Demographics*, March: 8 and 50–1.)

Table 1   The values of Turku Polytechnic and students
Table 2   The mission of Turku Polytechnic and students
Table 3   The vision of Turku Polytechnic and students

(The tables reported the mean scores of students' evaluations of strategic planning: Kettuen, J., 2003, 'Strategic evaluation of institutions by students in higher education', *perspectives* [*sic*], 7 (1): 14–18.)

Table 1   **General characterization of cottonwood and willow height classes in pre- and post-1998 photographs**

Table 2   Estimated levels of predation risk based on variables affecting the capability of a wild ungulate to detect a predator (viewshed) and terrain features that reduce the capability of a prey animal to escape (once detected)

(Ripple and Beschta, 2003: 304, refereed science journal article.)

Table II   **Management units (ANOVA results)**
Table III   **Summary of the ANOVA results for the management unit groups with regard to the Likert-scale items**

(Fitzgerald, T., Youngs, H. and Grootenboer, P., 2003, 'Bureaucratic control or professional autonomy? Performance management in New Zealand schools', *School Leadership and Management*, 23 (1): 91–105.)

Consider also the effect of the placement of titles for figures and tables. Figure 8.1 shows the same table twice with its titles and notes differently placed for each. The changes are minor but the second table gives a much more pleasing visual appearance than the first, since all the surrounding information fits within the same spacing as the table. The overall effect is of efficiency and consideration for detail which are both impressions that quantified data need to emit. A sanserif font has been used in the second example which also helps to clarify the visual effect.

Figure 8.1   The effect of repositioning table titles and explanatory information (tables from Oster, 2004)

Original version

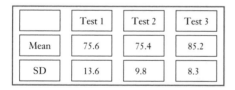

	Test 1	Test 2	Test 3
Mean	75.6	75.4	85.2
SD	13.6	9.8	8.3

($N = 38$, mean and standard deviation of tests administered at the beginning, middle and at the end of the year)

Table 1 Changes in pupils' understanding

Amended version

Table 1 Changes in pupils' understanding

	Test 1	Test 2	Test 3
Mean	75.6	75.4	85.2
SD	13.6	9.8	8.3

($N = 38$, mean and standard deviation of tests administered at the beginning, middle and end of the year)

8.5.2 Making inferences from the data

The convention is that any text accompanying quantified data should not repeat what is in the table. The raw data in Table 8.4 were presented without textual extension in a USA research report. Does it need any further explanation?

In contrast, the example in Table 8.5 used both text and table. Was the repetition justified by the need to emphasize the importance of the issues or because the journal in which it appeared has both academic and less specialized readers? Alternatively, did the text focus on what the researcher wanted readers to notice or did the researcher think that readers would have difficulty understanding the figures?

Compare Tables 8.5 and 8.6. In the latter, the author selected the less complex descriptive statistics of sample size and gender division for the text only. Items which were variables with which he would try to relate other results later in the article were reserved for the table only.

Finally, reflect on Table 8.7. It is from an article reporting research into the revisions which novice research article writers, who were non-native speakers of English (NNS), had to make before their articles were accepted in scientific journals. How much of this table might you have understood without the detailed, four page explanation that the article provided?

These contrasting examples show the choices researchers must make in deciding how to direct readers' attention to what is essential but which is not immediately apparent from the figures. Any expository text needs to take into account:

- *People.* How far is your audience likely to understand your data unaided?
- *Purposes.* How much do you want to influence the way your readers/listeners interpret your data?
- *Precedents.* What is considered the norm for the particular type of publication or presentation or subject? The social sciences, for example, 'however they may try to ape the natural sciences, have forever to face the difficulties posed by the fact that their subject-matter also has a voice' (Hughes, 1990: 138). Thus expository text can be used to illuminate the voices of those who have appeared only as mere numbers in a table.
- *Practicalities.* How much space can you allow for explanations? How many words can you save by non-repetition of data in tables and text? How close to the table can the explanation be set?

Table 8.4 Extract to demonstrate the presentation of a table without accompanying text (part of the table 'Trends in Teacher Flows In and Out of Schools', in Ingersoll, 2003: 10)

	1987–88 School Year	1990–91 School Year	1993–94 School Year	1999–00 School Year
1) Total Teaching Force – during school year	2,630,335	2,915,774	2,939,659	3,451,316
2) Total Hires – at beginning of school year	361,649	387,807	337,135	534,861
3) Total Departures – by following school year	390,731	382,879	417,588	539,778
4) Retirees	35,179	47,178	50,242	NA

My commentary
Note that the author used a clearer sanserif font for the table, in contrast to the rest of the report which was in Times New Roman. The cleaner lines visually convey the message that the data are factual, true and correct.

Table 8.5 Extract to demonstrate the presentation of a table with accompanying repetitive text (part of Table II 'Descriptive Statistics of Study Variables' with text, in Misra and Panigrahi, 1996: 7, 8)

	Variable	Frequency	Percentage
Gender	Male	421	41.5
	Female	594	58.5
Race	White	858	84.5
	Non-white	157	15.5
Marital status	Currently married	537	52.9
	Not currently married	478	47.1
Mother working	Yes	568	64.3
	No	315	35.7
Income (in 1991)	Mode = $40,000–$49,999		

Accompanying text
Descriptive characteristics of study variables
This analysis was based on 1,015 respondents ... and 58.5 per cent were female. The majority (84.5 per cent) were white and 64.3 per cent indicated that their mothers had been employed some time during marriage. Modal family income ... was in the range of $40,000–$49,999 ... Respondents were almost evenly distributed between currently married (52.9 per cent) or widowed/divorced/separated/never married (47.1 per cent).

Table 8.6 Extract to demonstrate the presentation of a table with accompanying non-repetitive text (part of the table and text analysing where students lived and were educated, in Westrick, 2004, 285–6)

Table 1 Demographic profile of years spent in environments of difference

Years	Expatriate years		International school years		Hong Kong International School years	
	N	*%*	*N*	*%*	*N*	*%*
< .5	103	19.6	20	3.8	44	8.4
5–1	22	4.2	24	4.6	50	9.5
1–2	31	5.9	40	7.6	75	14.3
... etc.						
Over 10	110	20.9	127	24.1	45	8.6

Accompanying text
Participants were recruited from the high school student body (*N* = 733) at the Hong Kong International School (HKIS), and the number that chose to participate represent a sufficient response rate (*n* = 526, 72%), with males representing a slightly smaller proportion (*n* = 256, 48.7% of the sample than females (*n* = 270, 51.3%). While HKIS hosts a student body of 40 nationalities ... and data were collected for this study on the 13 most common nationalities of the student body, nearly 70 per cent of students in this sample cite their citizenship as US, Hong Kong or Canada. Over a third, 38.7 per cent, of students in the sample claim nationalities in an Asian country. Demographic variables that relate to students' environmental exposure to difference are shown in Table 1 from three perspectives; the number of years spent living in another culture ('expatriate years'), the number of years spent studying at an international school, and the number of years spent studying at HKIS.

Table 8.7   Extract to demonstrate the presentation of a table with accompanying explanatory text (part of the table and text analysing revisions made to research articles written by non-English-speaking novices, in Gosden, 1995: 46–7)

Table 1   Overall Percentages for Categories of Textual Revision from NNS Novices (N = 7) FIRST to FINAL...drafts

		A	B	C	Di	Dii	Diii
#	N/T	−TD	+TD	(R)	RMd	RMc	RMp
1	31/95	0%	23%	6%	42%	26%	3%
2	50/89	14	20	8	28	20	10
3	54/100	2	48	4	24	11	11
...							
4–7	etc.						
Mean %	322/500	7	13	4	10	7	7
Standard deviation Rank		5	2	6	1	3	4

Accompanying text (extract)
In Table I, the individual NNS novices' drafts are numbered 1–7; A–D represent the four major categories of textual revision [codes explained on pp. 42–4 of the article]; the first column, N/T, indicates the number of revisions coded per total number of T-units (an independent clause together with all hypotactically related clauses which are dependent on it) counted in Results and Discussion sections. For example, NNS novice #1 made 31 textual revisions in categories A–D in the 95 T-units of the FINAL R&D DRAFT ... Individual novices' data and standard deviations indicate a wide range of textual revisions ... [so] it is suggested that the data in Table I reflect the linguistic and sociopragmatic concerns of 'expert' Research Article readers whose criteria these NNS novices are attempting to satisfy.

8.6   Supporting explanations

Explanations of the statistical techniques used should be adapted for your audience and the purposes of your documents. For theses, mathematical calculations and explanations of statistical techniques will normally be in the methodology chapter. In reports and books, they are most likely to be found in appendices. Refereed journal articles will have at least a paragraph and will have other information inserted at relevant points throughout. Populist media will usually have none, though intellectual magazines like *National Geographic* or *Scientific American* may include such information in separated, boxed sections.

   How much you write and what you write will depend on whether your aim is to try to make readers as comfortable as possible with your explanations or whether you are going for status with impressive 'gobbledegook'. The latter is best avoided; non-statisticians may be impressed but they can equally feel excluded. Statisticians will know that you are attempting to hide inadequacies.

The general aim is to provide enough information to enable non-statisticians to reach their own conclusions about whether or not the methods used were the right means to collect the data and to enable statisticians to judge if you used the methods effectively and correctly. Advantages and disadvantages of techniques should be given, especially for the less well known or complex techniques. For example, an article in the *International Journal of Manpower Studies* (which has a readership of academics from both quantitative and qualitative persuasions and of professionals with less interest in the methodology) had the following:

> the six variables were combined into a single, composite index. When deciding how to form the composite index, it was observed that 499 respondents had answered between none and three items, not enough to compute an index. These responses were dropped from the analysis. The index ... was then constructed by extrapolating the mean value of those that had answered four or five items from the six item scale. (Misra and Panigrahi, 1996: 10)

An article which stated its quantitative antecedents in its title, but which appeared in a journal that is not confined to quantitative research, contained the following explanation of techniques:

> For tests of bivariate correlation of IDI scores (Intercultural Development Inventory developed by Mitch Hammer and Milton Bennett in 1998 to measure the stages of development of intercultural sensitivity), the Pearson product-moment correlation coefficient is reported for variables expressed as continuous scores while Spearman's rho is reported for categorical variables. The unit of analysis of the correlation tests is the IDI score. (Westrick, 2004: 289)

Research reported in a journal article for education academics used data from health statistics. It therefore needed this explanation for readers not acquainted with health service tests:

> Public Health departments collect data about the residents of a Health Authority, mainly to estimate health care needs, for example the list size of a general practitioner. Their data are extracted from the census and are reported by electoral ward. Indices that have been used widely include those derived by Jarman (1983) [and] Townsend (Townsend et al., 1989) ... The Jarman Index combines eight measures of deprivation, while the Townsend Index, used here, combines four. The procedure used within the [area of this research] used normalisation of the raw figures. The purpose of the statistical transformation is to turn it into a bell-shaped curve with a mean of zero and standard deviation of one. (Conduit, Brookes, Bramley and Fletcher, 1996: 201)

Research on medical diagnostics required calculations and explanations, described as follows in an academic refereed article (Jones et al., 2000):

The use of sliding mode observers to reproduce fault signals is a promising innovation due to Edwards and Spurgeon ... Essentially, discontinuous injection signals are used to maintain some appropriately choosen switching function at zero. Such a scheme has been used to reconstruct faults in the components of the cooling system of a diesel engine as shown in Figure 4(a). Here the engine block represents a heat source. The thermostat valve divides coolant flow according to its opening level, α. The radiator acts as a heat sink to the atmosphere. Arrows dictate the direction of coolant flow. While the thermostat valve is closed ($\alpha = 0$), no coolant can flow through the radiator and coolant circulates through the left circuit. The coolant will only flow through the radiator when the thermostat valve is open. The bypass valve is used to bypass part of the coolant mixture. The location of temperature sensors is indicated with a cross. A thermal energy balance analysis produces the following equations.

$$\dot{T}_2(-k_1 - \dot{m}k_2)T_2 + \dot{m}k_2 T_3 + k_i T_b \tag{1}$$

$$\dot{T}_{2a} = (-k_1 - \hat{\alpha}k_{2a})T_{2a} + \hat{\alpha}k_{2a}T_3 + k_1 T_b \tag{2}$$

$$\dot{T}_3 = -\dot{m}k_3 T_2 + (\dot{m}k_3 - \hat{b}_{rad}k_4)T_3 + \hat{b}_{rad}k_4 T_{amb} \tag{3}$$

where $\dot{m}$ and $\hat{b}_{rad}$ are the coolant mass flow rate and the radiator heat transfer coefficient respectively. k_1, k_2, k_3, k_4 and k_{2a} are given by

$$k_1 = \frac{(\hat{b}A)_{bc}}{(\dot{m}c)_{bc}}, \quad k_3 = \frac{\alpha c}{(\dot{m}c)_{rad}}, \quad k_4 = \frac{A_{rad}}{(\dot{m}c)_{rad}}, \quad k_2 = \frac{\dot{m}c}{(\dot{m}c)_{bc}}, \quad k_{2a} = \frac{\dot{m}c}{(\dot{m})_{bc}}$$

8.7   Language and style

The words you select both inside and outside the tables and graphs are as important in quantitative as they are in qualitative and narrative research (Lindle, 2004: 2). Perhaps they are even more so for quantitative reporting in which you are confined to so few words in tables, graphs and charts. The 'mindset' of quantitative research reporting also errs strongly towards brevity (reinforced by publishing requirements, Chapter 14). Every word must therefore count (excuse the pun).

Almost invariably, the language and style will be conventional in all respects (5.3). The impersonal tone will dominate (5.3.3.6) because of the supposed inalienable objectivity of figures. An occasional personal appearance is acceptable, for example where you are reporting difficulties you found in your research methodology. Emotive expressive language is not usual and I have not found an example for this book (but to see how emotive statistics can be, read W. H. Auden's poem 'The Unknown Citizen: To JS/07M/378 This Marble Monument Is Erected by the State'.)

The conventional, impersonal style does not, however, absolve you from the necessity to realize that the words you have selected will still be transmitting 'feelings and

Table 8.8 Purposes of quantified data writing and presentation (version 2)

OVERT	%	COVERT	%
Simplifies evaluative processes	33.0	Provides incontrovertible numerical evidence	14.4
Enhances policy impacts	10.2	Masks subjectivity with apparent objectivity	23.0
Effectively demonstrates the applicability of data	11.0	Lessens researcher influence on the data	0.2

Analysis from the tape-recorded views of 1999 postgraduate management research students at the end of the author's class on quantitative presentation.

attitudes, unstated assumptions and embarrassing implications, as well as concepts' (Lanham, 1976: 34). You will already have taken normative decisions when you selected which variables to factor out, which correlates to search for or which sample to use, and these normative decisions continue with the language in which you choose to report your findings. The more you try to omit your emotions and attitudes and the more attention you pay to the figures rather than to the exactitudes of language, the less is the likelihood that you will convey the meanings you want.

For example, compare Table 8.8 with Table 8.1 which opened this chapter. You will see that the linguistic changes can create different understandings and attitudes to the categories. The researcher's preferences can be revealed in the language used. Visual changes could further alter readers' perspectives by, for example, removing the 'overt' and covert' classifications, putting data into ascending or descending order or adding shading to differentiate columns.

8.8 Appearances

In theses and research reports, you decide on the type, size and location of your quantitative formats. In published documents, the size and location are largely determined for you according to available space, page size and editorial requests. Within these limits, aim to achieve:

- tables, graphs and figures as near adjacent to related text as possible;
- a variety of formats, graphs, bar and pie charts, tables and figures, so that readers are not bored by repetition (but where the same tests have to be applied to several sets of data, you will need to report them similarly or consider how far data sets can be collated);
- alignment of text and data in columns;
- white space around quantitative formats (unless you are paying per page for publications, in which case you cannot afford the luxury of good looks);
- sanserif fonts for figures;
- colour to make results clearer, but keep to the same limited palette throughout a document; rainbows make the work seem less serious and can increase printing costs;
- the same settings for every quantified format: for example, titles always before, or always after, a figure; notes in the same font and size throughout.

The accompanying figures from an article on diagnostic schemes for biomedical and engineering systems illustrate many of these points. The figures were placed throughout the article but have been collated here as Figure 8.2 for demonstration purposes.

8.9 Ethics

Quantified results are superficially seductive in their impact, brevity and appearance. They ooze scientific respectability, especially as they are almost invariably combined with conventional, scientific style (1.3). Science is trusted. This was strongly evidenced in UK debates about education research in the late 1990s. Political demands for studies that measured outcomes from large samples arose after critiques of qualitative, small case studies (Tooley with Darby, 1998; Hargreaves, 1996). Similar demands appeared in the USA:

> Research on service-learning programs from the United States is often criticized as 'merely' anecdotal, relying too heavily on self-reports from participants and rarely using quantitative, rigorously designed research studies ... Scholars in the field of service-learning are searching for convincing, empirical evidence from well-designed studies to support claims about the outcomes of service-learning. (Westrick, 2004: 278)

Newspapers carry frequent exhortations that we improve our nutritional health following the latest scientific research, accompanied by impressive charts and figures that blind us to the facts that the samples were small, involved one gender and age group only, were researched in a different time and place to our own and contradicted other studies.

The likely impact from quantitative research, because of its scientific image, can create temptations that challenge ethics. These can be quite spectacular, as in the infamous case of the highly respected psychologist Sir Cyril Burt. His quantitative research on identical twins reared apart showed that intelligence was innate more than it was environmentally influenced. Relying on his so incontrovertible tables, the British government built the eormous edifice of their educational policy on academic selection from 1944 to 1964. Only in 1976 (five years after Burt's death) was it found that Burt had apparently invented his results, his named research assistants had not existed, there were inconsistencies in his reported sample sizes, and there were some remarkably convenient, but very unlikely, similarities in the results from varying studies.

Similarly fraudulent results were uncovered in 2006 in stem-cell research. Professor Hwang Woo-suk of Seoul National University claimed, in 2004, to have created the first cloned human embryo and, in 2005, embryonic 'designer' stem-cells, discoveries that promised cures for such diseases as Alzheimer's. A former research assistant revealed that he had been ordered to fabricate the data for these discoveries and an investigation found all the claims to be false, though who had falsified them was unclear.

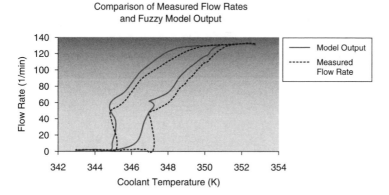

FIG 4. Characteristics of flow control valve.

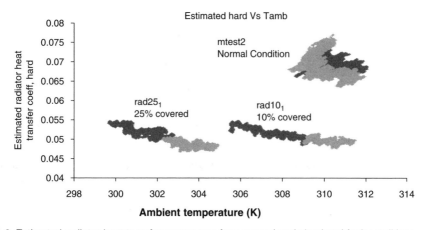

FIG 6. Estimated radiator heat transfer parameters from normal and simulated fault conditions.

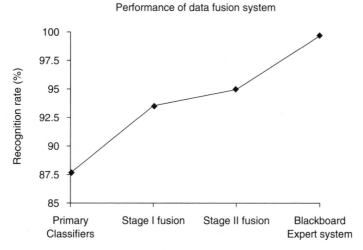

FIG 8. Improvement at each stage of data fusion scheme.

(Continued)

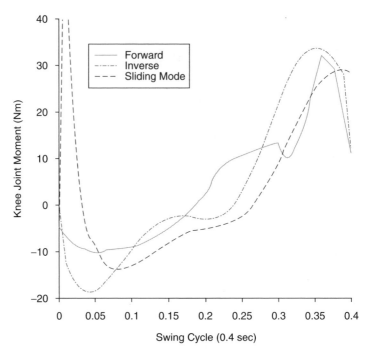

FIG 10. Evaluation of knee joint movement using 3 different techniques: Forward Dynamics; Inverse Dynamics; Sliding Mode Control.

Figure 8.2   Four figures collated from one article, showing variety of formats, sanserif font within the figures, column alignment and differing title fonts and formats (Jones et al., 2000). The originals also used colours which cannot be reproduced here.

Less spectacularly, in government statistics:

> The requirement for clear-cut conclusions, the pressure of work and the petrification of the original theoretical knowledge of the statistician, encourage such misleading practices as the automatic mechanical use of (perhaps inappropriate) significance tests at 95 per cent level of significance – without the proviso, however, that 1 in 20 of results so obtained is expected to be incorrect. (Hammersley, 1993: 160)

Obviously, readers of this book will not succumb to temptations to falsify data or fail to explain their tables' limitations or such factors as observer error in data collection and collation, but there are more subtle ethical dilemmas. Making public the researcher's background and relationship to the project is especially important because of the authoritarian appearance of quantitative research. Letting readers know the researcher's attitudes is, however, generally regarded as unimportant for quantitative data set in conventional scientific formats as the aim of this style is to demonstrate researcher neutrality (1.3). Feminist scholars regard this as androcentric, forcing women researchers (or research about women) to 'constantly repress, negate or ignore their own experience of sexist oppression and have to strive to live up to the so-called "rational" standards of a highly competitive, male-dominated academic world' (Mies, 1993: 67).

Whether or not you agree with this view, there is a strong rationale for realizing that subjectivity cannot be avoided and that this subjectivity should be openly admitted. The researcher will select which data will have most prominence, and will control the language in which the results are expressed (8.7), and is in the powerful position of being able to point out what conclusions should be drawn (8.5.2). Hence, for readers to judge the validity of data showing, for example, how many people suffered Gulf War syndrome, it is surely valuable to know if the researcher is or is not a pacifist; has or does not have a relative suffering from this possible disease; has been or has not been in the military; and is or is not paid by the government or companies marketing cures for Gulf War syndrome. Guidance on what should be revealed about a researcher, and how, is in 2.3.2.1 and 2.3.2.2. At the very minimum, this revelation of self should include a statement on who paid for the research and whether or not there is any conflict of interest for the researchers.

Such macro-issues are not the only ethical dilemmas to be solved. If you need to round figures up or down, what do you do about 10.5? Would 11 or 10 best prove your point? Or should you check back to your original figures and look for further decimal places to solve the difficulty? What do you do at the end of a long, tiring day of analysis and additions, when those final columns are just 0.3 per cent away from 100? Do you re-check the data or just add a casual 0.3 per cent to one of the existing figures? If the rank order data are not quite as conclusive as you hoped, do you leave them in rank order or just list them randomly so that the priorities you felt to be most important are less easy to distinguish from those that the research indicated were most important? Of course, I hear you say, 'I would not behave unethically', but next time you read quantitative data, inspect them with a more sceptical eye. Someone else might have been unethical.

8.10 Review

Now test the criteria in Box 8.1 on the following extract. It is from the methodology review of a well-written, erudite article in an international, refereed, academic journal, mainly read by university faculty but with also a substantial readership of practising leadership professionals. The extract consits of some text and a table.

Box 8.1 Criteria for evaluating quantitative formatting

- Are the data suitable for quantitative formatting? (8.3)
- Are the data appropriately reduced? (8.4)
- Does the accompanying text direct the readers' attention as intended? (8.5)
- Is there the right amount of information about how the data were collected and analysed? (8.6)
- Is the language precise? Do the words choosen predispose readers to particular conclusions? (8.7)
- Is the presentation ethical and is the researcher's context acknowledged? (8.8)
- Do the appearance and placement of the tables appeal to readers' interests and assist their comprehension of your data ? (8.9)

Table 8.9 Descriptive Analysis of Schools Backgrounds and Teachers Backgrounds (Ho, 2003: Table 2)

School Background	Percentage	Teacher Background	Percentage
1. Grade level		**3.** Gender	
Primary School	46.9%	Female	61.7%
Secondary School	53.1%	Male	39.3%
2. Types of School		**4.** Education level	
Government School	20.1%	Ph.D	0.1%
Aided School	73.9%	Master	7.5%
Private School	5.6%	Bachelor	46.0%
Others	0.4%	Post-secondary	21.4%
		Higher Diploma/Certificate	2.2%
		Diploma/Certificate	20.2%
		Others	2.6%
		5. Teaching Experience	
		< 5 years	27.9%
		5–9 years	26.3%
		10–19 years	25.9%
		20–29 years	14.4%
		> 30 years	5.5%

Extract

Questionnaires were sent to a sample of nine elementary and nine secondary schools that were selected strategically to include schools with heterogeneous student backgrounds. A total of 1056 teachers completed and returned the questionnaires … Table [8.9] displayed the school background and teacher background of the sample schools. (Ho, 2003: 61 and Table 2)

My reactions to the above extract are as follows. How do yours compare?

Visually, Table 8.9 and its accompanying explanation are a treat. You are not over-whelmed with explanation, so it is possible to reflect on the information for yourself. You can quickly absorb data that would be confusing if set out as a paragraph of text. The table sets the tone for the rest of the article; these are simple, descriptive statistics but one feels reassured that here is an author who will handle more complex data with *élan*.

But could the table have been more effectively presented? Consider my version of Table 8.9, rewritten as Table 8.10. I assume you can spot all the differences between the two tables:

☑ The sample sizes and date have been put into the table for easier reference and to add to the sense of veracity of the methodology.

☑ Readers can add up the percentages more easily since the tens, units and first decimal place columns are now aligned. So of course you will spot that the teachers' genders produced a 101 per cent teaching force and that teaching experience left 0.1 per cent unaccounted for. The

Table 8.10   Descriptive Analyses of Schools' and Teachers' Backgrounds (revised version)

Schools' Backgrounds N = 18	%	Teachers' Backgrounds N = 1056	%
Grade Levels		Gender	
Primary	46.9	Female	61.7
Secondary	53.1	Male	39.3
Types of Schools		Education Levels	
Government	20.1	PhD	0.1
Aided	73.9	Master	7.5
Private	5.6	Bachelor	46.0
Others	0.4	Post-secondary	21.4
		Higher Diploma/Certificate	2.2
		Diploma/Certificate	20.2
		Others	2.6
		Teaching Experience	
		< 4 years	27.9
		5–9 years	26.3
		10–19 years	25.9
		20–29 years	14.4
		> 30 years	5.5

latter is acceptable, the former is not. Decide if you will round your results up or down, tell the readers, and stick to this so your results will total the magic 100 per cent.

☑ The visually distracting and repetitious per cent sign for each item is removed and appears only at the top of each column. The data itself thereby become clearer.

☑ Visual absorption of the data is enhanced by the use of shading.

☑ The grammar has been corrected, plurals have been inserted where needed, and the title of the table now agrees grammatically with the headings in the table.

☑ Punctuation needed alteration: apostrophes were inserted.

☑ Capitalization has been standardized.

These last three may seem like minor matters but such accuracy in language infers that the writer is equally accurate in the quantitative material. All the other tables in the article were correctly set out so it's not possible to know how much of the format was decided by the journal or by the author or if there was insufficient time to proofread it. The alterations I have suggested are those that are all too easy for any of us to miss.

Reconsider the data in Table 8.9, the written text that accompanied them and the categorizations selected for the data. There appears to be a need for more explanations since the following questions seem appropriate:

? If nine elementary and nine secondary schools were in the sample, why are each of them not reported as 50 per cent of the sample in the table?

? Is there a distinction between primary schools (the designation used in Table 8.9 and English in origin) and elementary schools (the designation used in the text and North American in origin)?

? What does the category of 'post-secondary' include? The three categories of PhDs, masters and bachelors degrees would all be gained after leaving secondary school, so were the holders of these degrees put into one category or two? If this were not the case, then did the post-secondary group try and then fail to gain any qualifications? Or is there a 'post-secondary' teaching qualification in Hong Kong, since it appears from the other categories that diplomas and certificates are gained at school?

? What are the distinctions between 'government', 'aided' and 'private' schools?

? Are the numbers of schools selected from each group representative of the dispersion of each type of school overall in Hong Kong (this information might tell us how representative the sample is)?

? It appears from the text accompanying Table 8.9 that the sample of schools was chosen so as to ensure a 'heterogeneous' student body, but what does 'heterogeneous' imply in a Hong Kong context? It could be any one or more of social, economic, geographic, racial, regional or ability sets. An international readership is unlikely to be able to guess. Is each type of school in the survey similarly heterogeneous?

I am sure that there were rational explanations for all of these points, but the explanations needed to be given in, or close to, the table in order to reassure readers of the validity of the data. Given the unused space in Table 8.9, at the bottom of the first column, some explanations could have been inserted there.

BUT IT'S EASY TO BE CRITICAL OF SOMEONE ELSE'S WORK.

NOW WE HAVE TO ENSURE WE ARE AS CRITICAL OF OUR OWN.

Note

1   Chief education officers are the equivalents of North American district superintendents and Australian regional directors. Since 2005, the role has been abolished in the UK.

9 Qualitative Data

CONTENTS

9.1 Polyvocality

9.1.1 Definition

While quantitative researchers aim at reducing data to one voice, qualitative researchers must retain multiple voices and sources. This is polyvocality in which, somehow, everyone and everything must be allotted space and analysis. The polyvocal world that qualitative research seeks to convey is naturalistic, complex, varied, expansive and cacophonous. The cacophony can include the voices of respondents, readers (3.7) and the researcher (2.3.2) and even the silences between voices (Skultans, 2001).

The voices recorded may be those collected by social scientists and humanities' researchers from observations (9.4), interviews (9.5) and focus groups (9.6). These can also be the past voices released by historians and literati from archival, literary or archaeological sources; lawyers comparing case precedents and statutes, and artists discuss literature, sculpture or paintings reproducing the voices of the originators and those who have commented upon them (9.7). All of these can be presented in quantitative and narrative formats (Chapters 8 and 10); this chapter concentrates on using qualitative data qualitatively and, of course, ethically (9.8).

A good illustration of how polyvocality can be accommodated comes from research in museum studies. When an exhibition is mounted, the curators have to decide whose voices will be represented and how. The exhibition discussed in the extract below concerned the 'History of American Sweatshops, 1820 to the Present' in The Smithsonian Museum in Washington, DC. The topic was controversial with powerful interests likely to be offended. The curators coped with polyvocality as follows:

> The historical section employed a curatorial voice. But they felt that using only this voice in the exhibition would be a mistake. Therefore the El Monte section [a mock-up of a 1990s' Californian sweatshop] used the voices of the participants, be they workers or law enforcement agencies. The [section] 'The Fashion Food Chain' (which addressed a range of manufacturing alternatives) had the dry authoritative voice of a textbook. Furthermore, a video presented the industry voice, while a 'national leaders' section gave six individuals representing manufacturers, labor, government, community groups and others the opportunity to offer their written comments. (Dubin, 1999: 242)

9.1.2 Conventions and alternatives

Each researcher must choose their own balance amongst the voices to be reported. The parameters for this are outlined in Table 9.1.

9.1.3 Subjectivity and creativity

All the qualitative, polyvocal formats in Table 9.1 admit, and embrace, subjectivity. There is criticism that this means being 'blind to facts' (Hughes, 1990: 116) and accepting that 'sadly, qualitative, interpretive research data cannot provide facts and figures' (Fail et al., 2004: 333). The word 'fact', however, needs reconsideration. A 'fact', in qualitative data, is another voice, each voice producing part of the picture. Each voice is a complete 'fact' in itself and represents the truth as seen by that respondent, source or researcher. The perceptions of one voice may conflict with those of other voices but that does not make any of them incorrect. A 'voice' is a 'fact' about the situation being researched.

Your own individuality is one of the voices (2.3.2). This individuality should be openly confessed since it will guide not only the collection of your data but also the literary aspects of qualitative research reporting. The most basic way of confessing is in the author notes/bio-data (11.5) but these give you only partial absolution. The challenge is that your subjectivity changes, and no more so than when you are in the final writing-up stages and all the data are spread before you. Are you really the same person who commenced the research three years previously?

You attempt to convey emotively the empirical and rigorous facts that have been discovered during the years of your research, in what is termed in the social sciences 'creative analytic practice' (CAP) (Lewis-Beck et al., 2004: 212–13). Arguments rage over whether the creativity or the empirical facts should dominate, but in either case the writing or presenting cannot, and should not, be neutral. In the early

Table 9.1   Conventions and alternatives for qualitative data polyvocality

	Extent of raw data	Researcher presence	Intentional reader involvement	Format	Style
Conventional extreme	Up to 33%	Overtly absent. Covertly present in having chosen the data, format and conclusions	Nil – the researcher structures the document to point readers to unavoidable conclusions	Scientific (1.3.1). The tone is of distant, reasoned debate	Authoritative. Third person passive voice, past tense (5.3.3.5, 5.3.3.6)
Middle ground	A substantial portion, 33–66%	Overtly present; the researcher describes his/her own values so readers can judge the attitudes through which the data have been filtered	Partial – the researcher will draw some conclusions but will leave space for readers to empathize with the data too	Conventional literature and methodology critiques precede raw data. The tone is of justified, emotional researcher involvement	First person, active voice, present tenses (5.3.3.5, 5.3.3.6)
Alternative extreme	Virtually the whole document	Overtly absent. Covertly present in having chosen the data and format	Total – readers are expected to react and relate to the data and draw their own conclusions	Alternative (1.4) and dialogic, taking shape and form as the voices apparently materialize into text unguided and unchecked	Tense and voice as in the original data

2000s, however, admitting subjectivity can make some people downgrade your research, especially if you are female and/or of a colour other than very lightly baked biscuit (cookie) veering to white (as illustrated in Henry's 1997 paper). On the other hand, there are arguments that research is better if it is overtly subjective (Mehra, 1997: 70).

Much of this debate is about the collection of data and access to research subjects but there are a growing number of texts that address the issues of admitting subjectivity in writing and presenting (de Laine, 2000; van Maanen, 1988). In reporting your research, you have to decide:

- The distance to place between yourself and your subjects (Do you write in the impersonal passive, or the personal active?) (5.3.3.5, 5.3.3.6).
- The identification you made with those whom you studied (Do you use their language in your reports, or academic jargon?) (5.3.3.2, 5.3.3.3, 5.3.3.4).

- How much to include of what you experienced as a researcher, or what the research subjects experienced as observed by you, or as gleaned from your interviews (Which view is given most space and how?) (van Maanen, 1988: 106–8).
- How many different formats you can use to present facets of the data appropriately (de Laine, 2000: 189). This chapter and Chapter 10, on narrative data, outline some of the options.

9.2 Qualitative data writing and presentation: purposes

Decisions about the ways in which your research will report polyvocality can be guided by considering the purposes outlined in Box 9.1.

Box 9.1 Qualitative data writing and presentation: purposes

- To convey the reader to the research site. This creates 'the conditions that will allow the reader, through the writer, to converse with (and observe) those who have been studied' (Denzin, 1998: 324).
- To produce a rich picture of reality, detailed, extensive, reliable in its internal consistency and representative in the width of voices it reports. The whole must be believable.
- To provide the facts that make a worthwhile, substantive contribution to knowledge and comprehension.
- To communicate atmosphere, emotion and attitudes of both the subjects and the researcher. This can include political, social, economic, gender and religious affiliations.
- To demonstrate researcher reflexivity through the researcher's commentary on his/her effect on the data gathering and reporting.
- To transmit the direct experiences of the research respondents and of the researcher in interacting with the respondents, the literature or the history.
- To make the voluminous data comprehensible so that readers can enjoy the 'theatre in the round' experience. Categorization helps this (6.4) but qualitative researchers have to be cognizant that the lone voice still has rights to presentation (whereas erratics in quantitative data normally do not).
- To respect the sensitivities of respondents. Qualitative data reporting should avoid being intrusive and personal.
- To be artistically pleasing. Creativity is welcome.
- To create impact. It should affect readers emotionally and intellectually.

9.3 Qualitative data formats

For each document or presentation, the researcher has to decide which of the purposes in Box 9.1 will have priority and can then decide the format for the data. Examples of these are discussed below for data from observations (9.4), interviews (9.5) focus groups (9.6) and historical, literary and legal data (9.7).

9.4   Observation data

Observation is fun. For a while, researchers leave their usual environments for total immersion in that of others. This 'provides a degree of life experience that is lacking in most academic environments' (Hammersley, 1993: 197). The researcher is a TV documentary maker, recording without responsibility; a *doppelgänger* who becomes the shadow of those being observed, an actor with a walk-on, silent part. You become party to intimate thoughts and actions and intimate with parties you would never normally meet. After the fun comes nemesis. How do you convey your perspective, that of the observed and that of others in the scene who may not be the direct subject of the research?

9.4.1   Openings

Observation data always make an excellent opening. They are unrivalled for attracting reader attention. Observation immediately establishes verisimilitude and atmosphere with its rich data. It leaves options open as to whether or not the whole document has to be similarly directly reported.

The following example uses participant observation to take you straight into a Western movie. It makes the perfect beginning for an article about issues relating to farm workers' struggles on the Mexico/US border: 'The chair groans as I lean back and take a long draw from my cigarette. The tobacco crackles as the cherry ferociously consumes it like wildfire. I snap my jaw, launching smoke rings into the night. They quickly dissipate as the wind wisps them away' (Barnes, 2002: 55).

From that desert night, the next example, from semi-participant observation of inner-city policing beside an Amsterdam canal, appears to take us into a crime novel rather than a research report, a device calculated to make us want to read on:

> My first murder – this is not, I hasten to add, a confession – was that of a young woman whose suspected infidelity had caused her husband to stab her to death … It was a bitterly cold night and the eye witness account of the alleged murder became increasingly discredited as old bicycles, but no body, were brought to the surface. (from *Policing the Inner City: A Study of Amsterdam's Warmoesstraat*, Punch, 1979, cited in Hammersley, 1993: 181)

Both of the above examples used what was the ordinary in the circumstances observed. The extraordinary can be used to similar effect. Describing the life of chief education officers in England (the equivalents of district superintendents in North America), a job one might expect to tend towards administrivia, I choose to open the book with the observation data on an unusual meeting (see 11.10 'Reflections'; Thody, 1997a).

REFLECTIONS

How many of the purposes listed in Box 9.1 are satisfied by the above examples? It's interesting to consider how much can be achieved in even short sections of observation data.

9.4.2 A full picture?

The observer selects the focus of the scene to which readers' attention is immediately drawn but there has to be surrounding data to explain the context and its impact on the subject(s) observed. To decide on the amount of detail needed for this, consider the guiding principles of Chapters 2–4. How much can you assume that your readers will know? How much is it practicable to include without becoming tedious? What do you need to include to meet the purposes of conveying emotion, being creative and remaining sensitive to your subjects?

In the following two extracts, each author has choosen different ways to present a full picture.

Extract 1

Description of a Maltese school (from a masters degree thesis).

> The entrance to the school was through a side door which was situated in a rather disorderly small parking lot. There were no security measures, and on entry one found oneself in a large, fairly attractive corridor … This … actually 'felt' like a school since the corridors were closed to the elements and there was fresh paint on the walls … students' work adorned some of the displays on the walls and students and staff moved around purposefully and quietly. (Testa, 2004: 73)

Extract 2

Description of the debating chamber of an English local district council (from a research book).

> The walls of those council meeting rooms presented a cacophony of long since silenced local politicians weighed down with various grades of precious metal chains, elaborately gilded gowns and differential abilities of artists to depict them. The chief living politician sat within the arcs of paintings facing the horse-shoes, or circles, of councillors. Slightly below … sat the CEO whom I was observing, flanked by attendant officers … The outer circle was the public gallery, featuring, usually, no-one. (Thody, 1997a: 44)

9.4.3 Citation

Whatever observations you decide to include, you need to make their sources clear. In theses, research reports and academic texts, the origins of observations will be detailed in the research methodology chapters, sections or appendices (7.2, 7.4). Each observation can then be cited as, for example, (Obs. 24; site 3, Sept. 4, 2008). If the observations have been made by a team of researchers then the initials of each individual researcher who conducted particular observations may also be included in the parentheses.

In more populist media, citations should be incorporated into the observations. Each should contain enough information to allow you to check it if you wish so it still appears authoritative. In a business leadership book, for example, the authors illustrated their points with uncited observations but an internet search should enable you to test if they were true or not:

> Hugh McColl, former chairman of the Bank of America, once gave a powerful speech to a thousand of his top executives when his company was merging with the Bank of

America. He stated that the executives of the newly formed bank must immediately extend trust to the people who report to them, including any new people on the team. (Dotlich and Cairo, 2002: 23)

9.5 Interview data

Your readers have only the words of the interviews to help their understanding (and not even all of these). You, the interviewer, will have all the words and can recollect personalities, places, appearances and your interactions and emotions during the interviews to reach your conclusions from the data. You therefore have to meet the challenge of transmitting your wider knowledge through judicious selections from your data. Requirements for this are outlined in Box 9.2.

Box 9.2   Writing and presenting individual interview data: requirements

For definitions of formats see Table 9.1.

For all formats

Whether the source is face-to-face, telephone, email or written interviews, the extracts selected should:

- Be as short as possible because your fascination with the data is unlikely to be felt as strongly by readers.
- Be representative.
- Be entertaining.
- Be few since 'overuse of quotes can become tedious and the point being made can get lost in the words' (Darlington and Scott, 2002: 161).
- Respect confidentiality. Interviewees should have given permission for you to quote their words but other people to whom they have referred in their speeches have not.
- Be checked with the interviewees if possible (3.6.3).
- Cite the source (if anonymity has not been requested). For example, at the beginning of an extract, the interviewee might be identified by initials; at the end, the details should be placed in parentheses, such as (MH, 29 July, 2007; in his office) or (female attorney, 04/08/10, after the court judgement).

For conventional and middle ground formats

Data should tend to:

- Be interspersed with summaries; these help you to include more interviews than it is possible to quote from verbatim, and assist readers in keeping track of your themes.

(Continued)

Box 9.2 (Continued)

- Include commentary to indicate context, make comparisons and relate data to your research question.
- Be grouped into categories (6.4) for ease of assimilation and comparisons.
- Be verbatim but they will usually need 'aggressive' editing (Frisch, 1990: 84–5) to make sense of original transcripts. For example, punctuation will be inserted, sentences constructed, pauses ignored, extracts made to appear as if the interviewee always used correct grammar, cuts made and the order changed. This reconstruction should be admitted in the methodology review (Holliday, 2002: 101) but not for each extract individually.

For alternative formats

Data should tend to:
- Include contextual information in the interview extracts.
- Usually, but not invariably, be presented chronologically.
- Have minimal, or no, commentary.
- Be as close to verbatim as possible, e.g the silences should be indicated, as could be facial expressions, sighs and laughter; discourse is precisely as the subject spoke even where this does not quite make sense.

9.5.1 Conventional and alternative examples

The following extract (from a USA conference paper) demonstrates an effective conventional approach. The authors reported their interviews with trainee leaders to find out if writing case studies had helped the trainees' professional development. The researchers analysed the data into categories according to each possible effect of case story writing, such as 'Who am I writing for?', 'Groundhog Day', 'Relationships'. Each category opened with a summary of its main point, illustrated by short extracts from several interviews, of which this is an example:

> As participants struggled to develop their stories, many found that a major consideration was audience. An essential question for participants was 'Who am I writing for?' Certainly, this issue is consistent with what most authors experience … One participant aptly summed up this concern, 'I couldn't figure out what I wanted to write about until I could picture my audience' … Some later reflected, 'I wondered how much I should reveal about myself,' and ' … what will my classmates think of me' while others indicated that they needed to edit their stories because they were worried about making certain things public … One participant … became upset … when she realized she was expected to read [her story] aloud. (Ackerman and Maslin-Ostrowski, 1996: 6)

Summarizing the data as above absolved the authors of the necessity to attribute individual quotations and the group were sufficiently homogeneous in relation to the research question to make this acceptable. Had the authors been extracting variables for correlations, then they would have had to attribute quotations to individual speakers.

The following middle ground approach arises from a structured interview with a noted feminist scholar (Charol Shakeshaft in Collard, 1996). The transcript was a substantial part of the article but not its whole; the stilted language indicates editing.

Collard: Has the place of women in school administration changed since 1987?

Shakeshaft: It's complex. Women are receiving more principalships in the USA, but in other parts of the world, women's participation in school administration is declining. For instance, in Russia fewer women are school administrators now than held the position five years ago. We need to understand why the introduction of a free market system and a democratic political structure has decreased female participation in school management in the former USSR.

Collard: Are some women still being displaced from certain roles?

Shakeshaft: Women do not hold the majority of administrative positions in the USA, even though they hold the majority of teaching positions.

At the alternative extreme, the transcript of an interview formed the whole twelve pages of the article 'A conversation with Germaine Tillion' (Rice, 2004). Germaine (GT) was asked by the researcher (AR) about Muslim women and their position in society from her writings in 1966 and 2001. The conversation is less stilted than in the previous example; the occasional formal style appears to have been either because GT was not speaking in her native language or because it has been translated from her French.

AR: Does the relationship between mother and daughter differ from that between mother and son?

GT: Unfortunately, mothers are rather disappointed by their daughters and they treat them poorly. They treat their daughters badly, and they idolise their sons.

AR: And how do daughters react to this treatment?

GT: They are usually a bit angry with their mothers.

AR: Do you think that this poses a problem for them later, when they themselves become mothers? Do they perpetuate this tradition?

GT: They have the ambition of exacting revenge on society thanks to their sons.

AR: Through their sons?

GT: They absolutely want to have sons and when they have a son, they have won, and they dominate through the son.

One stage further is this attempt to report an interview completely verbatim. The interviewer is INT, the respondent is P:

INT: Okay can you just talk back and tell me about the different places you've lived in your life?

P1: Sure (.) um I was in Brazil for the first year of my life (.) just over a year ... I don't remember any of that (*INT*: Right).

P2: I think that was probably a very formative time (*INT*: Yes). (Taylor, 2001b: 37)

REFLECTIONS

In all four of the above examples, the researchers have edited the responses through inserting their own choices of punctuation. In none of them was there any indication of the tone of the speakers. Were the trainee leaders rueful or amused? Was Charol Shakeshaft emphasizing certain points or was everything said in the same neutral tone? Was GT angry? Did AR express incredulity that pushed the speaker towards particular statements? How long did P's hesitation last in her first response?

If you knew the answers, would it have affected your reaction to the data? If the writers had wanted to insert tonal references, how would they do this? For example, should you use bold or upper case letters to indicate that someone is shouting? How should you record silences and do they need interpretation? There are no precedents, so you make your own decisions.

9.5.2 Collating interview data

Collating material from different interviews helps with summarizing, comparing and the avoidance of repetition. From each interview, the responses related to the same topic are grouped and summarized. Minimal verbatim extracts can then provide evidence of the generality with any major deviations from the norm also reported.

In this example, the researcher states the main point and then uses verbatim extracts:

There was pressure to get married young and once married, there was pressure to have children.

May: I was married three months. I mean, in those days you tried to become pregnant as soon as you could ...

Karla: Did you feel pressure to become a mother?

Mary G: Yes, oh yes. You were married Karla, and if you weren't pregnant within three months, there was something wrong with you. (Kelly, 2001: 24–5)

In contrast, this example combines summary through reported speech with short, verbatim extracts:

B. Byron Price, at the time the executive director of the National Cowboy Hall of Fame ... represents an important perspective ... Price believes that *The West as America* [museum exhibition] forced a national debate about western art ... It really sharpened our skills ... This is exactly what some of the principals were after in his case. On reflection, Alex Nemerov observes ... 'We wanted to write really forceful labels' [for the exhibition] ...

But Nemerov had no continuing stake in the museum ... The situation was different for Truettner and Broun. Truettner admits, 'I was pretty scared' ... Broun too concedes that 'it made a lot of people nervous' ... Julie Schimmel argues that the urge to deconstruct accepted doctrines ... represents a generational impulse. (Dubin, 1999: 177, 178, 179)

Note that in a summary like this, the first time an interviewee's name is used, it appears in full; thereafter, only the surname is used. The dates of the interviews used in the above extract were stated in the footnotes earlier in the book, on the first occasion that data from an interview were used. Thereafter only the interviewee's name appeared. Places and dates of all interviews were in a summary list at the end of the book.

9.6 Focus group data

All the considerations relating to interview data apply also to group interviews but additional issues also apply. The reporting *must* summarize the views expressed (since finding collectivity is the object of a group discussion) but individual views must also be included in order to show their formative influence on what emerged. You will also need to demonstrate how the views interacted and influenced the progress of a discussion. Finally, the atmosphere in which discussion took place should be conveyed as well as its physical location.

Ways of combining these are shown in the following three extracts which also demonstrate different citation methods.

Extract 1

This example, from an MBA dissertation, mixes summaries, direct transcripts, present and reported speech, lists and paragraphed text, and reports the laughter that lightened the session. The mixture helps to hold readers' attention. The researcher was recording the discussion but was not participating in it (Horsley, 2004: 40, 43).

> The group reviewed what they considered to be the essential elements to be learned through team training ... They stated that:
>
> Team training must
>
> • clearly demonstrate the goal and purpose of activities
>
> • show how to measure achievement of these goals and review progress ... [nine further items concluded the list]
>
> Subject 3 said a key factor is
>
> > *'What is the purpose of the team? ... Clear objectives need to be signed off on by everybody ... because if you are training people who don't know what they are supposed to do that is just going to be frustrating.'*
>
> Subject 1 said [offering an example of unsuccessful team work] ...
>
> > *'Everyone was delegating to others to do the best that he was good at ... In a debating society* (roars of laughter all round) *like Xco if there is no leader to say where to go, there is no common goal.'*

All of them agreed that the big difference is that there must be a common goal, the mission must be clear for team training to reap rewards. Subject 1 stated that some huge organizations have a lot of politics where individuals have their own agendas and want to rise to the top at the expense of the team. If an organization is 'unclear, unfocussed and dysfunctional' teams fall apart.

Subject 3 said that teams must have both a mission and a vision which can be turned into measurable goals. A team must be able to measure its performance and in team training the goals are measurable.

Extract 2

In this following focus group example, the researchers themselves constituted the group of four speakers. Short extracts from a tape recorded discussion were presented verbatim to exemplify various aspects of the text. The transcripts were each shortened in order to convey the speakers' interactions. There was no commentary, or summary, as the text was part of a distance learning CD in which readers were asked to draw their own conclusions (Pashiardis, Thody, Papanaoum and Johansson, 2002).

In the transcript, the speakers are identified as follows:

Olof Johansson, Sweden	O
Zoi Papanaoum, Greece	Z
Petros Pashiardis, Cyprus	P
Angela Thody, England	A

Z: Of course excellency in principalship is not a matter of mere training.

P: [But] the good leaders that I have seen in Cyprus … had no training whatsoever in educational administration …

Z: They have a strong educational philosophy … Highly important is their theoretical and political thinking …

P: And they are good observers of behaviour. When I asked school principals in Cyprus about their preparation … [they] … said, 'Well I learnt through the mistakes of others, that is not to repeat them' …

A: It seems to me that in Cyprus and Greece, you are where England was in the 1970s, when we could say there were good leaders in schools but there wasn't any training then … By the end of the 1990s, there was national preparation, post-appointment and professional development … So … do we really need this training?

O: … we have had a strong tradition in Sweden for the last twenty years that we learn from our practice. Basically … those in … leadership positions come together to reflect and think about what they have done.

Extract 3

The final example comes from focus group research conducted through email. The challenge was to find how to convey the exchanges. The research team explained their decisions on their reporting format and followed it with email extracts. Note how they preserved the informal atmosphere of email exchanges and how they begin to link in their commentary at the end of the email extracts (Woods et al., 1998: 575, 577–8).

> In order to preserve the nature of the discussion, we present the e-mails in sequence as they were relayed, with some interconnecting explanatory narrative. We have edited some of the e-mails, taking out surplus material, but have otherwise left form and content intact ... There were, of course, more communications among us than this, including many, some of them lengthy, telephone conversations. There were also four full team meetings ...
>
> *E-mail from Peter to Barry, c.c. Team (1 December 1996)*
>
> Barry, I sent the e-mail above to Bob, then it occurred to me that your Tim [one of the research subjects] might be an example of 'enhanced transformation' ...
>
> *E-mail from Barry to Peter, c.c. Team (6 December 1996)*
>
> Not sure, but can the notion of 'enhanced transformation' be interpreted in a sense of adaptive professionalism ... ? Such people seem to be the contrast to the deprofessionalized group ... Tim emphasises that change was necessary ...
>
> *E-mail from Bob to Team (c. 12 December 1996)*
>
> [Here the article authors changed to reported speech form]
>
> Bob continued to process his data, and on 10 December 1996, circulated some material on an additional category ... During discussion, we decided that the typology should be focussed on changes to the teacher *self* ... and Bob's data were rich in this area ...
>
> *E-mail from Bob to Team (24 December 1996)*
>
> The work so far on this chapter includes the following ...
>
> Have a good Christmas Day.

9.7 Historical, literary and legal data

Dead, or inanimate, sources present demanding challenges for both humanities' and social sciences' writing and presentations. Superficially, there appears to be much licence in what can be reported and how, since the sources cannot argue with you or feel aggrieved. Deeper reflection finds researchers often faced with a plethora of data both from original sources and from those who have later commented on them. The written results can then descend into little more than a cursory survey, an annotated bibliography or extensive quotations with minimal linking text. Literati and historians face an additional challenge: they are expected to be able to produce literate texts. These are often bounded by 'essay' style; the beneficence of subheadings is not for these, and writers must perforce argue and theme their texts very rigorously (legal writers more usually adopt subheaded formats to help readers through the thickets of legislation).

The techniques for literary reviews will help (7.3) but research writing from historical, literary or legal sources consists of little else than literature review and so has to employ further devices to enhance understanding and deepen readers' enjoyment.

1 *Avoid swamping the text with citations.*

(a) Designations common to all sources should appear at the beginning of the text, as in 'Quotations from Oliver Goldsmith's journalism are taken from *The Collected Works of Oliver Goldsmith,* ed. Arthur Friedman, Oxford, Clarendon, 1966 ... The place of publication of all periodicals is London, unless otherwise stated' (Italia, 2005: notes p. xi).

(b) Select those items that must have citations (those central to the thesis you are expounding) but leave unsourced any material that could be deemed 'generally accepted' knowledge. In Worster's history of the mid-US dustbowl in the 1930s, he states, without overt verification, that 'One of the major obstacles to farmstead diversification was the high percentage of non-resident operators' (2004: 152). Later on the same page he quotes, and cites, a letter from the grandson of one of these operators that they were not interested in the land as a home but solely as a means to make cash.

(c) Use footnotes with end-of-text citations to produce an uncluttered text (12.4, 12.6).

(d) The sum of the text should exceed the sum of the quotations and examples. One or two per page is more than enough (12.5).

2 *Seek opportunities within the genres themselves.* Research about poetry and drama lends itself to reporting some of the findings as poetry and drama (Chapter 10). Issues of legal dispute could be presented as courtroom debates. Sections, if not the whole, could employ the language of the period being discussed in historical research (especially so in presentations in which you could be a character from the time). Intimations of these approaches were found in a book on crime fiction, in which the researcher regards himself 'Like a detective ... [who] retraces a chronological chain of cause and effect in order to make sense of the present' (Scraggs, 2005: 3). Research examining Canada's problems concerning environmental law used the analogy of a diagnostic check-up for its structure; the book was divided into three parts, 'Examination', 'Diagnosis' and 'Prescription' (Boyd, 2003).

3 *Avoid repetition.* Group together, in an opening chapter or section, the elements common to the whole. Italia's (2005) book on eighteenth century journalism, for example, has an introductory chapter about the emergence of periodicals before proceeding to chapters on individual magazines. Scraggs's (2005) book on crime fiction has an opening chapter surveying the history of the whole genre before launching into a thematic treatment.

4 *Utilize the visual wealth of your subject to break up text and for emphasis.* Worster's (2004) history of the 1930s' USA dustbowl has liberal photographic evidence, mainly spread horizontally across the tops of pages, matching the graphics for each chapter's title, which stretch across two pages on a grey, solid block. This 'horizontalism' is, in itself, a depiction of a great plain. The frontispieces of eighteenth century periodicals are reproduced at intervals throughout Italia (2005); the accompanying text interprets these for readers.

5 *Use structural devices to focus readers' attention.*

(a) The introduction must outline the whole of your document (11.10).

(b) Reiterate principal points at intervals to help readers follow your themes. For example, part way through a section discussing an 1894 South African statute, the researcher inserts the review that 'The three main concerns of the Act were *taxation, land tenure* and *local administration*'; each of these was then more fully examined before 'The rest of this chapter will ... primarily examine the terms of the ... council system' (Beinhart and Bundy, 1987: 139, 141, authors' emphasis).

(c) Ensure that each paragraph's concluding sentence is picked up in the opening sentence of the next. For example, in a text on crime fiction, a paragraph ended with: 'the prevalent literary view of the crime thriller [is] ... formulaic popular literature peopled with cardboard characters'. The opening sentence of the next paragraph reflected back to this with: 'This negative view of the crime thriller has a long heritage, however ...' (Scraggs, 2005: 106).

9.8 Ethics

Qualitative research is regarded as peculiarly democratic. Hence 'the "natives" or "insiders" with whom researchers are working must, ideally, collaborate in the construction of the final story that is to be told' (Swanger, 2002: 4). Some suggestions for achieving this are in 3.6.3. The ethical importance of respondent partnership is to balance the researcher's 'power regimes impacting ... [on] subjectivity' (Chaudry, 1997: 41).

Undertaking observation, the researcher, like a photographer, is the dominant personality, whether this is participant, semi-participant or non-participant. You are recording as an outsider what it is you think is seen by the insiders. Given your power, ethical observers should try to empathize with their subjects, to convey how they are likely to be reacting, to indicate where the researcher is situated physically and intellectually and to acknowledge all this in the text. This at least offers readers some chance to assess the data through their own subjectivities as well as those of the researcher and the researched.

A strong example of this can be found in a graphical cartoon used to report research on how the Chechen are coping as refugees in Ingushetia (Sacco, 2005). The researcher, as narrator, appears alone in the first frame, describing the context to the reader. In later frames he is drawn in the position in which he would be seen by those he is observing and interviewing. He wears spectacles and the glass obscures his eyes, almost as if he is conveying sightlessness to allow the reader to enter the scene. Each frame is meticulously drawn and includes detailed conversations; there is a connecting text in some frames but it is exquisitely flat and neutral.

Another solution to ethical challenges is to present more than one account of the same event, making sure that data which do not necessarily support your preferred view are also offered to readers. Interview and focus group data lend themselves to this, as does the presentation of varying recollections of events in history. For example, quoting from Sarah Bernhardt's own recollections of her life as told to her granddaughter, Otis Skinner's (1966: 49–51) re-creation of Sarah's life relates a touching scene in which the father of Sarah's son, deeply in love with her, tells of his intention to marry her. She dramatically refuses, having been persuaded by his family (unknown to him) that such an alliance would be disadvantageous to this man she loved so much. Alternative versions of this story describe scenes which indicate that the lover coldly refused her approaches and disowned the child.

9.9 Review

To ensure polyvocality in reporting qualitative research, select as many voices as possible; find ways to convey them briefly, sympathetically and ethically.

But this challenge of allowing polyvocality while keeping data manageable could be over. Simple, early twenty-first century technology enables all raw, unedited data to be placed on disks or internet files which readers can access as they choose through computers (though some form of codifying would be helpful). The researcher's text need contain only references to the coded data rather than summarized or edited extracts. Readers would then know which data you rejected as well as the references included. If the text itself is electronic, then the raw data can be accessed via hyperlinks. Readers might find the raw data tedious but the method would offer readers more opportunities to decide their own conclusions. It would thus reduce, but not entirely remove, researcher 'influence' since there still would have to be some text and the photos, videos and interviews still have to be designed and taken.

10 Narrative Data

CONTENTS

10.1 Definitions

Quantitative research reduces many voices to one. Qualitative research celebrates polyvocality. Narrative research produces its story from just one voice (though it may also use several including material from quantitative and qualitative sources). Narrative is normally associated with fiction, the creation of a reality that is believable but still fictional (Hayward, 1996: 67). In research, however, narrative *re*-creates reality, but to do so it adopts the formats more usually associated with literary fiction. You are telling a story, just as in all other forms of research writing and presenting (5.2.1), but in narrative you tell it *as* a story.

Since the mid 1990s, narrative has emerged from its ghetto of biography, fiction and history to take on what is claimed as 'a pivotal role in literary and non-literary discourse … applied to a variety of disciplines … [as] a way of making sense out of seemingly incoherent experiences' (Kruger, 2004: 109–10). These experiences now include research methods that collect episodes, accounts, life histories, personal journals, critical incidents, obituaries, letters, oral history and CVs (résumés). Even inanimate objects can inspire narrative (for example, Tim Dent's 2001 biography of a fruitbox). Narrative is deemed to be generalizable because 'writing that tells of one thing, necessarily tells of another' (van Maanen, 1988: 34). Any of these narrative data can be written up qualitatively (Chapter 9) and elements of them could be quantified (Chapter 8), but this chapter discusses their narrative formats.

To write narrative research as a story, the data are organized into a whole akin to a sequential plot, chronologically and/or thematically arranged. This then emerges in a range of styles, such as allegory (Friedman, 1998: 201), novellas, short stories, histories, poetry, biography, plays. It 'is like fiction [but] it is created out of the facts of experience' (Denzin, 1998: 328). It can *be* fiction but shaped by fact (for example, Ellis, 2003; Thompson, 2003; Thody, 1994b). This latter puts narrative research writing close to novels which use real events as their basis (such as Robert Harris's *Pompeii*) but sourcing, referencing and style keep it in academia.

10.2 Narrative's allure

The emergence of narrative as a means of both collecting and writing research is partly accounted for by the allure of story telling. It provides vicarious experiential learning in style and format to which we can easily relate and which do not demand that we take action. It 'invites the reader to join in solving a human problem, followed by an accumulation of meaning as the plot unfolds, and the relaxation of tension in a resolution of the central dilemma' (Barone, 1995: 66). Stories are 'bounded segments of the flow of behaviour and experience that constitute meaningful contexts for action' (Bauman, 1986: 3), 'uniquely powerful currency in human relationships' (Gardner, 1997: 42). More prosaically, stories link us to the comforts of childhood with comprehensible, familiar entertainment. They stimulate our imagination, lull us to sleep, provide a vehicle for disguised learning and offer a safe route for the emotions to be expressed (Thody, 1997b: 334).

In theory, narrative is the ultimate postmodernist alternative since respondents can tell their own stories without any, or only minimal, intervention by the researcher. In practice, the researcher has to intervene in the writing and presenting of narrative data and it is here that the challenges lie.

10.3 Narrative's challenges

Despite its attractions, narrative is somewhat distrusted (Barone, 1995), criticized for being at best partial and at worst 'downright misleading' (Evans, 2000: 27). Writing narrative brings 'the appalling problem of achieving understanding' (Skultans, 2001: 9). To overcome these apparent difficulties, challenges have to be met. These are summarized in Box 10.1 and then each is discussed more fully below.

> # Box 10.1   Challenges to be met in the writing and presentation of narrative
>
> ✝ Controlling voluminous data: *brevity is NOT the soul of wit.*
> ✝ Subjectivity: *personality is all.*
> ✝ Choice of formats: *the sky's the limit.*
> ✝ Fictional fact and factual fiction: *lies, damned lies and … stories.*

10.3.1   Controlling voluminous data: brevity is *not* the soul of wit

A businessman was asked to tell a story about the most significant innovation in his organization. This is a short extract from that story, the whole of which was used in a working paper reporting research into understanding innovation through narrative. The story was presented verbatim though the researchers would have chosen how to punctuate it.

> The furnace was the first [of its type] in the world. And we put that in, in 1992. The question is: why? … At one time our energy bill here was £20 million a year. We used to get a 22 per cent subsidy … The subsidy was going to be withdrawn. We're seeing an increase in our energy bill by 54%. You know £20 million! 54%! So how do you counter that? Well you can go on your knees, you can plead, you can kick … Anyhow what we decided to do was to go for this furnace. (Barnett and Storey, 1999: 15)

All this story tells us is that the company chose a radical new furnace in order to reduce a projected vast rise in energy costs. But this shortened version doesn't convey the full shock, the risk of the decision taking and the emotional impact. It does, however, exemplify this challenge; narrative data must be voluminous if they are to make their point.

They are voluminous because a story teller does not usually go straight to the point. Indeed the glory of narrative is as much in the journey as in the destination. Along the way a narrator will, however, often take a detour and usually these digressions can be removed as a first step in reducing the data. As the researcher, you use only the part of the story that illustrates your hypothesis and meets the needs of your report (6.3). Descriptive passages, for example, can often be deleted.

Volume also arises because conversational speech is usually 'chatty'. You need some of this in order to convey the emotions of the narrator but it can be conveyed by inserting punctuation (for example, the exclamation points in the above extract about the furnace) which the speaker will obviously not have included. Careful selection of particular parts of a narration can also help. In the above example, the repetitious phrase 'you can' gives us clues to the risks of the decision to be taken without annotation from the researcher.

Selecting themes around which to organize extracts from sources is another reduction device (6.4) but, within each category, the sequential nature of narrative has to be retained. For example, Samuel Pepys's seventeenth century diaries occupy very many volumes. From these, numerous researchers have selected extracts to produce manageable books on specific aspects, such as his administration of the navy (Kenyon, 1963). Historical writing lends itself very easily to chronological thematization and hence history articles are most likely to be simply subdivided into numbered sections.

Summarizing techniques will also be helpful (Box 6.1) but it is more important to retain the original tone and emotions rather than précis. Where you have multiple stories, you can at least consider reducing the total number as a last resort.

Much of the data reduction in narrative has, however, to come from the researcher's own commentary rather than from the stories being reported. This requires researchers to view themselves primarily as those who make it possible for others to be heard and as selectors of data that show their subjects, rather than themselves, in the most appropriate way. The cuts have to come mainly in the literature and methodology reviews and the conclusions.

10.3.2 Subjectivity, the researcher and the researched: personality is all

Subjectivity in writing and presenting narrative is as unavoidable as it is in quantitative (8.9) and qualitative research (9.1.3). The added challenge for narrative is that the subjectivities are few, often only the narrator's and the researcher's. The views presented will definitely be partial but partiality is an objective of narrative. Narrative is meant to be a first-hand account. Narrative does not present opinions (those are the domain of the quantitative survey or the qualitative interview); instead it presents the story of the opinion maker. It is a 'highly personal written account of real events' (Ackerman and Maslin-Ostrowski, 1996: 1).

From these accounts, you, the researcher, re-create the stories told to you. In that re-creation, your subjectivity becomes dominant. Thus in narrative, it is very important that readers are aware of the researcher's position (2.3.2). For example, a biographer of the actress Sarah Bernhardt was an actress herself and 'had a special place in her heart for Madame Sarah' (Otis Skinner, 1966: endpapers). She therefore often selected Sarah's own version of events rather than contradictory alternatives because 'I prefer ... [to] respect her wishes' (1966: 51). One anticipates, therefore, both empathy and sympathy and one needs to take these into account when evaluating the stories reported.

The power of the researcher to filter what narrative is presented through his/her own subjectivity has been criticized because 'the story that is told often turns the researcher into a masculinized hero who confronts and makes sense of the subject's life situation' (Denzin, 1998: 328). To avoid this needs large swathes of unadulterated original narrative, but readers' needs (Chapter 4) and word limits (2.3.1, 10.3.1) usually preclude this. The sensitivities, and subjectivities, of those whose story is being told must also be taken into account (Scott and Usher, 1999: 118). Narrative researchers therefore make selections but often present the information as if the researcher is not there and has not in any way biased the text, 'as if the quotations and document snippets are naturally there, genuine evidence for the case being made, rather than selected, pruned, and spruced up for their textual appearance' (Richardson, 1998: 353–4).

Oddly, criticism of narrative subjectivities does not appear to apply to the most subjective narrative of all, autobiography (for an example, see the Appendix to this book, Chapter 17). Autobiography, 'by virtue of its close relationship to the individual and unrepeatable life, elude[s] … constraints and categories … the genre is … lawless (Pilling, 1981: 116). Katharine Graham's autobiography as owner of *The Washington Post* (1997), for example, reports verbatim many detailed conversations that occurred years before the book was written. These do not appear to have been tape recorded, so how realistic is it to assume that what Ms Graham remembered was exactly accurate? Maybe she took time out to write down every conversation she had as soon as it was over, but this seems unlikely. Writing down conversations even later the same day relies on diminished memory. Some of her conversations had no witnesses. Nonetheless, the autobiography is regarded as highly authoritative and accurate. No such judgement would be applied to a researcher collecting the same, unvalidated data.

Researchers employing autobiography have, therefore, to be circumspect but auto-biography is a valuable way to carry a story line and to make a virtue of revealing the researcher's personality. For example, a conference paper on race and gender in leadership preparation was subtitled 'a retrospective journey along my faultlines' (Rusch, 2003). Woven into various paragraphs, the researcher gave the literature review the added interest of relating it to her personal life:

> My journey to the question of social construction of school leadership began at a time when my life was littered with other people's words … A doctoral student at the time, my living space literally was a maze of texts that represented the genealogy of leadership … As I tenuously worked my way through this intellectual labyrinth, I encountered Dorothy Smith's 'line of fault' … Smith's viewpoint was a defining moment in my journey to deepen my understandings … As an experienced female school administrator … Smith's theory exposed my line of fault … and for me, the earthquake had just begun … A friend, spotting my distress, agreed to join me. (2003: 1–2)

10.3.3   Choice of formats: the sky's the limit

There are no conventions for writing or presenting narrative data. Your choices are unlimited and there is plenty of scope for experiments with narrative language described as 'vibrant, suggestive, engaged and passionate' (Harper, 1998: 144). It's way beyond the cautious alternatives of Chapter 5 and the tentative creativities of Chapter 9. Narrative can, of course, be presented as stories with the usual defined beginnings, middles and ends but a much wider range of literary genres is possible. Three of these are discussed below.

10.3.3.1   *Narrative as poetry*
Poetry is unrivalled for enabling emotions to be conveyed. It's problematical for simul-taneously conveying factual research data. The following example (a two stanza extract from a ten stanza poem) was inspired by the collected records of farm labourers work-ing in the USA from 1942 to 1964. The researcher who helped to file the records in 2000, composed the poem to also reflect her own struggles as an outsider at the agency

where she was conducting the research, so she is trying to convey both her own subjectivity and that of the research respondents (Schwartz, 2002: 79–80).

> What should I do during the Revolution?
> Cover my face like stone?
> Steel myself against the cold?
> ... or steal myself (this is my role).
>
> And have you not made me your girl of war?
> Men of war make girls of war.
> I still feel the place where my hope tore ...
> with fear and guns and doubt and guns
> and anger and guns AND GUNS.

I feel that this poem would work best as performance poetry rather than written poetry, given the strength of feeling it conveys and the need for more explanation. The researcher-poet was transmitting emotional inferences from the data but perhaps insufficient of the data themselves for readers to understand her predicament.

An attempt to avoid the emotion but to add to the reading pleasure was tried in Woodley's (2004) narrative poem about a student's first reactions on going to university. His aim was to use poetic form 'as a process to aid my analysis ... rather than creating a transcript that others could use as the starting point for an interpretation of their own ... I hoped that poetry would be an appropriate form to help my data to sing' (2004: 49). Below is part of the data from his student respondent turned into a poetic song. It is a verbatim transcript but Woodley reformatted it.

> I turned up with my parents
> well my mother and step-father
> went in and just dumped my stuff in there.
> They took me out for a Chinese meal
> in the high street.
> It was a bit weird
> because by the time I got back
> and they left
> everyone had disappeared already
> and was down in the bar ...
> Although I did see someone in the bar
> who I'd seen in my halls
> when I first moved in, I'd spotted him down the corridor.
> He was chatting to a couple of girls so
> I went over and introduced myself,
> Said, 'Hello, I er ... I'm in the same halls as you'
> He just looked at me and said, 'And?'

Compare this with how the student's story might have been presented in its original form:

First year student: I turned up with my parents, well my mother and step-father went in and just dumped my stuff in there. They took me out for a Chinese meal in the high street. It was a bit weird because by the time I got back and they left everyone had disappeared already and was down in the bar … Although I did see someone in the bar who I'd seen in my halls when I first moved in, I'd spotted him down the corridor. He was chatting to a couple of girls so I went over and introduced myself, said, 'Hello, I er … I'm in the same halls as you.' He just looked at me and said, 'And?'

For me, the poem displays the disconnected confusions of beginning university life much better than the continuous paragraph. The poem's last two lines bring out the pure youthful, ironic insouciance so beloved of fans of *Friends* (iconic US sitcom 1994–2004); it could so easily have been the fictional first encounter between friends Joey and Chandler, but it was real. The researcher has interposed his own subjectivity only in the reformatting as the poem allowed him to convey more faithfully the 'orality of discourse … [with] a self-conscious artistry and literariness'(Woodley, 2004: 55).

I conclude these examples with an extract from a personally appropriate poem from Richardson's (1997) research on how academic life affects women. This appears in her commendable, seminal work on alternative ways of presenting research (1997: 203–4).

WHILE I WAS WRITING A BOOK

my son, the elder, went crazy
my son, the younger, went sad
nixon resigned
the saudis embargoed
rhodesia somethinged
and my dishwasher failed

[two more verses]

my friend, the newest, grew tumors
my neighbor to the right was shot
cincinnati censured sin
and my dracaena plant rotted
I was busy

Poetic licence allowed no capitalization and minimal punctuation. Both work much more effectively than could correctly presented prose from interviews. They convey the messages that writing overtakes all else in your life, that other claims on your time build up apparently faster and faster and that proofreading is extremely dull.

REFLECTIONS

Return to the poem in Box 1.1 and its alternative in Box 1.2. Was there enough information in the poem? Did it leave readers to work out for themselves what were the meanings of conventional and alternative? This illustrates the demands of narrative writing; readers can have to search harder for themes, meanings and data than in qualitative and quantitative formats. *But* narrative gives the greatest scope for readers' own deductions without researcher direction.

10.3.3.2 Narrative as drama

With a debate about holes to unravel, two philosophy researchers invented a group of quaintly named characters and put them in dialogue that aptly conveys the discursive nature of philosophy (Casati and Varzi, 2004). The result was snappy, entertaining and erudite, as the extracts below demonstrate (2004: 23, 25, 27). The debate arose because of the furore over the meaning of a 'hole' in the ballot papers for President Bush's election in 2000.

> *Cargle:* I know where Argle and Bargle went wrong
> *Dargle:* Concerning what?
> *Cargle:* Concerning holes. Argle claimed that holes supervene on their material hosts, and that every truth about holes boils down to a truth about perforated things ... But we still need an explicit theory of holes ...
> *Dargle:* Go ahead
> *Cargle:* For example, take this card – how many holes does it have?
> *Dargle:* Obviously zero
> *Cargle:* (punches a hole into the card): And now?
> ...
>
> *Enter Zargle (showing up with a suitcase full of newspaper cut-outs):*
>
> Wait a minute. In West Palm Beach the issue was precisely how to reckon the number of hole-creating processes. I have kept all the papers ... in some cases it appeared that a voter made a mistake and then tried to correct it ...
>
> *Dargle:* Fine with me ... [I think that] a hole can have two disconnected parts
> *Zargle:* My dear sisters, you have reached the usual impasse ... – you should have learned from Argle and Bargle – ... why don't we read again what they had to say?
>
> (End)

The selection of a play format was very suited to the purposes, readers and personalities of the researchers. It also enlivened the usual formats of conventional 'debate type' refereed articles. Such invented characters can also enable researchers to disguise their own opinions, and even to express more extreme opinions than they might otherwise admit. This can both avoid alienating readers and provide more chance for readers to decide their own conclusions.

I used the drama device in a 1990 refereed journal article reporting my research on the roles of English school governors. Socrates and his fourth century BC Athenian disciples discussed how twentieth century AD school governance reflected democracy. I chose to have them all meet in heaven debating in the style of Plato's *Republic*, from which I took some direct quotations (Thody, 1990a). Readers could not have guessed whose view I espoused:

> Well met, Socrates, you contemplate the earth below with close attention.
> Indeed yes, Glaucon, a new form of state arises there. School republics are being formed. Independent states claiming to be democracies ... They have guardians, called governors ... Like my ... guardians, these governors control admission to each republic ...
> Surely, Socrates, such detailed intervention in governance reveals overlapping of the executive and deliberative roles which you delineated? ...
> Intelligent observations, Adeimantus, but the governor/guardians are indeed to be 'watchdogs guarding a flock' (Plato, 145) ...

This would seem to militate against their roles as controllers, Socrates.
Certainly, Glaucon ... (Thody, 1990a: 42)

Drama created from a real conference presentation and its subsequent discussion was part of Richardson's report on research about women in academic life (1997: 197–202). The real-life expert on qualitative research, Denzin, appeared as moderator of the group, accompanied by two panellists and fifteen conference delegates. The effect was to take the reader right into the session.

10.3.3.3 Narrative as diaries

Real or imaginary diaries are one of the simplest forms of narrative writing since the order suggests itself and the chronology makes it easy for readers and researcher to keep track of the flow. The challenges lie in:

- deciding what to exclude from what are invariably exceptionally extensive records;
- providing research rigour by presenting sufficient detail for the picture to be coherent and verifiable against other records of the times;
- preventing readers becoming bored with the format of presentation dictated by chronology;
- making themes other than chronology significant.

Reproducing a diary in its entirety is a well established literary genre. Editing by the researcher will be determined by purposes, readers, practicalities and the researcher's personality (Chapters 2–4). Bell's editing of Virginia Woolf's diaries, for example, 'follows the manuscript as closely and completely as possible [with] minor concessions to the convenience of reader and printer concerning punctuation and layout (Bell with McNeillie, 1980: x). Hence we learn that a friend of Woolf's 'says he will get £300 as a lecturer at the School of Economics easily if he wants it ... then we went off on a "blowing" night to dine at Rose M's "pothouse"' (27 March 1926: 1980: 70). Such prosaics are scattered amongst passages that indicate Woolf's novelistic style, such as:

> Women in tea garden at Bramber – a sweltering hot day: rose trellises; white washed tables; lower middle classes; bits of grey stone scattered on a paper strewn green sward all thats [sic] left of the Castle. (3 September 1926: 1980: 105)

The Woolf diaries could afford to be comprehensive with a three volume spread, but for most some cutting has to be done. In Colville's (1985) diary of his time as a diplomat in Britain's Foreign Office during the Second World War, he tailored his entries to his likely readership. He removed

> a high proportion of the trivial entries which are of no general interest, but leaving in a few which may perhaps help to capture the 'atmosphere' of the time ... [and inserted] brief explanations on people and events which, if familiar to my contemporaries, are scarcely so now ... [Also excised were] many of the references to my private life and social activities. (1985: 16, 20)

Developing an imaginary diary offers much more scope for creativity and without the constraints of having to reduce data. It is also a device that collates what could otherwise be very fragmented data. I used this approach by inventing a nineteenth century school principal, Mr Thody, and describing his daily round of school management (Thody, 1994b). Each of the elements of the diary came from diverse documented sources since there are no records of any one principal of a public elementary school, so I imagined such a person. I used the third person but the present tense (5.3.3.5, 5.3.3.6) to combine observation and diary technique.

2.00–2.30 p.m. Seniors' geography [in the] gallery

Mr Thody examines the scholars' recall of his earlier lesson and then the remaining time is spent on Africa and Zululand again because of Matthew Arnold's preference for 'geography to be more than one's own parish' (1).

The managers' meeting
During this lesson, three of the school's managers cross the school room to commence their meeting in the vestibule ... [Mr Thody joins them] They agree with him to recommend ... that marching lines be painted on the floor of the Infants' School and that six chairs, a long pointer and an inkstand could be ordered (2) ...

2.30–3.40 p.m. Reading
Mr Thody hears the oldest children read ... [and sets homework] because then 'the parents get the impression that their children are well looked after' (3).

3.40–3.45 p.m. Good conduct and dismissal
Good conduct and achievement badges are awarded on the basis of last week's results ... because ... 'As long ago as 1804,' intones Mr Thody, 'Lancaster allocated 22% of this budget for prizes and rewards' (4).

(1)   M. Arnold, 1908, *Reports on Elementary Schools, 1851–1882*, London, 90–1

(2)   Gladstone Street School, Leicester School Board, England, Managers' Log Book Minutes, April 1883 [19D59/VII/34]

(3)   Gill, J. [1883, new ed] *Introductory Textbook on School Education, Method and School Management*, London, p. 108

(4)   Miller, P.J. 1973, 'Factories, monitorial schools and Jeremy Bentham: the origins of the *"management* syndrome" in popular education' *Journal of Educational Administration and History*, 2, p. 13

REFLECTIONS

To be deemed research, the above example required copious footnotes of sources. To establish the veracity of the research, the sources included primary documents from archives, secondary contemporaneous books and scholarly reflections from a later period. Remove the footnotes and the quotation marks and you have a historical novel – not an appropriate way to write research.

10.3.4 Fictional fact and factual fiction: lies, damned lies and ... stories

All research writing and presenting can be regarded as ' "fiction" in so far as they are at several removes from the original situation – they express a reality which distorts the social world from which the data is taken' (Holliday, 2002: 101). One stage further on is research presented as a 'non-fiction novel' (Zeller and Farmer, 1999: 16). As non-fiction, it details the reality researched. As a novel, it encourages readers to insert their own personal meaning from outside the text; the aim is to persuade readers to contribute answers to the research questions (Barone, 1995: 66). This comes from engaging emotions as well as rationality, a standard fiction technique.

From the opposite direction comes fiction based on fact onto which novelists graft imaginary characters and a story line. For example, Anthony Trollope's novel *The Warden* (1855) was a story about the effect on one imaginary man and his family of the very real nineteenth century abuses of charitable funds. Jane Austen's novels are praised for their accurate, but ironic, portrayal of life in eighteenth century England though the characters never existed. *The Archers*, a long running radio soap in England set in a mythical rural farming community, has an agricultural editor whose role is to check that all farming references are factually correct. Malcolm Bradbury's final novel *To The Hermitage* (2001) mixed the partly real eighteenth century journey to Russia of the philosopher Diderot with a parallel story of imaginary twentieth century travellers retracing his steps.

The fiction/fact mêlée is now so confused that it is often difficult to tell which genre you are reading. There are novels like *Life of Pi* (Martel, 2001). This is total fiction written as if it were fact, masquerading in the tone of a *National Geographic* article. The penultimate chapter is an extract from a mythical tape transcript presented precisely as you might in an appendix to a PhD thesis. Fortunately, the title page states that it is 'A Novel' otherwise the unwary might be deluded. Then there are short stories that give the appearance of being researched from oral history but are actually entirely fictional. Introducing a series of three stories about personal experiences in World War II, for example, the author writes:

> sons and daughters of ... veterans ... have approached me, asking if I know of anyone who would help them write down their father's memories while he is still able to voice them ... these personal memories usually go unrecorded ... the task of preserving the past is usually left to historians who weren't there ... and to writers of fiction ... Only in fiction can the ... human experience of war be laid bare. (Coonts, 2003: xii)

This introduces what emerge as three short fictional novels by techno-thriller writers, a genre one might term 'factual fiction'.

There is a fine line between this factual fiction and narrative research written as fictional fact. How is the distinction made?

10.3.4.1 Accommodating the fictional

In 'fictional fact' research writing and presenting, the researcher:

- can invent either the characters or the plot but not both;
- must provide detailed source references;
- must make clear what is, or is not, fictional;
- should preferably have some scholarly justification for fictionalization, in addition to its entertainment value.

For example, in the article, 'Tiffany: friend of people of colour' the author explains that Tiffany

> is a composite figure, not a real person. Wherever I have used just a first name in reference to someone, either the name has been changed or the person represents a composite. In one case, I used a last name for a composite figure ('Dr Lincoln') in order to summon particular mythic-historical associations. (Thompson, 2003: 25)

I used the composite figure technique in my article analysing a day in the life of a nineteenth century school principal (Thody, 1994b; extract in 10.3.3.3). I invented the school which he led since there were insufficiently complete records for any one school to provide evidence of styles of school leadership. The mythical school and imaginary principal existed within the real administrative district of the London School Board, one of the many local authorities for education that sprang up after the 1870 Education Act. Then the rest of the story:

> was created as far as possible from contemporaneous sources. It was constructed around a school timetable published in … On to these was built information from other management text books published during the century. Material published before the period to which this account directly refers was incorporated in the form of the headteacher's reflections on times past … It was assumed that the headmaster would still be using some of the methods of the past: headteachers today do not all use all the most recommended modern methods and Victorian school leaders presumably behaved similarly. One feature had to be invented – school lunch break since no books mentioned it but it seemed unlikely that the children went all day without eating. (1994b: 356)

Within the story itself, I had to use my imagination to fit all the elements from the real sources into a single day in the principal's life. The source of every element was footnoted as it occurred in the text, as shown in 10.3.3.3. Piecing the text together certainly required what is considered necessary for writing historical research: 'considerable imagination and resourcefulness … creativity and high standards of objective and systematic analysis' (Cohen et al., 2000: 163).

Fiction to teach research methodology was created in Ellis's (2003) *The Ethnographic 'I': A Methodological Novel on Doing Autoethnography*. She 'invented a fictional graduate seminar in which characters, based on composites of actual students, engaged in a dialogue about autoethnography' (cited in Lewis-Beck et al., 2004: 212).

10.4   Getting started

To try to have your non-fiction novel accepted as your doctoral thesis is possibly too risky as a first attempt at this genre (3.4.2). Research as story telling is a demanding art (van Maanen, 1988: 107). There are, however, some contained ways in which partial narrative can be incorporated into any research writing.

The narrative 'starter', like the qualitative opener (9.4.1), enables you to create a lively introduction but return to more conventional forms later. The following example was the beginning of a refereed journal article on racial power but its novelistic qualities help to attract readers:

> It was around the seventh week of class a steady pattern had been set in motion. We had talked about this pattern over coffee – two researchers eager to see talk about how this class was interacting with the whiteness literature … The class began with initial statements of disbelief, confusion, anger … The class watched a video, and then took a brief break … grab a Coke or a smoke … Randy was the first to speak. (Hytten and Warren, 2003: 65)

How much more enticing, atmospheric and thought provoking is the above extract than if the authors had continued to use the style of their own abstract: 'The essay is based upon an in-depth qualitative study of a graduate seminar dedicated to addressing diversity issues critically.'

Short narrative excerpts can be used at any point to illuminate data. In the following example, the writer could have said '1950s' African American Senate cafeteria workers resented other black people who had better jobs than theirs', but instead chose to insert a much more telling story from a black secretary hired in 1953 by a Senator from Missouri. Describing her first visit to the Senate cafeteria:

> The cooks would put [the food] on the plate and pass it to you. I was very uncomfortable, nervous. You could hear a pin drop. There appeared to be resentment. The [African American] cafeteria workers who I thought would be supportive were also very cold. As a matter of fact, my plate was shoved at me and I stepped back because I didn't want it on my clothes, and it all went on the floor. Well they were looking at me, but I had to deal with it. So anyway, I got another plate. (Ritchie, 2004: 75)

An alternative is to build short stories into conventional formats (1.3.1). A refereed journal article, for example, would have conventional sections on literature and methodology; the findings section would then be the gathered stories. For example, Marx and Pennington's (2003) refereed journal article on critical race theory recounted the reactions of a group of preservice teachers in exploring their attitudes to whiteness and racism. The article was presented, and subtitled, as stories by each of the researchers as they recounted what happened within each of their groups. The stories occupied almost half the article. The stories were in chronological form and the characters of both researchers and students were personalized. In my article with stories from three school principals about real, critical incidents in their careers (Thody, 1997a), each principal's story was recounted in full (about half the article). Each was separately set within the article's three sections, illustrating narrative as performance art, as research and as teaching. Each categorization (6.4) included the literature reviewing the academic rationale for adopting narrative.

10.5   Ethics

The ethical considerations applicable to quantitative and qualitative data apply here also but with two significant additions. First, it can seem difficult to present more than one view of a topic when the whole rationale is to present what is a very singular narrative. Secondly, there is the challenge of deciding how far 'entertainment' value should influence what is written or presented.

Singularity is difficult to avoid in narrative but an ethical researcher will try to present a holistic picture, selecting data that offer the necessary advantageous evidence while not discarding disadvantageous material. The word 'disadvantageous' is here intended to apply to the research hypothesis, rather than to the human subject providing the data. Where the two are inextricably bound up, the researcher should remember the laws relating to what can be allowed in print and the morality of wounding a respondent with what appears in publication. 'Entertainment' should be defined as meaning responsiveness to audience and purpose and ethically treated as suggested in 3.5.2 and 4.6. In addition, you should ensure that the variety that entertainment requires is used to present differing viewpoints and/or that you point out to your audiences where you might be considered to be biasing their attitudes to your work by the ways in which you have presented it.

10.6   Review

They were gathered around the computer. Frozen in disbelief though summer's heat seeped them through. Their narrative writing had been 'transformed from merely serial, independent happenings into meaningful happenings that contribute to the whole theme' (Ackerman and Maslin-Ostrowski, 1996: 12). They knew they could answer the siren call of narrative without brevity, allowing their personalities full vent and creating a novel masterpiece with a fictional cast. It was as much as they could hope for, 'a place to start' (David Helwig, *Considerations*). And a place to end.

11 Beginnings and Ends

CONTENTS

11.1   Why beginnings and ends matter

'Your first line doesn't make me want to continue with this,' intoned my final under-graduate year political science professor as he dropped my unread essay into the waste. Not surprisingly, every first line of my subsequent essays sparkled with wit; I got my scores and a lesson I never forgot.

As I moved on from final year essays, I realized that more than just the first line of the opening sections of documents and presentations made impressions too. There were also the:

- abstracts, executive summaries, key points, prefaces;
- acknowledgements, appreciations;
- keywords, descriptors;
- title and title page;
- introductions;
- contents lists;
- quotations;
- glossary.

The impact of these persuades people to pull your book off the shelf, lift your report from the pile of papers on already overloaded desks, prioritize your thesis or article or attend your conference paper when so many others beckon.

Producing endings likewise affects what people remember of you and your work. The last thing heard or read is what sticks in the mind but you're tired, deadlines loom, you've exceeded the word allocation and your findings sound brilliantly convincing to you. Nonetheless, you still have to spend time creating a great

- appendix;
- quotation;
- author notes or bio-data;
- bibliography, references, works cited;
- conclusion, discussion, summary, recommendations.

Each of your research documents or presentations will contain some of these beginning and ending elements but it's highly unlikely that all of them will be needed in any particular document. They will also differ in their appearance, their lengths and their locations in different types of research reporting. This chapter's contents are therefore presented alphabetically to emphasize that there is no set order, even in conventional documents or presentations. Researchers should choose which elements to include, and in which order, according to the principles of Chapters 2–4.

Box 11.1 outlines the design criteria for all the beginnings and endings listed above, each of which is elaborated in the rest of the chapter. Test the criteria against the examples in each section of this chapter.

Box 11.1 Design criteria for beginnings and ends

The beginnings should:

1. Encourage the audience to read or listen to your work.
1. Provide guidance on the contents.

Box 11.1   (Continued)

⊥ Establish a 'flavour' of what is to come through your chosen style.

⊥ Ensure that readers have appropriate information to understand what is to come, such as glossaries and contextual information.

⊥ Make sure that potential users will be directed to your work when conducting (electronic) searches.

The ends should:

⊤ Make readers/listeners remember you and your major findings.

⊤ Review the contents.

⊤ Ensure that readers have appropriate information to understand what has been written/presented. Hence, there should be a summary that repeats the main points, a bibliography to show the literary context of the work, and possibly appendices with raw data or research methodology.

Both beginnings and ends should:

⊥ ⊤ Demonstrate close and accurate attention to detail and exactness; these are professionally regarded as indications that your research document or presentation has been written in the same exacting way as the openings and closings.

⊥ ⊤ Be appropriate for audience, purposes, practicalities and precedents (Chapters 2–4) and adopt suitable style and tone (Chapter 5).

⊥ ⊤ Be produced after the heart of the document is completed. Working drafts, or notes, for beginnings and ends can be written as you start a document. They should be amended as you produce the rest of the document and only finalized as the last elements you write.

11.2   Abstracts, executive summaries, key points, prefaces

Are you interested in wind scorpions? Probably not but it's possible that you might be tempted by this *National Geographic* article's abstract that promises, 'Massive jaws, voracious appetite, and sprinters' speed attest that these aggressive desert dwellers are built to kill' (Moffett, 2004). This example encapsulates what these short synopses of your whole document should achieve, as outlined in Box 11.2.

Box 11.2   Objectives for abstracts, executive summaries, key points, prefaces

- *Outlines that guide.* The Literati website advises that sentence one of an abstract gives a rough idea of the whole, sentence two summarizes the main points of your argument and sentence three contains the conclusions. A possible additional sentence outlines the methodology. Keep it short by removing redundancies such as 'This article shows' and unnecessary qualifying words. Absolutes are permissible in abstracts; the cautions come later in a document.
- *Invitations that attract.* Hook the casual browser (reader or conference listener) into continuing to read your whole document (or listen to your presentation) by the supremely well written prose of the abstract, accurate to a nicety. Academics want to feel reassured that you are competent and the abstract should scream this. Wider readerships want to feel comfortable with your style. Hence, the 'hook' for a 2000 word article in *Traditional Boats and Tall Ships* was simply: 'For a brief period in the 19th century schooners rushed fresh fruit to Britain from the warmer climes in the south. **Tony James** tells the story of the vessels and the men who sailed in them' (2002: 40).
- *Keywords that guide.* These elements provide access routes for electronic searches. Hence you need to include all the keywords that web searchers in your field are likely to use.
- *Summaries that grab.* Summaries substitute for the whole document and are the only part of your document that you can guarantee everyone will read (apart from the title). They are the rapid reader's short cut when wanting to include you in a literature survey. Other researchers will cite you in only one or two sentences which can be culled from the abstract.
- *Compression that focuses.* Abstraction is a humbling experience, as you compress your 80,000 words into 150. The most important inclusion is showing what is special or unique about your research.

Given the important objectives of Boxes 11.1 and 11.2, impact is vital. Every word literally counts but you have relatively few words in which to summarize your work forcefully:

- *Abstracts.* Use about twenty words for a populist journal, 50 for a conference programme, 100–200 for a refereed journal and up to 400 for a thesis. Conventionally, abstracts are written as a text paragraph or sentence. These are often in a different font to the whole to distinguish them from the beginning of the text.
- *Executive summaries or key points.* Ideally, these should fit on one page of your report. They will be numbered or bullet pointed with usually no more than one or two sentences for each point. To each will be attached, in parentheses, the numbers of the chapters or paragraphs in the full report which elaborate the key point.

- *Preface.* Book prefaces are the author's apologia as well as the summary. They vary from one-liners to whole chapters. An example is the 'hazard warning' at the beginning of this book.

The impact of any of these brief openers increases according to its location in the document:

- *Articles.* Single paragraph abstracts can appear: in a collected list at the beginning or end of a journal (so think about the competition for readers' attention when writing yours); immediately after the title of an article and before its introduction; or at the end after the references and notes.
- *Books.* Abstracts can appear as part of the preface and/or on the covers. The front cover version would be just one sentence; a back cover version could be a longer paragraph. They are the most demanding to write and may well be done by publishers' editors who know best what attracts a market.
- *Conference papers.* Your abstract will be in the conference programme listings, competing with often substantial numbers of others. Such abstracts are usually required to be conventional and their layout is determined by the conference organizers. You, therefore, have only the wording with which to attract readers.
- *Reports.* Invariably the abstract appears as the key points summary on the front or second page but in massive competition for busy readers' time. As it may be the only part of your report which many people read, you do need to choose every word carefully.
- *Theses/dissertations.* These longer abstracts are usually set on a separate page after the title. They are the first part of your work that an examiner reads (3.4.2) so they really do have great importance.

The following three extracts (two abstracts and an executive summary) offer an opportunity for you to reflect on different styles. They are all conventional but my commentary indicates where the authors had choices to make. Reflect on whether or not you agree with their decisions.

Extract 1

The following abstract for an academic refereed journal meets all the objectives of Box 11.2, except one. Which one?

> This article presents the findings of a random national sample of 1,719 superintendents, using a 67-item survey instrument called the Superintendent's Professional Expectations and Advancement Review (SPEAR), which measures superintendents' occupational perceptions, career satisfaction, and job mobility. The study's major findings include that superintendents perceive the *quantity* of applicants for the superintendency to have decreased in recent years and are concerned about high turnover of superintendents. However, superintendents are less worried about the *quality* of applicants for vacancies. Contrary to popular perception, superintendents report significant career satisfaction, particularly in the nation's largest districts. The study concludes by offering possible explanations for the widespread public perception of a crisis in the superintendency. (Fusarelli, Cooper and Carella, 2003: 304)

Correct. You spotted that the abstract lacked the 'wow' factor that can make us want to read further. It doesn't tell us how special this study is. Is it the only such study? Has SPEAR been used before?

Extract 2

The next abstract is the perfect summary – but does it summarize too much? Some abstracters feel that the conclusions should not be revealed as has been done in this example; the abstract should confine itself to what the article intended to achieve, how and why, otherwise readers will not bother to pursue the full article. What is your opinion?

ABSTRACT The First Destination Survey of new graduates provides only a snapshot of graduate employment. This longitudinal study explores more fully the career pathways taken by undergraduates from two programmes and examines which skills acquired at university contributed to successful employment and development of their careers. It was found that 99 per cent of respondents made a successful transition from higher education to the workplace, with 56 per cent in a job related to their first-degree subject. Career pathways were diverse and half of graduates undertook further study/training at various stages to improve their career prospects. Skills identified as most useful were oral and written communication, teamworking, personal organization, self-motivation and subject knowledge. Areas recommended for curriculum development were subject-specific practical skills, information technology and additional support with careers advice and guidance. (Shah, Pell and Brooke, 2004: 9)

Extract 3

This executive summary headed a report on the evaluation of training programmes provided by the UK's National College of School Leadership for school business managers (bursars). What are its advantages and disadvantages?

This executive summary highlights the main points set out in detail in the *Bursar Development Programme Impact and Evaluation Report 2003/4*. The main focus is:

- the policy development leading up to the announcement of the Bursar Development Programme
- the case for school business managers
- the College's response in terms of the development of CPU programmes for school business managers
- the key challenges which face the programme.

(Bursar Development Programme at www.ncsl.org.uk as at 2004)

This summary is commendably brief and visually pleasing but it does not summarize the report; it only lists the main items in the report, so it's a contents list not a summary.

11.3 Acknowledgements, appreciation, forewords

Thankfully, 'acknowledgements' are beginning to be replaced by the much warmer sounding 'appreciation' (as at the beginning of this book) although these public admissions of gratitude can seem insincerely akin to your Oscar-winning speech. Through tears, you humbly mention everyone you cannot afford to offend. Less cynically, these are opportunities to spread gratefulness, which is rare in academic life, so give thanks in all your research documents and presentations for:

- *Funds* from research grant agencies or university scholarships. This shows that others thought your research was important and also ethically alerts readers to any possible bias that might arise from your source of funding. It is usually a condition of such grants that you acknowledge their help.
- *Information* from your research subjects, especially those whom you cannot thank personally (3.6.3).
- *Guidance on your research and/or your writing* from mentors, article reviewers, colleagues who read drafts, supervisors and publishers *but* point out that only you are to blame for any faults in the work.
- *Ideas* from other people's research to which you had privileged access. For example, 'I would like to thank J A Nunn, A Nelson ... for permission to cite their as yet unpublished findings' (Hodges, 1998: 230); 'I would like to give specific mention to Douglas Pye for generously sharing his ideas ... and for pointing me towards Fritz Lang's *Cloak and Dagger* with its mirror shots of offscreen space' (Thomas, 2001: Acknowledgements).
- *Education* from those who set you on the road to success, from your parents to your university.
- *Technical assistance* from secretaries, proofreaders, editors.
- *Earlier opportunities for your work to be presented*, at previous conferences for example.
- *Moral support and time to write* from your family or work colleagues.
- *Copyright permissions* to reprint material from the sources cited, together with the list of the sources.
- *The invitation to speak* from your conference academic hosts (usually at the beginning of your presentation).
- *Conference organizers* including the administrators, technicians, secretaries, caterers (usually at the end of your presentation).
- *Conference audience* for their responsiveness (always at the end of your presentation).

All these 'thanks' are simple good manners. They provide a little emotional warmth amidst the seriousness of even such solemnity as an article on race and class imprisonment inequities, in the *American Sociological Review,* as this example shows*:*

> Drafts of this paper were presented at the annual meetings of the Population Association of America, 2001 and the American Sociological Association, 2001. This research was supported by the Russell Sage Foundation and grant SES-0004336 from the National Science Foundation. We gratefully acknowledge participants in the Deviance Workshop at the University of Washington ... [names listed] ... and ASR reviewers for helpful comments on this paper. (Pettit and Western, 2004: 151)

More personally, in an article from a similarly peer reviewed social science journal:

> The authors would like to thank the students in Education and Culture for participating in this project; Anne Adkins and Kris Renn for helpful comments on early drafts of the paper; and especially Audrey Thompson for many conversations about their work and valuable suggestions for improving this essay. (Hytten and Warren, 2003: 88).

Scientists seem less effusive: 'This work is supported in part by the CVCP Overseas Research Scholarship Scheme and by Astra-Zeneca Limited' (refereed journal article on fibre optic research: Xu, Jones, Fothergill and Hanning, 2001: 614).

Book acknowledgements can be positively sparse, such as 'To Fred and Ximenia', or can expand over several pages. There appears to be no general rule.

Forewords (for books and occasionally for research reports) reverse the flow of thanks since they are an appreciation of you, or rather of the significance of the research you are presenting. It's valuable to ask someone who is important in the field about which you are writing to provide a short foreword in your book. This will celebrate its importance and support its provenance. For example, Frankhauser's (1995) book on the economics of the greenhouse effect has a foreword from the Director of the Centre of Social and Economic Research on the Global Environment, in which the research took place. He writes: 'In the space of only a few years, Sam Frankhauser's work has gained worldwide recognition … CSERGE is proud to have been the environment in which it was developed' (1995: xii).

11.4   Appendices

Appendices are temptations best avoided. They do, however, show awareness of audience since they can signal material of interest to minority readers only such as:

- Raw data for proof of conclusions in the document.
- Research methodology and/or sources for documents (see the Appendix to this book, for example).
- Calculations that would unnecessarily clutter the appearance of the main document.
- Anything not centrally germane (but remember the appendix question – if it's not central to the argument, why include it at all?). In Frankhauser's (1995) book on the economics of global warming, for example, appendices provided detailed information on how he created the models he used in his book. The models were almost certainly a central part of his doctoral thesis from which the book emerged, but the differing readerships relegated the models to the appendices for the book.

Whatever they contain, each appendix should be numbered (if there are more than one) and titled, both in the contents list at the beginning and at the head of the appendix itself. Each appendix should contain only one item. In the main text, there must be a reference to each appendix. This will tell readers the content of the appendix and explain why it's relegated to the back.

Research reports often carry more appendices than text. This can be justified in that it frees readers from all but the central essentials but still provides value for the money spent commissioning the report. Thesis and dissertation writers are the next most guilty of appendix fever, partly in the largely erroneous beliefs that appendices are not included in the word count or that appendices give an appearance of erudition. Articles rarely have appendices because of the limited word allocations. Those that do tend to be quantitative or scientific.

For example, in a quantitative article exploring the relationship between learning effectiveness and room types (Stewart and Hodges, 2003), only the one table showing the most important correlations appeared in the seven text pages and all other survey results were reported in prose. Sent to the eight pages of appendices were tables showing room capacities around the buildings, a copy of the survey instrument, tables giving the ratings accorded by the students for room quality and importance to learning, analysis of perceptions of quality between buildings, scattergraphs of quality versus importance and mean quality and importance. This use of appendices enabled each table to be set on full pages uninterrupted by text and the flow of the article was more easily maintained.

REFLECTIONS

Does the Appendix in this book (Chapter 17) contain appropriate material? Should it have been included at all? Should it have been placed elsewhere?

11.5   Author notes or bio-data

Conventionally the functions of author notes are twofold. The first is to establish the credibility of a research document from the author's experience in the particular field. For example, in an article on 'Belonging, identity and Third Culture Kids: life histories of former international school students', the principal author revealed that she

> has experience teaching in national and international schools in the UK, France, Israel, Nigeria, Switzerland and the US, and is a cross-cultural consultant with international schools specialising in the profile of the Third Culture Kid and transition. She currently leads the MA in Education: International Schools at Oxford Brookes University. (Fail et al., 2004).

The second function is to enable readers to contact authors for further discussion. Less conventionally, the notes should indicate the author's perspective so readers can judge the ethics of the research more effectively (2.3.2).

Select from your résumé whatever best establishes your credentials for that particular research. Then each document's bio-data will vary according to the principles of Chapters 2–4. Hence you can range across:

- *Theses/dissertations*. Your name only.
- *Research reports*. Short but formal. In a report on school governance for an English district education authority, for example, the bio-data could be:

  > Emerita Professor Angela Thody, FCCEAM, PhD, MEd, BA, PGCE, MACE, ILTHM of the International Institute for Educational Leadership, University of Lincoln, began governor research with her doctorate in 1990. Since then, she has evaluated governor training for private and public authorities, lectured to and about governors in many countries and published two books on the subject.

- *Books*. Short and less formal. For a book on school governance, my information could be:

  > Angela has enjoyed researching and teaching school governors since the mid 1980s. She's shown them how to control their principals (but she also lectures to school principals on how to control governors to redress the balance). She's a school governor

herself for both secondary and primary schools and presented a programme for governors on the teachers' TV channel.

- *Articles*. Their author bios are somewhere between the research reports and the books. For an article comparing English and Ugandan school governance, I wrote:

  Angela Thody is professor of Education Management at … Her research interests have focussed on school governance and she is currently directing a project on the role of school governors from industry. In her spare time, she is President of the Commonwealth Council for Educational Administration and Management. (Thody and Nkata, 1997: 77)

- *Presentations*. These bios mix the styles of research reports and of articles, but bear in mind that the chair of your session will be reading yours aloud. Provide the chair with your bio-data in a colloquial style; some slight humour is acceptable.

REFLECTIONS

Write your own author notes in each of the styles above. The author notes for this book are in 15.6 and 17.2. Are they appropriate in position and content?

11.6 Bibliography, endnotes, references

See Chapter 12.

11.7 Conclusions, summary, recommendations

Virtually all readers will pay particular attention to your conclusions and most listeners will awaken for your closing points. These provide your major opportunity to demonstrate the depth of your thinking and of your originality.

DON'T SKIMP ON WORDS OR TIME FOR CONCLUSIONS.

11.7.1 What's the difference between introductions and conclusions?

Very little, except for their locations. The conclusion below, for example, is from the article for which the abstract is given in Extract 1 in 11.2. Read them both to see what has been changed.

This article analyzed the findings of a random national sample of 1,719 superintendents, measuring their occupational perceptions, career satisfaction, and job mobility. Among the study's major findings, superintendents perceive that the *quantity* of applicants has decreased in recent years and that they are concerned about high turnover. However, superintendents are less concerned about the quality of applicants for vacancies. Superintendents in large districts were most mobile, spending fewer years in either the classroom or as a building-level administrator. Contrary to popular opinion, superintendents report significant career satisfaction, particularly in the nation's largest districts. Despite widespread public perception of superintendents lasting only a few short years, superintendent longevity is longer than commonly believed. While this study questions whether the superintendency is in fact in a state of crisis, there is clearly a concern among current superintendents about superintendent turnover and supply, if not the quality, of candidates applying for the position. The study concludes by offering possible explanations for the widespread public perception of a crisis in the superintendency. (Fusarelli et al., 2003: 324)

You're right: virtually nothing was changed, and that's how it should be. Repetition ensures more effective learning. Likewise in making *presentations*, the conference abstract, the introduction to the speech and its conclusions should all repeat. They should all be considerably shorter than for written documents and be presented in the most pithy and memorable way possible.

11.7.2 Components

Conventional concluding sections comprise one or more of the following:

- *A summary of the whole.* In long documents, such as books or theses, the summary can helpfully repeat the preceding chapters' conclusions though this can sound rather pedantic. For example, the conclusion to Thomas's book on interpreting spaces in American films is as follows:

    > In Chapter 1 we saw how the significance of various spaces within [the films] *My Darling Clementine* and *Party Girl* assumes and depends upon the viewer's familiarity with ... historical facts and cultural myths ... In Chapter 2, our exploration of the theme of scandal in small-town melodramas uncovered the way that ... films ... give us sympathetic access ... in Chapter 3, our close reading ... of *Advise and Consent* revealed parallels between women and homosexual men. (2001: 120)

    (Note how she uses the inclusive 'we' and 'our'. For comment on this style see 3.7, 5.3.3.6.)
    In shorter documents and in presentations, one is forced to be more succinct and thus emphasize only the most significant points. Whichever approach is selected, the aim is the same – to assist the readers' and listeners' recall by repetition.

- *Links to the literature* can be generalized or can discuss particular authors (the latter would be a requirement in a thesis), as in this example from the conclusion to a working paper:

    > In this paper we have sought to build on the work by Buckler and Zien ... We have agreed with them that ... But our work differs from theirs in two main ways. First, the focus of our attention has not been on the symbolic. (Barnett and Storey, 1999: 26–8)

- *Recommendations/implications* for theoretical, methodological and practical developments as appropriate for readers/listeners. These are not easy to draft (Darlington and Scott, 2002: 178) or to have accepted. To help the process:

    (a) draft possible recommendations as you write from the start of your research (2.2); this means you will constantly refine the ideas to make more impact;

    (b) make realistic suggestions in the light of what you know about the possibilities for implementation;

    (c) offer various options rather than just one closed recommendation;

    (d) work out the practical implications of your recommendations (not usually needed for a thesis);

    (e) present them appropriately (Chapters 2–4);

    (f) show that they arise from your research but demonstrate how they could fit other contexts.

- *Discussion of the findings (conclusions)* showing how your outcomes prove or disprove your hypothesis or question (stated in the introduction: 4.3.2, 11.10) and showing what your findings have added to the literature (7.3) and methodology (7.4).

- *Final thought-provoking statements.* Here you can even express a personal opinion since 'there comes a moment when ... the significance of the unreflectively utilized viewpoints becomes uncertain and the road is lost in the twilight' (Max Weber, 'Objectivity in social science', in Shils and Finch, 1949: 112).

In *alternative* approaches, conclusions shouldn't exist – literally. Readers should be left to make up their own minds. Even the most dedicated postmodernists, however, would only very rarely follow this route so you can expect to include at least a short conclusion even in the most alternative of documents. Omitting a conclusion is found most suitable in research documents that reproduce entire conversations or narratives.

The following example demonstrates all that a conventional concluding section should combine. It reflects back to what has gone before in the document and forward to a shining future.

> There are examples of positive and negative personal experiences [in the data] just as there are examples of positive and negative findings in the literature. Sadly qualitative, interpretive research data cannot provide facts and figures to parents of Third Culture Kids to reassure them that their children will grow up as well balanced individuals with a deep sense of belonging and strong sense of identity. The data do, however, illustrate the comments and claims made in the literature, and what is important in that the data provide a springboard for discussion. They provide case studies for examining the issues so that readers can see to what extent they identify with those speaking ... It is hoped that they will be used as such, and that they will help current international school students prepare for the future. As Socrates said, 'An unexamined life is not worth living.' May research in the area of Third Culture Kids provide an opportunity for current international school students to examine their own lives with reference to those who have gone before them. (Fail et al., 2004: 333–4)

11.7.3 Location

It seems obvious to put conclusions at the end. With, however, large numbers of papers to scan for a research project, one can only be grateful to authors who decide to put their concluding summaries into the introductions. This is exemplified by the following extract from the first paragraph of an article about parents' involvement in their children's education in Hong Kong:

> The purpose of this paper is to identify teachers' perspectives on the most important institutional factors that affect parental involvement in the local context ... The findings indicate that teachers exhibit a low level of acceptance of parental involvement in school governance. Teachers generally did not accept parents as having authority to 'make decisions' in ... issues such as school management, budgeting and staffing. (Ho, 2003: 58)

When key points of research reports and abstracts commence documents, they fulfil much the same function as putting the conclusions in the introduction (11.2).

11.7.4   Style and tone

- *Caution* is required in all but the most populist media (5.3.3.1) however unassailable the data seem and however much the policy makers want definition (3.5, 3.6.2). Hence, for example, 'the results indicate a strong actuarial prediction of a school's educational achievements ... The meaningful variables underlying this relationship remain to be explored. Educational support ... is likely to be one source but there may be others' (Conduit, Brookes, Bramley and Fletcher, 1996: 204).
- *Constancy* of style is needed so that the concluding sections fit with the rest of the document. In a first person ethnographic paper, for example, the researcher ended with:

  > My field study at the Center for Environmental Resource Management was a very rich experience for me. Working there allowed me to interact with people of wide and varied backgrounds ... During my time on the border [between the US and Mexico] I was able to appreciate the interconnectedness of such phenomena as economic development, industrialization, pollution ... and poverty. (Kadel, 2002: 41–2)

- *Presentations* offer the opportunity to be much more authoritative and to change style. You want to provoke debate and have an immediate opportunity to argue with protagonists. You want to wake up your audience before lunch.

11.8   Contents listings

This book has three sets of contents listings, the overview, the analysis and the index, a format also found in, amongst others, the MLA *Handbook for Writers of Research Papers* (2003). The varying contents lists recognize that different readers have different purposes; the books may be used as linear text or as 'dip-in' reference. Babbie's (2001) text on *The Practice of Social Research* also has three, a one page outline, a nine page detail and a twelve page 'holographic overview'. This latter is each chapter's content in text form and an explanation for the rationale behind each chapter. This creates:

a context in which you can hold and make sense of the many details on social research which follow ... Second ... referring back to this chapter can help you keep the forest in focus as you become familiar with individual trees ... Third, after reading the entire book, you can use this chapter as a review. You can return to the big picture. (2001: 1)

Conventionally, contents lists appear at the beginning of documents:

- *Books* will generally have only one short list; reference texts may use a longer, but simplified, index as their contents' listing, as in *Key Ideas in Educational Research* (Scott and Morrison, 2005) and *The Sage Encyclopaedia of Social Science Research Methods* (Lewis-Beck et al., 2004).
- *Theses* will have one, detailed, list since they have no index.
- *Research reports* incorporate contents into key points (11.2).
- *Academic articles* must include a contents list but as a sentence or two outlining the whole paper, at the end of the introduction (11.10).
- *Populist articles* rely on the abstract or opening sentence.
- *Presentations* must review what's coming at the beginning and should then return to that list at intervals during the talk and again at the end. This reminds the audience of how many points have been covered (easy to do with PowerPoint and the repetition aids learning and alertness).

I would advise having a contents list even if your approach is more alternative. All readers and listeners are likely to find some guidance helpful. But a serious alternativist would eschew contents lists and leave the readers to discover their own pathways through a document.

11.9 Glossaries

Glossaries have a number of purposes.

First, they can contain anything with which your readers might be unfamiliar. For example, in a book reporting research on the economics of the greenhouse effect, a glossary of chemical symbols was provided (Frankhauser, 1995: x). In a book on chemistry, these would not be needed.

Secondly, they may list abbreviations which are frequently used in the text. Frankhauser's (1995) book, for example, had a long list including:

AEEI   Autonomous Energy Efficient Improvements
BAU   Business as Usual
CETA   Carbon Emission Trajectory Assessment
CGE   Computable General Equilibrium
CRRA   Constant Relative Rate of Risk Aversion

Thirdly, they can explain words that are in common use but whose usage in your text differs from the ordinary. The following extract, from a chapter reporting research on animals' long-distance travels and their consequent spatial awareness, illustrates this and also shows how a glossary can be incorporated into the text rather than being separately listed. The writer has used italics and repetition to build up the readers' understanding.

> Free-ranging animals do not typically spend their life roaming about erratically. They rather tend to display distinct bouts of *sedentariness* in relatively small stretches of space that they go all over repeatedly ... a *home range* ... [when] an animal leaves a home range forever to settle into a new one ... [this] is called *dispersal* ... *return migrations* ... are periodical trips back and forth between two established ... home ranges ... a short lasting foray away from ... and to ... its home range is an *excursion*. (Bovet, 1998: 239)

Finally, glossaries can contain explanations of words that are not in common use outside your own country (3.6.4). For example, in a book that is about the English political system, but is likely to have an international readership, it would be necessary to explain that the abbreviation LA means local authority. The glossary explanation could be that 'England and Wales are divided into local administrative units responsible for most of the services in their areas, such as planning, refuse collection and museum provision. They are led by councillors elected by the local voters.'

Glossaries of one page or less are usually at the beginning of a book; longer glossaries are better placed at the end.

11.10　Introductions

> Imagine that you are swimming in a lake ... Somewhere between a diving board and the mouth of a small river, you find a submerged rock ... I guess you will remember this episode and the general spatial context in which it happened. But how much practice will you need to remember the rock's exact location ...? laboratory rats [could] after a dozen training trials in the Morris place navigation task, which represents the laboratory version of this holiday [swimming] game. (Schenk, 1998: 145)

And so, you are personally swept into a chapter about rats' spatial recognition and, without noticing, you absorb the learning. Thus did this psychology experiment use the introductory device of the comfort of a personalized story to reassure readers that they could cope with learning from an academic textbook.

Academic books for readers largely outside of academia will have similarly enticing introductions, and can afford some imprecision in language and a novelistic style:

> THE TIME: SPRING 1997. The place: outside the Russian embassy, a few blocks from the White House. The stakes: the future of East–West relations. A tense standoff drags on for days, while diplomats and other top-level negotiators scramble to defuse the situation and avert disaster. (Dubin, 1999: 1)

Is this a James Bond thriller with its terse opening phrases that ignore grammatical rules? No, it's a book about museums. The 'standoff' was about Romanov family jewels and where they should be sent following a museum exhibition in Washington.

From the initial entrapment of your readers, we move to the more prosaic context setting that is an integral part of most introductions, as this example demonstrates:

> The realities of globalization and increased local diversity challenge people around the world to develop the ability to live peacefully with those of many different cultures. Not surprisingly, intercultural sensitivity is increasingly seen as an important objective for local and national school systems. (Westrick, 2004: 277)

Then it's on to the outline of the contents (if there is no contents list). Like the context, this can sound prosaic but clarity is welcome to readers. This example is from a refereed journal article on discourse in poetry:

> In this paper, I will first briefly look at some of the debates around transcription, including the importance of using the recording as the primary document. Then I will outline my method of poetic transcription ... After this, I will look at how the creative process of writing can sensitize the writer ... This issue of reflexivity leads on to a discussion of how suitable poetry is for representing discourse. (Woodley, 2004: 49)

Next you add definitions and lead up to your research topic, as in this example. It is from a refereed article on medical signal processing in an engineering journal; the principal audience is not, therefore, medical and needs some explanations.

> Medical diagnosis involves the integration of stored knowledge with new data ... Often the quality of the data is not known, and it is not clear whether enough data exists to provide an acceptable level of confidence in the diagnosis. Associated with this is the pressure to conduct the diagnosis in few sessions with limited resources while keeping patient inconvenience and discomfort within bounds. Attempts to add automation to the diagnostic processes should take these issues into account. It has been shown ... that schemes based on blackboard technology ... and which use fuzzy logic ... can be appropriate ... While the broad objective of engineering and medical diagnostic systems is the same ... it is legitimate to ask how much common methodology is possible. (Jones et al., 2000: 357)

Finally, check Table 11.1 to see that your introduction is effective.

Table 11.1 Effective introductions

Content	Style
Context of the research	Grab readers' attention
Topic/research questions or hypothesis	Avoid jargon (5.3.3.4)
Outline of the document/presentation	Shun abstractions
Significance of the topic (including its relationship to national and international trends in your field)	Move from the general to the specific as fast as possible
Your influence on the research (alternative postmodernism) or your role in it (conventional modernism)	Make readers feel it matters to them (3.7)
Seminal terminology	Show why it's worth reading the whole document

and

REMAIN SHORT

REFLECTIONS

Which of these two introductions to an academic book for both academic and non-academic audiences would encourage you to continue reading?

1   I looked. Increasingly I began to watch. His every move that is. Mr Big couldn't even go to the bathroom without my being there somewhere in the background. In the shadows. If I had known how long it would take, I would never have started but long before I finished, I knew his every hidden thought ...

2   This book reports an investigation into the roles of chief education officers as evidenced in a longitudinal observation study of nine CEOs over nine years. The observations recorded every minute of activities during thirty-six days, including comfort breaks and confidential discussions on covert planning.

These were two possible introductions I considered for my book reporting non-participant observation research (Thody, 1997a). I rejected both and settled on a single paragraph semi-narrative with methodology:

'I'll walk you back to your car,' offered the chief education officer (CEO) to my profound relief. The inner city, 2300 hrs, in November 1986 was not my usual beat. Not so unusual though for the CEO of the education department of an English local education authority (LEA), attending a late-night community protest meeting about the neglect of the interests of one racial group at the expense of another. Being the executive's shadow, I followed whither he went, noting the surroundings, the events, the people and his role in it all. I was in the first months of non-participant observation research on strategic leadership. One CEO had been observed. The second observation was in progress. Still to come in this investigation were nine years and seven more CEOs. (Thody, 1997a: 1)

11.11   Keywords or descriptors

Some journals and abstracting services require keywords for your paper, article or thesis, normally a maximum of six. These are mainly to direct electronic searchers to your document, so in choosing these:

- avoid words already in the title (searches will also scan the title);
- test your selected descriptors on a search engine before finalizing your choice (if no responses are found, the chances are that the phrases are not in sufficiently common use to attract hits; if tens of thousands of responses materialize, then find something more exclusive);
- keep phrases as short and precise as possible;
- use your full allocation of keywords.

REFLECTIONS

Which of the following examples appears to best meet all the above requirements for keywords?

1 'Incorporating a public health approach in drug law: lessons from local expansion of treatment capacity and access under California's proposition 36'

   Keywords: Proposition 36; California Drug Abuse and Crime Prevention Act of 2000; drug abuse treatment; drug abuse policy
   (Klein, D., Miller, R.E., Noble, A. and Speiglman, R., 2004, *The Milbank Quarterly*, 82, 4: 723–57)

2 'A typology of student engagement for American colleges and universities'

   Keywords: student engagement; involvement; Carnegie Classification; typology; NSSE; *Q* factor analysis
   (Pike, G.R. and Kuh, G.D., 2005, *Research in Higher Education*, 46, 2: 185–209)

3 'Gaze patterns when looking at emotional pictures: motivationally biased attention'

   Keywords: attention; pictorial stimuli; gaze; emotional valence; emotional arousal
   (Calvo, M.G. and Lang, P.J., 2004, *Motivation and Emotion*, 28, 3: 221–43)

11.12 Quotations at the beginnings and ends of texts

When there are quotations at the beginning or end of a document (or a section of a document), it strangely appears acceptable *not* to give the precise source or date, not to use quotation marks and not to use sources from the discipline of the research being reported. For quotations cited in the text, these would be unforgivable errors. I can only assume that these conventions recognize that opening and closing quotations are superfluous and just serve as light hearted digressions to attract attention.

To appeal effectively, quotations used at the beginnings or ends of research documents should be 'particularly interesting, vivid, unusual, or apt' (MLA, 2003: 109), brief and singular, and an explanation of their connection to the text should be immediately following or preceding the quotation. I like to see them correctly attributed (see 5.1 for example) but that's not conventional.

All these points are illustrated in this example from a conference paper on the use of case story as a teaching method. It opens with:

> *Pursue, keep up with, circle round and round your life ... Know your own bone, gnaw at it, bury it, unearth it, and gnaw at it still.*   Henry David Thoreau

> The purpose of this paper is to describe ... an approach ... called case story ... A case story is ... a ... description of real life [i.e.] 'close to the bone'. (Ackerman and Maslin-Ostrowski, 1996: 1)

In contrast, an article on the challenge of interpretation and reporting of silences from narrative was anything but silent in its opening. This was decorated with three quotations, to none of which did the text refer directly:

> *Not everything that can be thought can be said.*   Ludwig Wittgenstein

> *For the silence which at every point surrounds the baked discourse seems, by virtue of Wittgenstein's insight, less a wall than a window.*   George Steiner

> *To speak is to sow, to be silent is to harvest.*   Latvian saying

> (Skultans, 2001: 3)

Hughes's (1998) history of swearing went further and opened every chapter with six quotations.

Where quotations are overused like those above, they lose impact and distract readers from your own views. The impression is that the author found many fascinating quotations but could not be bothered to fit them appropriately into the text. The quotations appear to be sourced from general literature rather than academic texts and can make readers feel that the writer is being showily erudite. The quotations just waste your word allocation.

All these caveats also apply to the use of quotations to begin or end presentations. It's better to avoid them and deliver your own words instead. If you must use them, put them on slides and allow the audience to read them in silence. Alternatively, deliver them with panache worthy of a good actor and then explain their relevance to your presentation.

My excellent copy-editor, Brian Goodale, kindly and rightly, took me to task about my views on these quotations. They are, he tells me, correctly termed epigraphs and postscripts and 'come from a gentler age when learning was less evidential ... [and the rules] stem from 100-year-old [publishers'] guides'. Brian felt that my 'antipathy to these elements seemed to jar with [the book's] ethos ... Epigraphs are a bit pompous but they do remind the reader that there is wisdom outside their particular box of commodified knowledge' (Goodale, 2006: 8). I am grateful to Brian for providing readers with a choice as this is indeed the book's ethos.

11.13 Titles and title pages

11.13.1 Titles

When asked for his advice on titles by a neophyte author, W. Somerset Maugham (twentieth century prolific English novelist and short story writer) is reported to have asked the enquirer if there were any drums in his story, to which the answer was negative. Maugham followed this by asking if there were any bugles in the story. The bemused author again responded negatively. 'Well then,' stated Maugham, 'call it "No Drums, No Bugles".'

Maugham's suggested title accords with the most generally accepted advice – that titles should accurately reflect what is in the document. 'No Drums, No Bugles' also grabs attention, is memorably short and lends an air of 'must-read' mystery, all of which are needed in titles. Unfortunately, with the advent of computerized databases, web searching and the global market for research, Maugham's advice would prevent your intended audience retrieving your work electronically; on a book spine, it might lead to your work being shelved in musicology; on a research report, it would be regarded as unnecessarily facetious (unless perhaps the report concerned the needs of school bands in US high schools). The title might, however, be suitable for catching the attention of a conference audience who would have a short abstract as clue to your content.

In creating a title, you are writing an advertising slogan to sell your research. It will encapsulate your product and persuade people to 'buy' it. Following the advice in Chapters 2–4, and from casual, amused observation, I have produced the following for guidance.

THODY'S FIRST TITLE HYPOTHESIS

The smaller, more captive and more academic the audience, the closer the document or presentation to the original research, and the narrower the topic, then the longer and more literal will be the title.

This is *not* a rule but an emergent convention. Thus, in descending order of length, beginning with the most extensive, will be the titles of the following:

- *Theses and dissertations*

  'Within category variation as used in spoken word recognition: temporal integration of two time scales'

  (McMurray, B., 2004, Unpublished PhD, University of Rochester, NY)

'Team training for school senior leadership and governance: a possible model from a business corporation?'
(Horsley, G., 2004, Unpublished MBA dissertation, University of Lincoln, England)

- *Conference papers*

'Student willingness to enroll in a community college English course: the influence of student gender and reading assignments'
(Johnson, B.B. and Newton, R.M., 2003, Paper presented at the Annual Conference of the Universities' Council for Educational Administration, Portland, OR)

- *Research reports*

Evaluation of North East Lincolnshire LEA Governor Support Services
(Thody, A., 1997, for North East Lincolnshire)

- *Refereed journal articles*

'Are district judges equipped to resolve patent cases?'
(Moore, K.A., 2001, *Harvard Journal of Law and Technology*, 15, 1: 1–39)
Note for conventionalists: APA guidelines stipulate 10–12 words.

- *Conference presentations*

This is the most varied genre, ranging from the impossibly long to the naively short. The variations often arise because some presenters will attempt to build the conference theme into their titles whereas others will assume that their title fits the theme without further reference.

- *Books*

These often have two titles. The one for the spine has to be short enough to fit horizontally in enticing capitals, has to be able to be easily deciphered vertically and must be self-explanatory in its shortened form. The one on the cover is an extended version.

> *LIFE AND DEATH* (on the spine)
> *LIFE AND DEATH: PHILOSOPHICAL ESSAYS IN BIOMEDICAL ETHICS* (on the cover)
> (Brock, D.W., 1993, Cambridge: Cambridge University Press)

> *GENDER DIFFERENCES IN MATHEMATICS* (on the spine)
> *GENDER DIFFERENCES IN MATHEMATICS: AN INTEGRATIVE PSYCHOLOGICAL APPROACH* (on the cover)
> (Gallagher, A.M. and Kaufman, J.C., 2005, Cambridge: Cambridge University Press)

- *Generalist magazine articles*

'A stormy star', 'Cocaine country', 'Elephant hunt'
(*National Geographic,* July 2004)

Following the admonition that article titles should not be 'poetic, cryptic or clever' (Sadler, 1990: 19), my further observation research led to:

THODY'S SECOND TITLE HYPOTHESIS

The closer the discipline is to the natural sciences, the less likely are cryptic titles and colons.

Hence *The Canadian Journal of Economics* (2004, vol. 37, no. 2) has uncompromising article titles including:

'Sources of aggregate labour productivity growth in Canada and the United States'
'The determinants of bilateral trade'
'A cost–benefit analysis of R&D tax incentives'
'Lumpy consumer durables, market power and endogenous business cycles'

In contrast, the *Review of Religious Research* (2004, vol. 45, no. 4) offers:

'Spires, wheelchairs and committees: organizing for disability advocacy at the judicatory level'

Finally, *International Studies in Educational Administration* (2003, vol. 31, no. 3) provides:

'The room that nobody wanted: an exploratory study into the importance of room quality to learning'

Using the above two title hypotheses and the success criteria in Box 11.1, consider your comments on the following article title which appeared as set out below, in the journal *active* learning in higher education (journal and article titles are in the same punctuation and fonts as in the originals) (Saunders, Brake, Griffiths and Thornton, 2004). Compare your views with my comments which appear after the title.

Access, astronomy and science fiction

A case study in curriculum design

This example emphasizes words that do not immediately appear 'academic'; 'science fiction' raises subconscious thoughts of leisure reading, thus enticing busy academics with thoughts that this article might not be too 'heavy'. The main title would have the advantage of possibly capturing a wider audience making an electronic search and expecting futuristic novels or stargazing, but the subtitle would also pick up its directly intended audience. The layout attracts attention by its varying font sizes for emphasis.

The article which followed recorded the development of a new curriculum imaginatively including the popularity of science fiction, to encourage access to higher education by people who would not usually want university education. The title not only encapsulated this content but also reflected the 'flavour' by encouraging access to the article by readers who might have flicked over the page had the title been 'A case study in curriculum design using popular literature to attract under-represented groups in higher education'.

The 'advertising slogan' feel to this title could presage an article that uses more of a soundbite approach to our learning. The combination of the cryptic and the literal is entirely appropriate for the journal in which it was placed; the journal is about improving teaching methods in higher education and is a mouthpiece for the Institute for Learning and Teaching in Higher Education which was formed in the early years of the twenty-first century.

The value of the title becomes even more apparent when it is seen in the contents list of the journal, reproduced below. If you were not a specialist in any of the topics listed and did not know any of the authors, the 'Access' article's title implies more lively content than the others.

Beyond first destinations: graduate employability survey
Anita Shah, Katherine Pell and Pam Brooke
Access, astronomy and science fiction: a case study in curriculum design
Danny Saunders, Mark Brake, Martin Griffiths and Rosi Thornton
Teaching business IT ethics: a professional approach
Mark J. Taylor, Eddie Moynihan, Jenni McWilliam and David Gresty
The Revised Approaches to Studying Inventory (RASI) and its use in management
Angus Duff
The postgraduate chameleon: changing roles in doctoral education
Tony Harland and Gabi Plangger
The impact of training of university teachers on their teaching skills, their approach to teaching and the approach to learning of their students
Graham Gibbs and Martin Coffey

Note: the above title demonstrates the increasingly popular alternative of non-capitalized format for titles. Conventionally, 'title case' means that the first and last words, all other principal words and all words that qualify the principal words will be capitalized. Lower case will be for the definite or indefinite articles, prepositions, co-ordinating conjunctions.

11.13.2   Title pages

Having selected a title, you remain only to place it on a page – but placement has differing impacts too. The bare essentials are the title itself and the author's name, but

Leadership Training for Voluntary Sector Managers – the Public Sector Learning Experience?	Is There Really a Teacher Shortage?
An investigation into what a hospital might learn from leadership training employed in the public services	**A Research Report** **co-sponsored by** Centre for the Study of Teaching and Policy and The Consortium for Policy Research in Education **CPRE**
by A. N. Author	by **Richard M. Ingersoll** University of Pennsylvania
A dissertation submitted in partial fulfilment of the requirements for the degree of **Master of Public Administration** **University of XXXXX** **June 2008**	**September 2003** ***(Document R-03-4)*** **ctp** Centre for the Study of Teaching and Policy **UNIVERSITY OF WASHINGTON**
Commentary The above is from the school of 'I must shout at the readers or they won't understand what I am saying.' So let's embolden everything, add underlinings, use the whole page and add a subsidiary explanation to the title. Verdict: OK for elementary school but not for a masters degree.	*Commentary* The above has a much more adult appeal achieved through such devices as right justifying the text and utilizing rules as page dividers.

Figure 11.1   Contrasting styles of title pages

other elements have to be included. Figure 11.1 and Figure 2.2 show all the elements and demonstrate the varying effectiveness of different means of presenting the same elements.

11.13.3   Chapter titles

Your document should appear as a connected whole. Hence:

> ## THODY'S THIRD TITLE HYPOTHESIS
>
> The smaller, more captive and more academic the audience, the closer the document or presentation to the original research, and the closer the discipline is to the natural sciences, the more will chapter titles be statements of fact.

For example, Arnold's (2001) research that produced a textbook on *Fashion, Desire and Anxiety* had chapters titled:

'Status'
'Power and Display'
'Violence and Provocation'
'The Eroticised Body'
'Gender and Subversion'

Hughes's (1998) research on the history of swearing, an erudite topic, seriously addressed but published with both general and academic readership in mind, arranged its chapters chronologically and added an impression of their main themes with elements of the cryptic:

'Unlocking the Word Hoard: the Germanic Heritage'
'Paynims and Charlatans: Swearing in Middle English'
'Schismatic Vituperation: the Reformation'
'The Reign of Decorum: Augustan and Victorian Attitudes'
'Quakers to Convicts: Swearing in the New Worlds'

Almost entirely cryptic in its chapter titles was Dubin's (1999) study of debates about American museums, a book that could equally attract the professional and amateur specialist. His chapter titles breathed contestation in themselves as an embodiment of the book's theme:

'Museums as Contested Sites'
'Crossing 125th Street: *Harlem on My Mind* Revisited'
'"The Troubles" in the New World: The Uncivil War over *Gaelic Gotham*'
'War of the Words: Psychoanalysis and Its Discontents'
'A Matter of Perspective: Revisionist History and *The West as America*'
'Battle Royal: The Final Mission of the *Enola Gay*'
'The Postmodern Exhibition: Cut on the Bias, or Is *Enola Gay* a Verb?'

(Note: italicized as in the original.)

11.14 Review

Against the success criteria in Box 11.1, test this book's:

- *Beginnings*. Title, title pages, appreciation, hazard warning (preface), contents lists, lists of figures, tables and boxes.
- *Ends*. Bibliography, epilogue, appendix.

REFLECTIONS

How, and why, would you alter the beginnings and ends of this book?

12 Citations: Bibliographies, Referencing, Quotations, Notes

CONTENTS

12.1 Uses for citations

Citations attribute ideas and extracts to their sources:

- *In text* as references, quotations and footnotes.
- *At the end of texts* as bibliography.

Box 12.1 explains the uses of all these types of citations.

Box 12.1   Uses for citations

⚔ Defensive

To show that your research is justified by other work in the same field, that the sources cited are not imaginary and that you have used appropriate works from varied sources.

📚 Archival

To record the sources you used for your own future reference.

🎖 Altruistic

To provide readers/listeners who want to research the same area as yourself with accurate and effective directions to the sources you used.

🏆 Promotional

To gain grades in national research assessment exercises which rate you according to how many times your work is cited. There are rumours of citation cartels in which each member cites you if you cite them in return.

👪 Sycophantic

To win friends, and to flatter your mentors, supervisors and examiners, cite their work, paying 'ritualized obeisance to the reigning authorities in a field or accord[ing] newcomers a nod of recognition' (Thompson, 2003: 27). *But* don't cite work that is not relevant to your research just because you want to please the author.

🔒 Protective

To avoid plagiarism by giving credit to the authorities whose work you have used.

12.2   Major citation systems

Citations follow the precedents of one of about 400 assorted formatting systems or variations of these. Box 12.2 lists some of the principal ones or recommended variants of these and provides an example of the same article and book in each format.

Box 12.2   Citation and style systems: examples

System	Most usual in:
APA (American Psychological Association)	Psychology, social sciences

Thody, A. M. (2000). Utopia revisited or is it better the second time around? *Journal of Educational Administration and History, 32* (2), 46–62.

Thody, A. M. (1997). Leadership of Schools: Chief Executives in Education. London: Cassells.

(Continued)

Box 12.2   (Continued)

System	Most usual in:

Bluebook   **American law**

Angela M. Thody, *Utopia revisited or is it better the second time around?* 32 (2) J. ED. ADMIN. & HIST. 46–62. (2000) (discussing the revival of nineteenth century ideas for twenty-first century education leadership).

ANGELA THODY, LEADERSHIP OF SCHOOLS: CHIEF EXECUTIVES IN EDUCATION (Cassells 1997).

British Standards 1629 and 5605   **Any**

THODY, A.M., 2000. Utopia revisited or is it better the second time around? *Journal of Educational Administration and History*, 32 (2), 46–62. .

THODY, A.M., 1997. *Leadership of Schools: Chief Executives in Education*. London: Cassells.

Chicago   **Natural and social sciences, technology, humanities, law**

Thody, Angela, 'Utopia revisited or is it better the second time around?' *Journal of Educational Administration and History* (2000): 32 (2) 46–62

Thody, Angela M. 1997 *Leadership of Schools: Chief Executives in Education.* London: Cassells

CBE (Council for Biology Education)   **Biological sciences**

Thody A.M. 2000. Utopia revisited or is it better the second time around? J. Ed. Admin. & Hist., 32 (2):46–62.

Thody, A.M., 1997. Leadership of Schools: Chief Executives in Education, London: Cassells.

Harvard   **Social sciences, some humanities, journalism**

Thody, A.M., (2000). 'Utopia revisited or is it better the second time around?', *Journal of Educational Administration and History*, vol. 32, no. 2, pp. 46–62.

Thody, A.M., (1997). *Leadership of Schools: Chief Executives in Education*, Casssells, London.

MLA (Modern Languages Association of America)   **Languages and humanities**

MLA has two guides: *Handbook for Writers of Research Papers* (for those up to undergraduate level) and *Style Manual and Guide to Scholarly Publishing* (for postgraduates and professional writers)

Thody, Angela. "Utopia revisited or is it better the second time around?" Journal of Educational Administration and History, 32 (2) (2000):46–62.

Thody, Angela. *Leadership of Schools: Chief Executives in Education*. London: Cassells, 1997.

Oxford   **British law and some humanities**

A.M.Thody, 'Utopia revisited or is it better the second time around?' *Journal of Educational Administration and History*, vol. 32, no. 2, 2000, pp. 46–62.

A.M. Thody, *Leadership of Schools: Chief Executives in Education*, Cassells, London, 1997.

(Continued)

Box 12.2   (Continued)

Vancouver   **Medical sciences, engineering**

Thody A.M. Utopia revisited or is it better the second time around? J. Ed. Admin. Hist. 2000; 32 (2): 46–62.

Thody A.M. Leadership of Schools: Chief Executives in Education. London: Cassells; 1997.

REFLECTIONS

Amuse yourself spotting the minute differences amongst the examples in Box 12.2. Add to your enjoyment by imagining reasons for the differences.

Arcane, archaic, absurd, incredibly detailed and irrational as these systems seem, they each achieve the objectives of standardization as an aid to understanding and accessing references and of saving you the trouble of devising your own. Follow the dictates of one of them to ensure you cite correctly.

1 Find out what system is required at the start of your research. Enter in-text and bibliographical references in this format from day one of your research. Do not wait until the text is complete before entering the citations correctly (2.2.4).

2 Obtain the guide to whatever is the required system. These are readily accessible from numerous websites. Find the latest versions by inserting the systems' names as keywords in a search engine. Universities, journals and publishers usually have online and hard copies available. Each system's guide is immensely detailed and it is not possible to report them here.

3 Use bibliographical management software and let it put all your references into the right format. In 2005 software such as *Reference Manager*, *ProCite* (in need of updating and rumoured to be out of use from 2006), *Papyrus*, *Biblioscape*, *GetARef*, *EndNote* and *APA* were all available, each with varying advantages and disadvantages. More and better software appears continuously so each of the above systems will have several versions. Many universities have the full versions of such software available for all their staff and students but less extensive and cheaper versions can be purchased for PCs. All the systems will store your references in fully cited formats, will allow you to sort references by author, date, title or other indicator and thus search similarly, will enable you to select the references you need for a particular project and will print ready formatted bibliographies. The more expensive systems allow importation of references directly from other sources such as electronic databases, and can establish templates, help with foreign language texts, check that you don't duplicate entries, offer a wide range of citation systems and help you to set up your own, and automatically insert references into your texts. The differences amongst systems relate to perceived ease of use for your subject area and technical capabilities. Guidance on which to buy can be found on retailers' websites as well as demonstration versions. Users often post independent reviews on

the web. Many universities have externally accessible user guides which are also helpful when trying to make up your mind which system would best suit you. Those in academic careers (or intending to pursue academic careers) should learn to work with one of these systems from now (expect costs of around $400 or the same in UK pounds at 2005 prices; UK prices are usually higher than those of North America). Those with just one thesis between them and qualification for careers outside of academia or other research environments should use their university's provision or buy the student versions of their chosen reference management software (about $100 or £100 at 2005 prices). Useful websites to consult develop apace. In 2005, I found:

- www.biblioscape;
- http://information.net/ir/reviews/sofrev12/sofrev12.html;
- www.arts.gla.ac.uk/www.ctich/Resources/bibliogr.htm;
- www.ukolug.org.uk/content/public/links/refmanlinks.html;
- www.library.rdg.ac.uk/resources/endnote;
- www.citewise.com/endnote;
- www.adeptscience.co.uk/products/refman/procite;
- www.refman.com.

12.3   End-of-text citations: bibliography, references, works cited, further reading

12.3.1   Aims

Bibliographical aims are outlined in Table 12.1.

Table 12.1   Bibliographical aims

Aims	Achieved by
To help others find your references and to assure readers that the works you cite are real	Providing as much information as possible about each reference (*but* amuse yourself with Ian McEwan's novel *Enduring Love* to find out how easy it is to fake a credible sounding bibliography)
To show that you know the rules of academic discourse (1.3.2.1)	Following citation system precedents, and contributors' instructions, slavishly (2.3.1, 12.2). Nothing upsets we academics more than a misplaced comma in a bibliography (3.4)
To produce an easy-to-follow list	(a) Using the same citation system for all entries (b) Allowing indentations, white space or graphic devices to signal the beginning of a new entry (c) Clearly differentiating citations from the text. So start a new page for the bibliography. Insert a space at least double that of the paragraph breaks when displaying a quotation in the text. Use different font size and type for the references from that used in the main text (d) Arranging entries in alphabetical order of authors' surnames (e) Opting for minimal punctuation if a citation system is not specified

12.3.2 Definitions

Table 12.2 explains the different types of end-of-text citations.

12.3.3 Locations

Even in these postmodernist times, end-of-text citations appear at the end of the text usually, but not invariably, before any appendices. Case and statute lists for law texts, and filmographies and picture credits for other subjects, may be at the beginning of the text.

The following apply to academic documents:

- Theses and research reports invariably have citations grouped at the end of the document.
- Books may have listings at the end of each chapter, or grouped by chapter headings at the end of the book, or the usual alphabetical full listing at the end of the book.
- Science and social science articles generally have end-of-article lists.
- Humanities papers and books generally footnote citations instead of listing them at the end of the text.
- Literature studies often use the titles of works and/or authors' names in the text and then list the references in full at the end or footnote them.

Professional and populist media have very short or no bibliographies. You put the titles of works and/or authors' names in the text but without any full referencing.

12.3.4 For oral presentations

For academic and professional audiences, the bibliography will be with the accompanying paper. If there is no paper, put references on your PowerPoint slides in very small print (if people are interested, they can ask for details and the references show that you have 'done your homework') or give out the list of references. It's a compliment to the audience, showing that you anticipate that they will be knowledgeable enough to want further references, and it shows you have authorities behind you.

For wider audiences, offer a short list if anyone wants a copy. Those who come to collect one from you at the end are always good for a post-presentation discussion.

12.4 In-text citations (what to put in those brackets)

12.4.1 Professional and populist texts

You won't find the niceties of bracketed citations in these. The few in-text references are incorporated into the sentence flow. For example, in an article about nineteenth century fruit schooners, we find that:

Table 12.2   Types of bibliographies

Title	Most usual in	Contents
Annotated bibliography	Academic textbooks; presentations, lectures	Includes comments on the value of particular sources and brief notes on their contents, for example, Wertheim, M. (1999) *The Pearly Gates of Cyberspace: A History of Space from Dante to the Internet.* London: Virago. An accessible discussion of various frameworks – philosophical, scientific, literary, artistic – for understanding space in different historical periods. (Thomas, 2001: 126)
Bibliography	Dissertations, theses and academic books	Everything you have read in the course of preparing the research, whether or not you have used quotations from them in your text
Bibliographical guide	Equivalent to annotated bibliography	
Essential (or primary) reading	Books for less specialized audiences; sections in textbook bibliographies	'Works considered to be of particular importance to contemporary understandings of topics most central to this book' (Thomas, 2001: 125)
Further (or suggested) reading	Academic textbooks	Sources you would recommend to those who wish to study the subject further; these must contain a significant amount of material directly and overtly on the same topic, or in the same field, as your work
Filmography Picture credits	Appropriate theses, books	Film media listed by title, occasionally by director
Recommended reading	Equivalent to further reading	
References	Articles, papers, research reports, academic textbooks	Everything from which you have quoted or to which you have referred in your text or presentation
Resources	Books for less specialized audiences	Non-text sources, organizations, occasionally websites from which readers can obtain further guidance but which may not have been referred to directly in the book
Secondary reading	Books	Sources used by the author, containing some pertinent material but insufficient to interest a reader wanting to take the subject further
Selec(ted) bibliography	Books for less specialized audiences; presentations	Major sources only
Sources	Equivalent to bibliography	
Works cited	Equivalent to references	

'We'd have fruit on deck when we left St Michael's (in the Azores),' remembered George McVeigh, mate of the Salcombe schooner *Emily*, 'and the skipper would look at it every morning. If it was ripening too fast he'd clap every bit of sail on … There was big money in fruit brought in fast and fresh.' (James, 2002: 40)

There are no clues about who was George McVeigh or from where his words were sourced except for a general reference at the end of the article: 'An excellent collection of fruit schooner models, photographs, pictures and information can be seen at Salcombe Maritime Museum, open daily Easter to October.'

12.4.2 Academic texts

In-text citations can be like wedding confetti – scattered liberally and indiscriminately in the hopes that they will bring joy. They won't, and 'there is a lot to be said for anything that discourages people from referring to work they have not read or from contriving references to barely significant works they have' (Knight, 2002: 198–9). Guidance on in-text citations (what to include, where and in what format) is in Box 12.3.

Box 12.3 In-text citations: what, where and how

- Put parentheses at the ends of sentences as far as possible (so that text flow is disturbed as little as possible).
- Group authors commenting on the same topic into one set of brackets.
- Keep the information within the brackets as brief as possible; you need only as much information as will lead readers to the full reference at the end of the text.
- Use punctuation only where it is absolutely vital to separate items that might be confused, such as dates and page numbers, but not names and page numbers. In this book, the publishers prefer a comma between names and dates, so I acquiesced to their conventions rather than being alternative!
- Whatever format you use, it must be constant throughout your text.
- Parenthesize seminal sources and sources for direct quotations only, 'the rightful acknowledgement of all intellectual debts' (Sadler, 1990: 21).

This book's Epilogue (Chapter 16) conveniently demonstrates examples of all of these in the same Harvard notation as for the other in-text citations throughout this book.

Usually, you must follow the system formats for the type of publication you are writing. A few of the many differences amongst these systems are discussed below, but *always* check what you are required to do and if variations are permitted.

1 *Do you include the date?* Is it:

   (a) (Thody 1997: 234) or
   (b) (Thody 234)?

   Social sciences, natural and applied sciences generally use (a). Dating is significant for disciplines in which changes are frequent. Humanities generally use (b) since seminal works can have lengthy currencies so in-text dating is less important. Dates are used if there is more than one source from the same author.

2 *Are multiple authors listed chronologically or alphabetically?* Is it:

   (a) (Thody 2005; Dettman 2008; Austin 2009; Johansson 2012) or
   (b) (Johansson 2012; Austin 2009; Dettman 2008; Thody 2005) or
   (c) (Austin 2009; Dettman 2008; Johansson 2012; Thody 2005)?

   Social sciences, natural and applied sciences generally use (a) or (b) since evidence of recency is considered vital to proof. The forward or reverse order varies by type of publication or personal choice. Humanities generally use (c) for reasons explained in item 1 above. To trip you up, the *British Journal of Psychology* requests (b), so always check.

3 *Are multiple authors listed by names or summarized?* Is it:

   (a) (Thody, Pashiardis, Johansson and Papanoum 2003) or
   (b) (Thody et al., 2003)?

   The first time you cite the work, all authors are listed in the order in which they appear in the original source. Thereafter, use the summarized 'et al.' (from the Latin, 'and others').

12.5   Quotations in the text

Always follow precedent. Where none is specified:

1 Keep quotations minimal – normally no longer than three lines, beginning and ending with single inverted commas.
2 If more than 60 words, indent from the text, leave a line space above and below and do not use inverted commas.
3 Quotations of a paragraph or more should not be used unless really vital.
4 Quote rigorously correctly and cite the sources.
5 When amending a quotation to make it more relevant to the work in hand or to make it grammatically correct in your location, put any new material in square brackets [ ]; use ellipses (three dots), with or without brackets (…), to show where words have been omitted.
6 Don't overuse quotations. One or two per page is more than enough.

For quotations at the beginning and end of documents see 11.12.

12.5.1 Quotations in foreign languages

1 Provide the original and the translation for at least the first quotation. This enables readers to see the approach that has been used for translation. Thereafter use originals sparingly or not at all, otherwise the whole becomes unwieldy.

2 Use where the translation does not quite convey the sense of the original, where a point is disputed, or where the issue is seminal.

The following is an example.

Extract

From O'Riley, M. (2004) 'Place, position and postcolonial haunting in Assia Djebar's *La Femme sans sépulture*', *Research in African Literatures*, 35 (1): 71.

> colonial ideology produces ... 'post memory', through which the ... tensions of colonial history return as staged scenes (*Les Nuits de Strasbourg*, 1997):
>
>> À cause [...] de cette lumière qui n'aveugle plus, qui nous auréole – comme si pour toi, spectatrice de toujours aux yeux ouverts, au visage tendu par l'attente, nous nous mettions tous, y compris les gardes et leur material bruyant, à jouer quelque répétition de spectacle antique pour la cité assoupié.
>>
>> Because [...] of this light which no longer binds, but which haloes us – as if for you, wide-eyed spectator of all time, face tense from the waiting, all of us, including the guards and their clamouring materials, began to rehearse an ancient show for the tired city.

12.6 Notes

12.6.1 Conventions and alternatives

Conventionally, notes are the written equivalents of 'asides' in oral presentations, interesting but not vital to the flow of the argument. They are strongly discouraged in social sciences. They are most likely and frequent (but not invariably) in law, literature, languages, history, music, drama and theology since these subjects use notes for bibliographical citations. Brevity and simplicity are seen as the heart of good note writing but some subjects need exceedingly lengthy notes (for example law, where many words need qualifiers, legal proofs are essential and notes can occupy whole pages).

Alternatively, notes are a positive enhancement to a text, 'the original hyperlink of the always virtual, always expansive, universe of knowledge' (Willinsky, 2000: 175). To expect the conventional minimal and brief footnotes is to believe the outdated view that research is unproblematic with unequivocal findings. Eloquence, elegance and extensiveness are encouraged in formulating these snippets.

Whether you adopt conventional or alternative approaches, notes have the same functions outlined in 12.6.2 below, and the same locations. They can be placed at the bottom of each page of a text as footnotes, thus keeping them as close as possible to the section of text to which they refer, or conclude a text as endnotes. In either case they are termed 'Notes' though your PC helpfully distinguishes them as footnotes and endnotes.

12.6.2   Functions

1   For bibliographical references

Notes create a much smoother text flow, and easier access to bibliographical information, than do in-text citations in parentheses, as Box 12.4 shows. In Box 12.4, method (a) would be a major annoyance in historical or legal texts which need so much referencing and added notes, that to insert Harvard style would leave the text in total disarray.

Box 12.4   Comparisons of citations in the text and citations in notes

(a)   Conventional social science format (citations in the text)
The references in brackets appear in full in the bibliography at the end of a book.

> Writing up research, or its oral presentation, is a 'site of contestation' (Lewis-Beck et al., 2004: 1197), one which can be regarded as problem solving with its own subprocesses and mental events (Flower and Hayes, 1981; Kellogg, 1994).

(b)   Conventional humanities' format (citations in the notes)
The references appear in full at the bottom of the page or at the end of a chapter, as shown in the notes following the quote.

> Writing up research, or its oral presentation, is a 'site of contestation' (1), one which can be regarded as problem solving with its own subprocesses and mental events (2).

---

(1)   Lewis-Beck, M.S., Bryman, A. & Liao, T.F. (eds) (2004) *The Sage Encyclopaedia of Social Science Research Methods.* Thousand Oaks, CA: Sage, p. 1197.

(2)   Flower, L. and Hayes, J.R. (1981) 'A cognitive process theory of writing', *College Composition and Communication,* I(32), pp. 365–87; Kellogg, R.T. (1994) *The Psychology of Writing.* New York: Oxford: University Press.

Method (b) works well the first time a reference is made. If the same sources are used again and again later in the text, readers have to search back, sometimes over several pages of labyrinthine notes, to locate the earlier full reference. When the number of notes exceeds fifty, this can become tedious, as the following example shows.

Extract

In Thompson's (2003) article on racism and anti-racism, some data came from a certain Pratt. This group of notes appeared on p. 29 of the article (given here in reverse order):

80   Pratt, "Identity," 53
75   Pratt, "Identity," 14

67 Pratt, "Identity," 39

66 Pratt, "Identity," 35–36

The trail back to the elusive Ms Pratt lay, first, two pages earlier:

38 Pratt, "Identity: Skin Blood Heart," 47

The trail ended two pages earlier still, in a footnote:

12 A relational voice and a confessional stance are not mutually exclusive – Minnie Bruce Pratt's powerful interweaving of the two in "Identity: Skin Blood Heart" (In *Yours in Struggle: Three Feminist Perspectives on Anti-Semitism and Racism,* by Elly Bulkin, Minnie Bruce Pratt and Barbara Smith (New York: Long Haul Press, 1984), 11–63)

Of course, you might have read note 12 the first time the reference appeared and have remembered Ms Pratt, but it's just as likely that one of the later references caught your eye first.

In the style of notes used in the above example, the writer used the main word of a book's title to identify it repeatedly. Some writers use instead:

- op. cit. (abbreviation for the Latin *opere citato*, 'in the work cited'), meaning 'I have referred to this author somewhere before in the notes and it's up to you to work out where'; or
- ibid. (abbreviation for the Latin *ibidem*, 'in the same place'), meaning 'I have just referred to this source in the previous note so just look behind you for it.'

I would advise avoiding both.

2 *For explanations of unusual terms or unfamiliar phrases, where there is no glossary (11.9)*

For example, in an article about nineteenth century school principals (Thody, 1994b), the term 'headteacher' was used. This was explained in note 3 on p. 356:

The term 'headteacher' ... emerged in the latter part of the nineteenth century, developing first from its usage in the public schools for upper class children ... Prior to 1870, the word 'schoolmaster' was more common ... In this article, 'headmaster' or 'headteacher' is generally used ... The modern, international term, 'school leader' is also utilized occasionally.

An anti-racism article needed likewise to explain its terminology. The text and note were:

In principle, "white identity" approaches to antiracist education move beyond the kind of multicultural pedagogy that is satisfied with exposing students to non-European cultures (40).

_____

(40) I use the terms "white identity", "good white", "allies", "developmental" and "stage theory" approaches to whiteness more or less interchangeably insofar as these orientations focus on the affirmation of a "good" white identity.

(Thompson, 2003: 14, 27)

3 For information that enhances, but is not vital to, the main theme

In an article on interview methodology for research on Roman Catholic motherhood, interviewees' biographies are in the notes (Kelly, 2001: 31). These were not deemed central to the research because the writer had only eight respondents and was not correlating her conclusions to particular life experiences.

In Rice (2004: 162–89), the researcher begins with bio-data about the person being interviewed which is then enlarged with a note:

> Germaine Tillion (b. 1907) is unquestionably one of the most significant figures in contemporary French thought … As an ethnographer … Tillion gathered notes to inspire … *Le harem et les cousins* (2).

---

(2) *Le harem et les cousins* is a feminist work that deals with the Neolithic origin of women's subservience and reveals that this condition is not unique to Muslim societies.

4 For secondary arguments

In a biographical article narrating the life of an object, the researcher uses this note to cite another authority on a different aspect of his topic:

> Of course, Baudrillard makes a very strong argument about the importance of objects as signs of status, a semiotic value that is not reducible to their economic or exchange value.

> (Dent, 2001: 19, Note 4)

By commencing with the phrase 'Of course' the writer appears to imply that if he did not mention Baudrillard, then his readers would wonder why not.

In a historical article about Canada's involvement in the South African War, the researcher introduced a doctrine and explained it in a note:

> Canadian constables' national identity … was based upon social assumptions … [which] differed markedly from the patrician nationalist definition promoted by Canada's 'imperialists'.

> [The accompanying footnote was:]

> See Carl Berger, *The Sense of Power: Studies in the Ideas of Canadian Imperialism 1867–1914* (Toronto, 1970) for an incisive analysis of their ideas in which he argues that their imperialist ideology was but another form of English Canadian nationalism.

> (Miller, 1995: 78)

5 For acknowledgements (11.3)

In an article discussing American political leaders, the researcher describes a social event and supplies a note:

A 1974 *New York Times Magazine* feature on Davis recounts Rumsfeld and his wife ... witness[ing] Davis's impromptu hallway improvization of Elvis, in response to which Donald Rumsfeld remarks on Elvis's weird smile. Has he ever seen his own?

[The accompanying footnote was:]

James Conaway, "Sammy Davis Jr. has Bought the Bus", *The Sammy Davis Jr. Reader*, ed. Gerald Early (New York, 2001), 352, 354. Thanks to John Gennari for hipping me to this essay.

(Lott, 2004: 117, 122)

6   For fun

This is for information that is not central to the particular item but which lends it some colour, or provides anecdotes the author could not bear to leave out but could not think of a justification to include.

An example of this appears as Note 8 in an article on the effects on policy of gubernatorial changes in US states (Fusarelli, 2002: 157). You can almost hear the writer laughing here. It would make a wonderfully colourful aside in a lecture. It would certainly wake up the audience.

> 8   Williams ran one of the most inept gubernatorial campaigns in Texas history, Williams appealed openly to Texas's macho cowboy past ... Williams, an old-fashioned oilman from Midland, made several public relations mistakes ... He refused to shake Richards's hand [another candidate] ... made references to her past problems with alcohol ... made ... troubling sexist comments, including jokingly comparing bad weather to rape ... [He admitted] to being serviced by prostitutes and not paying income tax ... many conservatives ... were embarrassed.

7   For methodology information

In an article on Canadian history, Miller (1995) discussed how difficult it had been to find sources for the article as many records had been destroyed. A Note (7) then explained how the researcher had created the study:

> (7) Consequently the reconstruction of the experiences of this unit, and more particularly the Canadian component, has had to rely upon Baden-Powell's Papers in the National Army Museum, London; the S.B. Steel Papers, at the Glenbow Museum, Calgary; and various newspapers and published memoirs.

12.6.3   Asides in presentations

These have functions 2, 3, 4 and 6 from the above list and an additional one:

WAKING UP THE AUDIENCE

A presentation of longer than one and a half hours (less if you are not a good speaker or have no visual aids) needs a break. It's generally accepted that fifteen to twenty minutes is the longest span of listeners' concentration possible during oral presentations. Use some of the following ideas for 'asides':

- *Insert an audience activity related to the lecture such as a discussion with neighbours.* I saw this humorously engineered by Professor Michael Hough (Wollogong University, Australia) at a conference presentation in Hobart (Tasmania) in 2000. He instructed us to argue about his ideas for three minutes with anyone nearby who did not look like an axe murderer; he timed us exactly (just in case our neighbour was unkindly disposed towards us).

- *Insert an audience activity unrelated to the lecture.* During a two hour presentation in Sweden, I slid in a few fun questions about the town and university where we were located. The audience could talk and relax while guessing the answers.

- *Have a physical activity break.* Lead the audience in brain-gym exercises (rubbing your temples, swinging your arms across each other) or engineer the need to move around the room (such as running a mini-questionnaire that results in everyone having to relocate to a specific survey group). Yes – people will laugh and maybe think you a little odd but they'll learn more readily. (NB Collect the mini-questionnaires at the end and you have more data for your research.)

- *Give a practical demonstration.* In his 2004 professorial inaugural lecture, Martin Barstow, Professor of Astrophysics and Space Science (Leicester University, England) demonstrated a spectrograph built by his team for the Faulkes robotic telescope on Maui (in Hawaii, USA). He could just have given us the results obtained but the demonstration provided a change of pace. This, in itself, operated as an 'aside' but the information from the demonstration was also an 'aside', showing us how his results had been obtained. Only the results themselves were central to the lecture. To view the lecture in PowerPoint, see http://www.star.le. ac.uk/~mab/inaugural.

- *Add sound or video clips.* These should not carry the main points of the lecture but should reinforce them while giving the audience a chance to relax. Thus, in his inaugural lecture in 2005, Mike Cook, Professor of Health Care Leadership at Anglia Polytechnic University, England, used three film extracts to illustrate his investigation of whether leadership was the solution for modernizing health and social care. The extracts were from *Carry On Doctor*, a 1960s English comedy, from the dramatic *Apollo 13* and from the children's film *Monsters Inc.*, each appealing to a different sector of his audience and showing differing interpretations of leadership (the lecture is available on DVD at Anglia Polytechnic University Library). Note that using video is not an easy option; it took Dr Cook careful rehearsal and timing to ensure that the clips operated flawlessly at the right moments.

Asides should be as carefully planned as the rest of a presentation:

- They make a welcome break for your audience *but* signal to listeners when you are introducing an aside. You can remark, 'Just as an aside … '; 'Taking a break from my central theme reminds me of a story …'; 'Returning now to my main points … '.
- They can confuse audiences who are less familiar with your native language than you are but they can also give them relief from the need to translate everything you say. You can also learn a short aside in the audience's principal language.
- Beware of too many asides; you, and your audience, lose track of your theme.

- Avoid the temptation of personal reminiscences unless you want to be classified as being in your 'anecdotage'.
- Time your asides when you are rehearsing your presentation and don't let them overrun.

12.6.4 Hyperlinks

In electronic publications (CD-ROMs, CDs or web pages), hyperlinks perform the same functions as do notes in print media.

The advantages of hyperlinks are:

- They can point to much more extensive sources, and to sources which you have not collected specifically for the research being presented on your website. The bibliography, for example, can contain hyperlinks to the full text or abstracts of the literature cited. Methodological comments can be expanded to show raw data and calculations. An author note (11.5) could be the link to your full curriculum vitae.
- You can create interactive notes since the links can point readers to ongoing chat rooms.
- Hyperlinks disturb the text flow much less than do any form of notes and referencing in print media.
- You are absolved from many of the challenges of summarizing note information.

The disadvantages are:

- You are absolved from many of the challenges of summarizing note information, but the burden is then passed to your readers.
- It's difficult to avoid the temptation of excessive hyperlinks because so much information is readily available.

12.7 Review

Correct citation helps to prove the validity of your research. You prove the validity of citation by following conventions.

Part IV Publication:
Reference guides

13 Becoming a Presenter

CONTENTS

Advice on presentations has appeared throughout this book where information in other chapters has been noted as appropriate for both writing and presentation. This chapter provides additional advice relating solely to presentations, such as invited keynotes, conference papers and lectures and with some relevance to radio and TV interviews and programmes. For advice on the oral 'presentations' that constitute doctoral vivas (note 1, Chapter 5), see Trafford and Leshem (2002a; 2002b; 2002c).

13.1   Challenges and opportunities

The fun of research afflicted me when I had to use my research about school governors to present a TV programme in which two teams of governors competed to see which was better at interviewing a potential school principal. The producer assumed that experienced governors would be better at this than new governors, that the failures of the beginners would make entertaining TV, and that the programme should be slanted to show only the mistakes of the neophytes and the successes of the experienced. Research told me that the connections between experience and naiveté were not so clear cut and that undermining new governors' confidence was not an ideal way to proceed. Should I therefore allow the ethics of presentation to override the ethics of conveying what I had discovered from my research? After much argument, we inevitably compromised. We showed the newcomers' one major success and the oldies' one major failure (my research perspective) while leaving the weight of the evidence to support the producer's view. And all this argument was for just fourteen minutes of TV on an education cable channel.

For me, the event encapsulated the challenges of oral research presentation in any form – invited keynotes, conference papers, lectures, radio and TV interviews and programmes:

- Time is short.
- Audience concentration span is limited (3.4.3).
- Listeners' memories are fleeting for the content of a speech but lengthy for its success or failure as a performance.
- Most spectators want entertainment with their education while others will regard entertainment as anathema (Chapters 3 and 4).
- Your academic career needs solid respectability (1.3.2.3) but combined with memorable performance that will encourage repeat invitations for you as a speaker.
- Data have to be even more reduced than for text (Chapter 6).
- The intricacies of reasoning and proof have to be simplified to be readily conveyed in speech.
- Oral presentation provides much better opportunities to inspire and enthuse an audience than does text.
- You can reach a much wider audience than is ever likely to read your thesis or articles.
- You are more likely to impact on policy making through presentation than through publication for academic audiences.

13.2 Conventions and alternatives

The challenges and opportunities outlined in 13.1 spawn the inevitable debates, which roughly divide along modernist/postmodernist lines. Note, however, that the two views do overlap in some respects and that the two are not necessarily mutually exclusive.

First consider conventional presentations. The oral equivalent of the most conventional written text (1.3.1) is the formal, word-for-word reading of a paper or keynote speech or the dictation of lecture notes, delivered by a speaker from a front-placed lectern without deviation or hesitation. Audience questions are permitted at the end. A copy of the full paper is usually provided, typed APA style. PowerPoint slides displaying the text may be used.

Now ponder alternative presentations. These will vary as much as their written counterparts (1.4.2). An extreme version would be a team of researchers opening, in costume, in a barber shop quartet that summarizes their main points about, for example, the effect of peer assisted learning in musical composition. Students who took part in the research would present their compositions with commentary from the team. Listeners would be invited to try peer assisted learning by working with partners in the audience to draft questions for the research team. Posters around the room would summarize the main points of each stage of the research and listeners would be invited to walk around these and to talk with the member of the research team stationed at each poster. A summary of all the main points on one sheet of bright blue paper would be provided. Listeners would be offered a CD of the full paper if they left their contact details with the researchers or would be referred to a website or publication. A much simpler alternative would be to distribute copies of the paper to the audience, give them twenty minutes to read it on their own, and then move into discussion groups, each led by one member of the team.

How each of these styles can operate in practice is reviewed in Table 13.1.

13.3   What's effective for both conventional and alternative presentations?

Preparation ➲ *Precedents* ➲ *Practicalities* ➲ *Personality*
➲ *People* ➲ *Purposes* ➲ *Production* ➲ *Post-presentation*

13.3.1   Preparation

1   Planning follows the advice in 2.2.2, 2.2.3. The template (2.2.4) for a presentation is always:

(a)   Introduction – outline the main points you are going to tell the audience.
(b)   Centre – tell them the main points and insert reminders of the whole outline at intervals.
(c)   Conclusion – remind them of the main points that you have told them. The repetition in the above helps learning. The research findings are the heart of the presentation. Unless literature and methodology are the topic for the event, then these elements are usually minimal or omitted for a practitioner audience (3.5).

2   Plan time for breaks, asides and audience participation (12.6.3).
3   Incorporate some visual assistance. Slides should normally have no more than six points on each, in about 24 point font. Equipment needs checking and double checking to see that it will work. Assistants need precise instruction.
4   *Rehearse, rehearse, rehearse.* The need for this diminishes slightly as you gain experience, but it remains vital so that:

(a)   You can confidently move away from your notes on stage and make eye contact with an audience rather than having to be glued to your text.
(b)   You can keep to time – and the shorter the time for your presentation, the more you need to rehearse to ensure that every one of those precious ten minutes is used to best effect; please don't try to just read your paper very very quickly and face the chair's axe halfway through. For such short speeches, learn the whole thing but keep your notes handy as back-up.
(c)   You keep your anecdotes under control (12.6.3).
(d)   You tell jokes snappily without forgetting the punch line.
(e)   Everything you need is close at hand and working.

Rehearsal will need to be done mentally on the journey to the conference or solo in your hotel bedroom. You may see the presentation arena before you have to speak but it's extremely unlikely that you will be able to practise there (Box 2.4).

5   Produce the materials to be distributed (13.3.2).
6   Go to see the room in which you will be presenting in advance of arriving for the actual presentation. Listen to other presenters in the same room – then decide if you'll need a microphone and how you may need to adjust because of the positioning of a lectern or projector.

Table 13.1 Comparisons between conventional and alternative presentations

Views on the conventional	Attitudes to alternatives
'I take the view that a "lecture" should be different from a "speech". The calm, rigor, matter-of-factness and sobriety of a lecture declines with definite pedagogical losses, when the substance and manner of public discussion are introduced, in the style of the press' (Max Weber, 'The meaning of ethical neutrality', cited in Shils and Finch, 1949: 4) (see also Box 1.1, first verse, in this book) 'Most of the lectures were dull and uninspiring … Sometimes they were inaudible. One of the lecturers used to sit behind a desk, leafing through pages of notes. If anyone asked her to speak up, she'd say one word very loudly and then relapse … Teaching didn't appear to have a high priority' (Clare, 2004b: 19). The comments refer to Bristol University's lectures in English Studies in a department commended for its teaching excellence by government assessments	'Performance promises a far richer and more subtle science of culture than the analytical text can establish. But it makes different demands. It requires a narrative, drama, action and a point of view' (Paget, 1990: 152, cited in Darlington and Scott, 2002: 166) (see also Box 1.1, second verse, in this book). For example, when there are controversial points to be made, a presenter can metamorphose into an invented character. I have variously appeared as a nineteenth century school principal, an astronaut, a judge. The 'character' can speak what the researcher may not wish to risk. This device shifts potential blame and distances the researcher while also being entertaining and presenting a definitive point of view
The speaker can be identifiable and memorable but must not overshadow the data	Steven Pinker of Harvard, who teaches a core science class, is 'Known as the "rock professor" for his long hair and easy style, he uses cartoons, videos, music and poetry to enliven lectures. He closed his first class by quoting *Hamlet* and opened another with [a song] from *The Wizard of Oz.* "He's incredibly charismatic"' (Arenson, 2004: 23)
The subject matters, not the speaker. The value of the work should speak for itself without tricks or artifice	The visual impact of a research presentation affects readers' and listeners' perceptions of its importance. Images 'allow us to make kinds of statements that cannot be made by words … [they] enlarge our consciousness' (Harper, 1998: 147). These images include the visual appearance of the speaker as well as the visual aids used in the presentation. Both of these must be planned for and managed just as much as should the content of a presentation
It's vital that a conference paper be read in its entirety. Only then can the audience fully appreciate the rigour of its reasoning. To do less than this is insulting to the audience (a professorial viewpoint recorded at the conference reported in Box 1.1)	Just as literature has coined the term 'performance poetry' for works that are better spoken aloud than read individually and silently, so, I think, should conference papers and keynotes (and lectures) be performance research' . Such events should

(Continued)

Table 13.1 (Continued)

Views on the conventional	Attitudes to alternatives
	be regarded as academic theatre. The 'lines' should be written as if for a play, not a paper. Costume, music and sets all need attention. Rehearsal is vital
PowerPoint raises the floor but lowers the ceiling (apocryphal). The audience can centre on the slides rather than the powerful presence of the speaker. The presenter can centre on the slides too and not notice that the audience has fallen asleep	PowerPoint enables everyone to produce unrivalled visuals, movement and sound but the pictures and settings are now becoming standard. Go outside the restricted icons and search the web for images; design your own slides. Blank out the screen periodically during presentations so the audience redirect attention to you. Insert activities in addition to watching PowerPoint
Conference presentations are 'passive dissemination' that enable a little learning but 'the effects are small' (Gomm and Davies, 2000: 141) 'Few presentations are remembered six weeks later' (Knight, 2002: 202) Audience participation should be permitted through controlled questions at the end when they have heard the full arguments	Conference presentations should actively involve the audience (12.6.3 🖾). For example, as described in 1.4.1, we presented research on European education management in the style of an ancient Greek symposium (Pashiardis et al., 2002)
Presenters are central; there has to be audience belief in these gurus, the 'contemporary witch doctors' of our day (Clark and Salaman, 1995)	The polyvocality of qualitative and narrative research (9.1, 10.1) lends itself to a presenter literally speaking in different voices as each viewpoint is presented. A group of researchers can act out the research, playing the characters who were the respondents as a readers' theatre production. Audio or visual recordings of the actual research subjects can be used. Any of these devices enable the real voices to be heard and vividly show where opinions collide or coalesce
The research presentation needs to face an academic research audience to be taken seriously	One author did readings to the homeless she had researched at one of their drop-in centres. This also served to validate the research as the audiences nodded and smiled as they recognized themselves. She read sections of her research and the audience asked her to read the bits about themselves. This enabled her to give feedback to participants who would not otherwise have read the research (Darlington and Scott, 2002: 175)

7 Be prepared with back-up materials. Slides showing your data should be available should you need them to help answer questions. A few OHT slides could be kept in reserve for a PowerPoint failure. Have whiteboard and marker pens in case all the equipment fails. During your rehearsal, decide which points you will omit if the chair or other presenters eat into your time allocation.

8 Always pack your presentation materials in your hand luggage should you have to travel by air to that important conference (or have them on a data stick on a neck cord).

13.3.2 Precedents

1 The issues about breaking with conventional precedents do apply (2.3.1) but risk is more tenable in presentation.

(a) If you're new to conferencing, you need to make your mark quickly, so doing something a little different from the norm will gain attention. Your audience will already have sat through numerous sessions of identically presented research, so anything distinct will be a welcome break. Just make sure that you distribute copies of your impeccable, and conventional, academic paper to go with your oral extravaganza.

(b) If you're a seasoned presenter or keynoter, please try to break with the interminably (and terminally) dull reading of papers that are too often the norm at academic conferences. You can afford to – and for professional audiences you have to – if you want repeat invitations.

2 (a) Copies of your full paper should be provided at an academic research presentation (usually about twenty) unless the paper is to be issued in the post-conference publication, is in the conference programme in full or is supplied on a CD by the conference organizers. Conventionally, your full paper will be in the exact form in which it was accepted by the conference committee, including even the double spacing. Much more effective communication results from such tiny changes as a more eye-catching cover (Figure 2.2), reverting to single spacing (which will cost you less to reproduce), using a sanserif font, dramatizing subheads in bold, creating greater visual definition for tables, and setting off the text effectively by surrounding white space.

(b) If the presentation is reporting research in progress, then issue a single summary sheet with your contact details and a short bibliography.

(c) For presentations to audiences outside of academia, a summary sheet as in (b) can be given out or offered to anyone interested (12.3.4).

(d) For paying audiences, set the fee to cover the cost of giving them a copy of your book. If you are part of a wider conference, then you issue order forms for your book.

(e) It is helpful, but rarely done, to duplicate copies of any quantified data referred to in your presentation since the details are not always sufficiently clear on PowerPoint or tables have to be truncated to fit on the slides.

(f) If the texts of your lectures have to be on your university's virtual campus, then don't repeat them exactly; enliven them with additional visuals, interactive activities with the students, and enthusiastic and dramatised elements.

13.3.3 Practicalities

Box 2.4 has dealt comprehensively with the issues but these additions are specific to presentations.

1 Plan and rehearse well, and well in advance. The night before is only for last-minute rehearsals. Alternatives take much longer to plan and prepare than do conventional formats.
2 Avoid death by PowerPoint (17.2.5) and overuse of PowerPoint's wonderful movement and sound options – but do use some of them.
3 Check and adjust for your time allocation. However short your allocated time, you can assume that the chair's introduction will shorten it still further, as will announcements about fire exits, toilets and refreshment breaks and other speakers who will overrun their time.
4 The room layout is unlikely to be conducive to discussions. If you want interaction with your audience more than just through end-of-session questions, then arrive early and rearrange the furniture into a circle shape. If this is not possible, then you yourself need to walk around the audience or at least emerge from behind your desk/lectern barrier.
5 Ask the audience to signal if they cannot hear you at the back or cannot see your slides clearly. You may need to do this more than once during a presentation: watch for signs of restlessness on the back rows. If possible, check prior to your presentation that the screen can be seen clearly from all seats (yes, that means going to the room during a meal break and checking all the seats yourself).
6 In a small room, you can usually see if anyone is significantly visually or hearing disabled and lacks a reading or signing assistant, in which case you need to read out loud the information on your slides or ensure you face the listener needing to read your lips. With a large audience, you may need to ask if anyone has such needs. This can cause embarrassment but that's better than not being able to communicate.
7 If your paper is in the previously issued conference proceedings, don't expect that delegates will have read it. If you have copies to distribute, don't give them out until after your presentation. If you are the keynote, then the conference organizers should ensure there are sufficient copies.

13.3.4 Personality

Personality has been covered at length in 2.3.2 but it has additional importance in presentations.

1 There are no hiding places for your personality when you are making a presentation. Even if you do not consciously plan the impression you will make on the audience, they will subconsciously assess you using seemingly unimportant signals from your clothes, your body language, the confidence with which you handle your visual aids and notes, your tone of voice and whether or not you make eye contact with them. This assessment will largely precede anything you say and can influence how your research is rated.[1]
2 Your apppearance should accentuate your message.
   (a) If you are male, white haired and white bearded, you can get away with anything because you look like everyone's idea of a professor and will gain immediate respect even before you speak. If you lack these attributes, then wear

scruffy jeans and holey sweaters for UK sociology conferences; smart casual at most other UK academic conferences; suits for academic conferences outside the UK; very smart for all professional, public or political conferences. For whichever type of audience, serious clothes indicate how seriously you view your research. Look as if you have deliberately chosen what you wear rather than thrown on your gardening or relaxation clothes.

(b) Accessorize. Wear your datastick on a neck cord (for academic conferences) or flash the latest electronic device (for professional conferences). Display your conference badge: these are usually omitted after day one at UK conferences but are always worn elsewhere (keynote speakers often won't wear one since they assume that everyone knows who they are). And wear one brightly coloured or unusual clothing item, so you will stand out against drab conference settings and you can be located afterwards by those anxious to speak to you.

(c) Women have the advantage of being able to wear cosmetics; these help give you facial definition when on stage in a large hall. Women have the disadvantage of being assessed by the largely male elite of academia. I overheard a female associate professor incurring the disdain of a male professor because she used nail varnish which, he said, 'showed she didn't put enough time into her research'. She had a strong publication list and had led a flagging journal into peer reviewed status.

3   If you're a risk taking, extrovert personality, then brighten up presentations as in 2.3.1 (list item 13) and as suggested in Table 13.1 (alternatives). If you're an introvert risk averter, just try a catchy opening to an otherwise conventional offering as proposed in 2.3.1 (list item 14) and 2.3.2.2.

13.3.5   People

Audience has been discussed in Chapter 3 but now they're visible, how should you adapt?

1   While waiting for your presentation to begin:

(a) If you are the first or only speaker, chat to audience members as they come into the room while waiting for you to start. Try to avoid greeting friends over-effusively (it makes others feel left out). Make eye contact with as many people as possible (but beware, there are some countries where cultural norms make this difficult) (3.6.4.2).

(b) If you are one of several speakers, introduce yourself to the others, check the order and timing with the chair, look interested throughout all the other speeches and look at the speakers, not the audience. If the others encroach on your time, pass a reminder to the chair asking when you are to start, look at your watch prominently, shuffle your papers.

2   Audiences are generally weary, enjoy the social life of the conference and want to absorb your message as easily as possible. Try the techniques of 12.6.3. Also, vary your tone, move around the room physically, maintain eye contact, smile and look interested in your audience.

3   Academic audiences are the ones most likely to expect a paper to be read in its entirety. Doing so saves you from stage fright and from spending time preparing

a presentation; it's risk-free and no-one will have time to ask you questions; it gives the conference audience some much needed time to catch up on their sleep (and being academics, they have learnt from their students how to sleep with their eyes open). Some academics consider it respects their intelligence by assuming that they can absorb all the intricacies and interstices of your paper. Some will feel annoyed that you have not bothered to prepare a presentation. One way of satisfying both groups could be to distribute copies of the paper at the beginning of the presentation. Give your audience twenty minutes of your presentation time to read it; then have a discussion with them. If time is short, distribute a summary to stimulate discussion. Have prompts ready to start the discussion just in case no-one should ask a question. If you do read your paper, speak it with meaning, speak it without too much haste; speak it enthusiastically and speak it without constantly looking at the paper.

4 Practitioner audiences are highly unlikely to want a paper read to them. If you do this, expect some to get up and leave and others to express polite hostility.

5 Questioners come in four varieties:

(a) Those genuinely seeking information or wanting to add information to your ideas. These will be the briefest questions usually. Offer to meet them for further discussions afterwards, they're valuable.

(b) Those who speak because they want everyone to know who they are.

(c) Those who speak so they can show that they know the presenter personally.

(d) Those who just love the sound of their own voices and ideas.

All the last three generally have long questions. You can't cut them short but respond only to the very last point they raise. Resist the temptation to address them by name (this cuts out the rest of your audience).

6 When answering questions, keep the rest of the audience engaged by looking around the room, not just at the questioner.

7 If you're new to presenting and/or your paper is at the end of the day or the end of the conference, your audience is likely to be small. Put as much effort into your speech as you would for a larger audience. It's polite to do so, it's good practice for you, it's enjoyable – and who knows how important may be the few who come? I spoke before two people at my first paper in 1988. As a risk taker, I stuck to my prepared format of discussing observation methodology by actually doing it – watching and recording the audience by writing on OHP sheets, opening my bag to reveal (and share) the emergency rations of chocolate bars I keep with me on observational forays (in case my subjects should be on diets or never eat during the day), and then letting my micro-audience evaluate my performance as if they too were observation researchers. Fortunately, that audience was powerful and adventurous; they were academics who not only approved the presentation but helped my later publication (as one was a journal editor) and academic career (the other appointed me as an external examiner). They must have put the word around too since my subsequent audiences grew rapidly, keynote requests abounded and my final conference paper in the early 2000s was packed to the doors and overflowing and the audience happily joined in the singalong which summarized the research findings.

13.3.6 Purposes

Inspire, intrigue, impress, impart electrifying ideas: see Chapter 4.

13.3.7 Production

Production is the meat of Chapters 6–12. For presentations, you need a few additions:

1   Distribute confident smiles and larger than life gestures: you're on stage.
2   Use body language, tone, sound levels to emphasize particular points.
3   Don't stand in front of the projector or screen.
4   Look all around the audience.
5   Style should be conversational rather than declamatory.
6   Disperse the visuals throughout the presentation.
7   Where there is more than one presenter, keep to your agreed plan for how long each should speak.
8   Know your paper well enough to present it without looking at it other than with cursory glances or with prompts such as your main points only on PowerPoint slides.
9   Show conviction and enthusiasm about your ideas or no-one else will be convinced.
10   Oral presentations offer opportunities for enticing methodology reviews since what was done can be 'acted out'. Scientists can have their equipment working, as in the brilliant inaugural lecture from Professor Martin Barstow of Leicester University, England, in 2004 (12.6.3). He recalls that it took several hours of nail-biting suspense to ensure his spectrograph would produce the required public demonstration successfully, a reminder to all public speakers that good presentations require extensive preparation. A simpler performance came from two email researchers at a US educational conference in 2001 who had not met until their conference presentation. They used this to their advantage by standing back-to-back to deliver their presentation as if they were still emailing. Thus we could see the advantages and disadvantages of the research methodology without it being spelt out for us.
11   If you're running out of time, leap to the final summary. Don't try to cover everything by speaking more quickly.

13.3.8 Post-presentation

Invite anyone who wants to talk to you to stay on longer. If you have copies left of your conference paper, don't throw them away; leave them on a table in the conference registration area (2.4).

REFLECTIONS

To make your mark when attending someone else's presentation, sit three or four rows from the front and at the extreme edge against the wall. When you then stand to put a question, turn sideways so both the audience and the speaker can hear and see you, and state your name clearly.

13.4 Review

Effective presentations need:

- preparation – planning, templates and rehearsals;
- awareness of precedents and conscious decisions on which to follow;
- adaptation to practicalities – keep to time, rearrange the furniture if necessary;
- involvement of your own personality, be that as a risk taker or a risk averter;
- realization that you must meet people's needs – academic and professional audiences require different approaches;
- achievement of purposes to educate, enliven, excite and elucidate;
- an enthusiastic production that shows you think that your research matters;
- post-presentation contacts with interested members of your audience.

As for the other topics in this book, there are choices for you to make between high risk alternatives and lower risk conventions. The decision will depend upon what you want to achieve, as this final story illustrates.

In 2004, the UK's public broadcasting station, the BBC, presented a highly success-ful series of wildlife programmes, *Britain Goes Wild*. Live transmissions were made every day for fifteen days following native species (such as foxes, badgers, peregrines) as they went about their daily living routines. An enormous amount of natural history research made this programme possible. It was presented by well known people who could be classified as 'interested and aware amateurs', rather than the actual researchers, and its format was unashamedly, and unusually, that of a soap opera. It used cliffhangers and disputes more usually used by the drama department. These were to intrigue viewers and make them return the next day to discover the denoue-ments such as whether or not the wagtails were still all right after nesting beside the main road. The series deliberately used language to connect with the interests of view-ers, referring to wildlife 'families' and 'communities'. It drew between three and four million viewers daily, even competing successfully with the Euro 2004 football on another channel. Despite its success and its impeccable research credentials, it was attacked as oversimplified and because the presenters were overfamiliar with their audi-ence. Many still preferred a more scientific, sober view.

Your choice?

Note

1 Even stars of the international lecture circuit can be afflicted by the conservatism of academics. Baroness Susan Greenfield, CBE, Fullerton Professor of Physiology at Oxford University, England, Director of the Royal Institute of Great Britain, awarded the Faraday Medal in 1998 for contributions to public under-standing of science, a renowned authority on novel neuronal brain mechanisms, elegant and fashionable in appearance and in enormous demand for her outstandingly interesting but erudite presentations to many different types of audiences, was rejected for membership of the prestigious academic Fellowship of the Royal Society (of eminent scientists) in 2004. It was rumoured that her liveliness and her miniskirts implied a less than appropriately serious approach to her subject in the eyes of the staid gatekeepers of the Royal Society.

14 Getting into Print

CONTENTS

If you're serious about getting published, always follow the conventional routes outlined below. There are no alternatives.

14.1 Start-up

Your work environment

1 Find a mentor at your university, one who is publication active and genuinely willing to help you. Ask advice. Listen avidly.
2 If you work in a university, refuse extraneous work tasks that cannot be directly related to your publication/research agenda. If that's not possible, make every task lead to publication opportunities. Stewart and Hodges (2003) took a work task that they had to do (room use survey) and produced from it an excellent article 'The room that nobody wanted: an exploratory study into the importance of room quality to learning'.
3 If you're employed elsewhere, or are a student, then substitute publication for one of your existing hobbies. It is fun to see your name in print (but 5.1 still applies).

Connections

4   Accept all requests from more senior staff to publish jointly with you; curb your annoyance that someone else is benefiting from your work.

5   Ask already published authors to write with you; you do most of the work; they get their name up front and you get a better chance of acceptance.

6   Network like crazy in your professional association and at conferences. Locate editors at conferences. Pick up those leaflets requesting papers for special editions of journals.

7   When publishers' representatives come to your university, make sure you book a session with them. Ask their advice on what is wanted and *follow it*. After you've had success publishing a book they want, they are more likely to accept your ideas for others.

Learning the trade

8   Attend conference sessions discussing how to get published. Ask questions of the presenters. Make yourself known to them personally at the end of a session.

9   Accept all requests to publish even if it is only for newsletters. They are all good practice.

Can't think what to publish?

10   An undergraduate dissertation should have at least one article buried in it; doctoral theses should run to several or a book. Publish during or immediately after writing, otherwise findings will be outdated.

11   Look around you. My work responsibility for training school governors led to two books, a PhD, three chapters and fifteen articles.

12   Twin track. Research projects always produce more data than will fit into one article. Use the rest for further publications. Write separate articles on the literature or methodologies used. Don't use the same material that you have already substantially published, either in other journals, in chapters or on the net. *Social Science Quarterly* has already added a caveat to their contributors' instructions that:

> papers already 'published' through electronic means and *whose publication in SSQ would substantially reduce the value of the copyright* should not be submitted and cannot be published. (2004, 85(2): 521)

The last words

13   Don't be humble. You have good research to publicize.

14.2   Journals

14.2.1   Which ones?

1   Go for print, rather than the less prestigious electronic journals which are rarely refereed. Even those that are refereed tend to be regarded as less significant than those traditionally published. *But* this is a rapidly developing field and, by the time this book is in its second edition, this advice could change substantially.

2 For academic ratings, go for peer reviewed journals, read by academics. Sad to say, this is deemed 'shouting into a gale for all the impact most articles have' (Knight, 2002: 201) since academic journals are equated with 'obscure' (Gomm and Davies, 2000: 135). Ignore such gloom for your career's sake (4.4.1). Go for the top journals in your field. If rejected, you recycle downwards.

3 For wide impact, go for practitioner journals which have larger audiences. They want 'short, clear, practice focused, human interest and topical pieces' (Knight, 2002: 201).

How do you tell the difference between academic and practitioner journals?

- *Academic journals.* Usually A5 size, lengthy articles, fully referenced, matt paper, contributors' instructions, an academically impressive editorial board.
- *Practitioner journals.* Usually A4 size, short articles, illustrations, few references, glossy paper, no instructions, one editor.

14.2.2 Submitting

1 ALWAYS follow the contributors' instructions PRECISELY. You may not see any rationale in the instructions but the editor does, so OBEY. These instructions 'are necessary if the system is to function properly, and are intended to make for fair means of quality control and for a smooth transition from an author's manuscript to the printed journal article' (Sadler, 1990: 1). Most journals now have their contributors' instructions online. You can also view past copies and sample articles, so you have no excuse for incorrect submissions.

2 *Never* exceed the word limit. Guidance in the *Social Science Quarterly* for example, states unequivocally that:

> Submitted manuscripts should not be longer than twenty-five pages total, double spaced throughout (including indented material, tables, references and notes) with 1" [2.5 cm] margins and 10 CPI font … First time authors sometimes wonder if they should send in a paper they know is too long, hoping that the readers [reviewers] will tell them where to cut. Seasoned authors know that readers almost never suggest places to cut but bring up new issues that should have been treated in the first place.

3 Read several articles from your targeted journal. Present in the same style, font, title format and referencing. Try to cite at least one article from your chosen journal in your own article. All this will make your article 'resonate with the interests of a particular community of practice' (Knight, 2002: 200). You are more likely, therefore, to have your early papers accepted in journals in your own country.

4 Always cite references and bibliography in the required format (Chapter 12).

5 Send your article to the *named, current* editor (so the editor will believe that you read the journal currently). Check if your work should be sent to the general editor, a specialist editor, a country editor or the editor for a special edition.

6 Send the required numbers of copies. No editor has the time to make the extra copies. Increasingly only electronic submission is requested, so this obviates the need for multiple copies.

7 Send a letter with your submission politely requesting consideration for publication. Don't send your résumé, recommendations from anyone for you or for the work, or

your estimate of how important your work is. Don't send enquiries about whether an editor would be interested in a topic or not; you should know this from the journal.

Despite such advice:

> Editors in a wide range of disciplines constantly complain that 15–40% of the unsolicited man-
> uscripts they receive either do not conform to the journal's stated technical requirements or are
> wide of the mark in terms of the type of article appropriate to the journal. (Sadler, 1990: 8)

As a past editor myself, I can sadly only echo that with feeling.

14.2.3   What happens once your paper is submitted?

Hurdle 1 – the editor

Editors (3.4.4) want 'papers ... which enhance the journal's reputation ... [which] other researchers will want to read, and which will influence their ... activities' (Murray, 2001: 1). The Editors of the *Canadian Journal of Economics*, for example, an elite academic journal,

> seek to maintain and enhance the position of the CJE as a major, internationally recognized jour-
> nal and are very receptive to high quality papers on any economics topic from any source. In
> addition, the editors recognize the Journal's role as an important outlet for high-quality empirical
> papers about the Canadian economy. (Contributors' Instructions, 2004)

Editors scan your article to see if it is worth asking referees (reviewers) to spend time on it. Editors look at the abstract (11.2) to find out background and aim and to check that the findings do prove what the paper sets out to prove. They then skim the whole paper to see if the structure's logical and it's reasonably grammatical and correctly spelt. Only if your work passes all these tests will it be sent on to the reviewers.

Hurdle 2 – reviewers

Journal editors usually select the reviewers (3.4.5) but some ask for your recommendations. The *American Sociological Review,* for example, states:

> you may recommend specific reviewers (or identify individuals whom ASR should not use). Do
> not recommend colleagues, collaborators or friends. (Contributors' Instructions)

Usually, there will be two or three reviewers. The comments you receive from them will *always* give faults and will usually reject the paper unless some revisions are done. *So do them* with as good grace as you can muster. Do not argue with reviewers.

> [They] put a lot of work into reviewing papers and authors should learn from their comments, and
> improve their manuscript. Never take the attitude that the referee is wrong. (Murray, 2001: 1)

Hurdle 3 – wait time

Be prepared for a long delay in hearing if your article has been accepted by peer reviewed journals. A good journal should acknowledge receipt of your article very quickly but it can take up to six months for it to be reviewed and the reviewers' responses sent back to you. If you have not had an acceptance or rejection within six months, you could write a very gentle letter asking if they have had time to review it yet. The *American Sociological Review* states that the median time between submission and decision is approximately 12 weeks – but note the use of 'median' and 'approximately'. Professional journals are more likely to take one or two months maximum.

Don't try to speed the process by sending the same article to two journals simultaneously. It's considered unethical and a waste of reviewers' time.

Hurdle 4 – paying for publication

1 You will receive no payment for articles in peer reviewed journals; professional journals may pay; newspapers and magazines will pay.
2 You are not generally charged for publication but some journals require a submission fee to cover editorial and refereeing costs (for example, the *American Sociological Review* charges $15 submission fee, 2004; the *Canadian Journal of Economics* charges a fee). In some cases, the fee is refunded as a reward if the article is accepted or as compensation for rejection.
3 Some charge you for publication at a rate per page (generally the scientific journals). While 'there are undoubtedly a few journals who operate this system quite honourably, there is a fine line between this practice and … "vanity publishing"' (Sadler, 1990: 13).
4 Some journals in the natural and applied sciences offer some free pages and then you pay to go beyond that. Alternatively, they offer free and rapid publication to those willing to stay within the free page limit. Some will charge only if the article is the result of sponsored research. Sometimes journals will take payment from authors who want their work published quickly but this can't be done unless the journal is enlarged for an issue. The author pays the enlargement cost and then gets priority access – a rather questionable practice.

14.3   Chapters in edited books

1 You have to wait to be asked to write one of these, hence the importance of networking and other start-up activities (14.1, 4–7).
2 Once invited, draft your chapter following the editor's guidelines. Don't write the full chapter until you are sure that the editor has had the book accepted for publication. This can be a lengthy process. During this time, you have to hold back your material from other possible publications.
3 You may receive a small fee payable on submission of your manuscript (in the UK) or a part of the book's royalties (more usual in the USA). Note, however, that the more famous the editor, the less likely is any payment (you just get the kudos of having been asked). Professional associations publishing post-conference compendiums of papers are unlikely to pay either – they plead poverty.
4 Book chapters are not highly rated in university assessment exercises (1.3.2.3) but they do make your name more prominent, improve your chance of being asked to join research projects and keep happy your network contacts.

14.4 Books

1 Academic books and e-books 'will not reach large audiences, will seldom make your reputation, and certainly will not make you rich' (Knight, 2002: 202). They will cement a reputation and give you personal satisfaction and some ratings credibility.

2 To convince publishers that your proposed book will sell, check their catalogues to see if you fit in with what they publish and that the same subject is not already published. Then follow their guidelines for the information they need from you in order to judge the value of your proposal. Sage, for example, requests:

(a) working title;
(b) book type and synopsis (topic, scope, aims, price, length);
(c) style;
(d) table of contents (a paragraph on each chapter);
(e) the intended market;
(f) competing titles;
(g) writing plan;
(h) short curriculum vitae.

3 Seriously consider any changes requested by the publisher even if they don't immediately seem to accord with your ideas.

14.5 Success and rejection

1 *Success.* Give yourself just a few minutes to savour it before going straight on with the next publication. Maintain your momentum.

2 *Revisions requested prior to publication.* First, remember that you are not alone. The editor of *Educational Administration Quarterly,* a major US journal, reported that only 3 per cent of articles submitted were accepted without revisions being required, and this was the same whether the writers were senior or junior faculty. Senior faculty 'persisted in making revisions and resubmitting the manuscripts until they were published' though juniors were less willing to do so (Lindle, 2004: 2). Most manuscripts submitted to *EAQ* needed at least two rounds of revisions before publication. Secondly, just follow the advice and make the revisions as quickly as possible. Thirdly, revision requests are not a guarantee of publication even if the revisions are done.

3 *Rejection.* Recycle the document to another journal or another publisher *but* alter it first to fit in with their requirements (Chapters 2–4; 13.2.2).

14.6 Extending the audience for your research and publications: using the web

Back up your publications with organizing access to you and your research via the web.

1 Get to know the databases for your discipline. See if they accept publications or abstracts or may allow hyperlink access to your work. Find out if you retain ownership of your material so posted.

2 If you're published in a journal, check that your article is on the database.

3 Seek to publish in journals with both print and electronic versions.

4 For your theses, register with a company that provides thesis abstracts if your university does not arrange this.

5 Put your publications on your own website.

6 Make available material from your research that would be difficult, or expensive, to access any other way. Ó'Dochartaigh (2002) suggests a bibliography of the online sources you have used so readers can just click on the links you found for quick access. In the written version of your document you could refer to this and where it can be located rather than putting the whole thing into the thesis. In addition, you could provide an annotated bibliography of the print sources you used, photographs, or raw data in full, if you are willing for others to access them. Such material can be put on your own website or that of your organization or appropriate specialist sites.

7 Keyword search engines, such as Yahoo, Google and Lycos, allow you to chose one or two subcategories into which to place your web pages. Go to the web page for your chosen subcategory, or the link on the main page that asks you to submit a site, and use the 'suggest a site' link. You get a form to fill in. It may take some time before your work appears and search engines don't guarantee inclusion.

8 Use email lists only if they are very subject specialist and if they regularly mail you. If so, then contact them to request including your materials.

14.7 Ten top tips: publish or perish

1 Be utterly conventional in the way you submit research for publication whether the content be alternative or conventional.

2 Make publication your number one work and leisure activity.

3 Write everything for which you're asked.

4 Ask everyone you can for help.

5 Write about everything you do.

6 Read articles in your targeted journal before writing your own. Adjust your own style to the journal's.

7 *Obey* contributors' instructions, editors' demands, publication deadlines, grammatical rules, citation requirements, word limits, reviewers' advice, publishers' requests. Until you are very, very well established, *don't argue*.

8 Produce several articles, chapters and books from the same research project but always alter the style, tone and format to fit the audience and aims of differing documents.

9 Thank those who have in any way helped you to get published.

10 One day, you'll produce a top-selling academic blockbuster. Meanwhile, enjoy immense satisfaction from seeing yourself in print.

15 Standing on the Shoulders of Giants – Without Violating their Copyright

Lora Siegler Thody, BA (Pennsylvania) JD (Rutgers) and Serena Thody, LL.B (Leicester)

CONTENTS

This chapter provides a general overview of the US and UK copyright issues within intellectual property legal principles that you should be aware of, both to protect your own work and to avoid violating the copyright of others. There are similarities in the laws for other countries, for example, Canada, Australia and the European Union. This chapter can be used as a reference point for other countries but local laws should always be checked.

The format of the chapter as FAQs illustrates an alternative style for academic writing. The coding is for ease of reference. Where answers apply to both the UK and the USA, the text is black. Specific USA points are shown on a grey background *while specific UK references are noted in italics.*

The authors of this chapter are not engaged in rendering legal or other professional advice, and this publication is not a substitute for the advice of a lawyer. If you require legal or other expert advice, you should seek the services of a lawyer or other professional.

15.1   General

15.1.1   What is copyright?

A copyright owner acquires a 'bundle' of rights applying to their original work, including the right to reproduce, modify (i.e. to create what is known as a derivative in the US *and an adaptation in the UK*), distribute, publicly perform, or publicly display the work. Copyright ownership may also grant protection of 'moral rights'. In the US, the law prevents the 'intentional distortion, mutilation, or other modification of the work which would be prejudicial to the artist's honor or reputation'. However, only certain categories of work are protected: the work must be in an edition of 200 or fewer signed, consecutively numbered copies and consist of paintings, drawings, print, sculpture, or photographs.

In the UK, protection of moral rights is construed more widely, with Article 6bis of the Berne Convention providing authors with the right to 'object to any distortion, mutilation or other modification of, or other derogatory action in relation to, the said work, which would be prejudicial to his honour or reputation'.

A copyright owner may transfer, assign, or license the copyrighted material to others (see also 15.3.8 on joint authors).

15.1.2 What is covered by copyright? What is not?

Copyright covers many different 'works of authorship' including but not limited to:

- literary works (including articles in newspapers, journals and magazines);
- non-fiction prose;
- computer software;
- documentation and manuals;
- compilations;
- research finding presentations, e.g. graphs, charts;
- training films and videos;
- maps, diagrams, cartoons, illustrations, photographs.

The work in question must be an original work, but it does not have to be a completely original idea (as is required to obtain a patent). The material must not be copied directly from something else (or virtually copied, with just a few minor changes). For example, original writing on research findings is copyrightable, even if the area is already subject to much prior research and writing.

Copyright does not cover company marks such as the NIKE® swoosh or names such as DISNEY®. These are protected by trademark law and permission must be sought before using trademarks in presentations or printed materials. Simply referring to trademarks in text would be acceptable, but use capital letters to identify them and add the ® or ™ as it appears in the owner's format. Photographs are covered by copyright owned by the photographer and/or publisher, and may also be protected by trademark law for the subject of the photograph, e.g. a celebrity's image.

Copyright also does not cover inventions, although architectural designs and drawings are copyrightable. Inventions can be patented under a different set of laws.

15.1.3 Where is a copyright valid?

US citizens and foreign nationals residing in the US receive automatic copyright protection for works created in the US. The protection extends to any country party to the Berne Convention for the Protection of Literary and Artistic Works, or party to the Universal Copyright Convention. Most countries are signatories to these conventions including the US, the UK, the EU, Canada and Australia).

Similarly, UK copyright protection arises based on residency in the UK or the UK citizenship of the author. Foreign authors (non-UK nationals) resident outside the UK have protection in the UK under treaties to which their country is a party (e.g. the Berne Convention).

15.1.4 When does copyright arise?

As soon as the work is 'fixed in a tangible form'. You do not need to put a © on the work *at all in the UK* and not unless it was created before 1 March 1989 in the US. Tangible form means 'fixed in any tangible medium of expression, now known or later developed, from which they can be perceived, reproduced, or otherwise communicated, either directly or with the aid of a machine or device' and can include writing down on paper, typing, entering into a computer, or even dictating into a tape recorder.

15.1.5 How is a work protected through copyright? Do you have to register formally?

You do not need to register formally to receive copyright protection. In the US, you cannot bring an action for infringement and cannot recover damages or attorney's fees without registering. If you do register, your work is also placed in the United States Library of Congress.

There is no registration requirement in the UK to be eligible to bring a suit for infringement and damages.

15.1.6 How long does copyright protection last?

In the US, copyright protection lasts the life of the creator plus an additional 70 years (if work is created after 1 January 1978). For joint works, the copyright protection lasts for 70 years after the death of the last surviving author. For works created prior to 1978, the protection lasts 95 years from date copyright was secured. Where the work is a work made for hire, copyright protection (owned by the employer) lasts 95 years from date of first publication or distribution to the public, or 120 years from date of creation, whichever expires first.

In the UK, copyright protection lasts for the same periods as in the US except in the case of a computer generated work, for which the duration is 50 years from date of creation. Further, 'publication' in the UK is an issuing to the public in any EU country.

15.2 Violation of copyright

15.2.1 When do I need to get permission to use extracts from others' publications?

If you intend to use any copyrighted material, you should seek permission from the copyright owners. You need to be certain to request permission from all owners (for example, an article in a magazine may have copyright owned by the author, the magazine itself and perhaps a photographer). Printed materials usually contain contact information on how to request permissions. Many websites have links to copyright terms that provide the owner's policy on use of their materials and possibly even the form of attribution (look for links such as 'terms of use', 'legal' or 'site guidelines'). If you cannot find help at those links, use the general 'contact us' link to seek permission.

Obtaining permission from copyright owners mitigates the risk of copyright infringement liability, ensures appropriate recognition for the original creator, and avoids any royalty claim on the quoted material. If you are granted permission to use copyrighted information, adhere carefully to the correct form of attribution requested, do *not* change any of the material being quoted, and follow any guidelines to the letter (for example, the permission may allow print use but not online publication).

15.2.1.1 What should the permission request/clarify?

When requesting permission to use copyrighted material, you should clarify the following:

- title of your publication;
- publication details, e.g. publisher, author(s), frequency of publication (note that you may need to request a new permission for each and every update, new edition, etc.);
- media, for example, print, CD, online (request everything needed);
- what exact material you wish to include;
- reason for including the material, for example, why it is important to your work;
- any changes you wish to make to the appearance of the material;
- the suggested attribution that you will include.

Many copyright owners are pleased to have their material included in another work. However, but if you receive an initial negative response you may be able to persuade original copyright owners to allow permission to reproduce their work by offering some form of compensation: for example, a one-time payment, a copy of the finished book, or even just full and prominent attribution including details of how/where to purchase the original work.

If you cannot locate or persuade a copyright owner, do *not* include the material. Remember: if in doubt, leave it out!

15.2.2 If I download free information from the internet, I'm not violating copyright – right?

This is probably the most common misconception about copyrighted material! Just because information is free to view, it does not mean it is free to be copied. Copyright protection became attached to the created material as soon as that material was in a 'fixed form' – whether that is written in pencil or HTML coded to appear on a website. Even apparently public information, such as government forms, may be covered by restrictions: for example, it may only be publishable for use in non-commercial publications and an attribution must be included.

Many websites have links to copyright terms that provide the owner's policy on use of the materials and possibly even the form of attribution (look for links such as 'terms of use', 'legal' or 'site guidelines'). If you cannot find help at those links, use the general 'contact us' link to seek permission (see 15.2.1).

15.2.3   Is government information copyright?

Information published by the government, in print or online, may also be subject to copyright under certain circumstances. In the United States, works created by employees or officers of the United States federal government, in their capacity as such, are not copyrightable and are in the public domain. (Such material also is excluded from being the subject of copyright when included in another person's work.) Thus, most works published by the US government are free of copyright restrictions. However, works published by the US government may contain other material which is subject to a third-party copyright: careful inspection should be made for a statement notifying the user of this fact. Works of state and local governments in the United States can be the subject of copyright protection.

In the UK, government materials such as legislation are subject to the special category of Crown copyright. However, the government has determined that in order to increase public access to legislation, a waiver of this copyright will be applied if certain conditions are met. These conditions include reproducing only the official version of the legislation, using the most up-to-date version, not using the material in a derogatory or misleading manner, and providing appropriate attribution.

15.2.4   Can work in the public domain be used freely?

If work is in the public domain (for example the copyright has expired, see 15.1.6, or never existed), the material can be used freely. Anything you add to it (for example, building on research findings in the public domain) would be copyrightable to yourself, but the original portion you built on would remain in the public domain for others to use.

15.2.5   What is plagiarism?

Plagiarism is passing off as one's own the words or ideas of someone else or using someone else's work without crediting the original source.

Plagiarizing material is not only unethical, it also likely violates legal copyright. As mentioned above, this applies to printed materials and online materials. Simply reprinting text downloaded from a website is plagiarism. Paraphrasing might be considered acceptable but only if it is not extensive. Merely changing a few words or altering the organization of the work would fall under the definition of plagiarism. Plagiarism can result in successful infringement proceedings, including significant monetary damages to the original owner.

The best approach is to emphasize sources clearly that are not your own original work by the use of quotation marks, indentation of text, italicization, or other means, and to provide the proper citation to the original source.

If you use your own material from another book, thesis or article this, of course, would not be plagiarism, *but* there could be copyright implications if you have assigned your copyright in the first material to a publisher and now you are producing a competing work.

15.2.6   What is fair use or fair dealing?

The US fair use doctrine provides a limited exception to copyright protection. The doctrine allows a limited use of copyrighted material (e.g. quotes, criticism, parody, news reporting) for use in educational or scholarly works (in teaching or research). There is no set limit on the amount of material which may be so used: some uses which have been considered too much in the US were the use of 300 words, three sentences, 0.8 per cent of content, one paragraph, eight sentences, and thirty-one lines. The courts determine the applicability of this exception on a case-by-case basis, examining the character of use, amount used, and effect on the market of the copyrighted work.

In general, use of copyrighted material in teaching, preparing teaching materials or research, for classroom use or discussion, or for other not-for-profit purposes, would fall within the fair use doctrine, but there are a number of other requirements to consider concerning spontaneity (no time to get permission) and cumulative effect (copying several pieces of the same source).

Fair dealing in the UK includes use for research or private study, use for criticism or review, and use for preparation of teaching materials or as an example in a classroom. Copyrighted materials cannot be used for commercial purposes without permission even under the fair dealing doctrine.

If a book is to be published for sale, fair use is unlikely to apply, so you should obtain permissions to reprint long portions of copyrighted material (see 15.2.1) and provide full attribution for quotations. Remember that if you include copyrighted materials in a thesis or research study that is subsequently published for commercial purposes, fair use will no longer apply.

15.3   Your own copyright

15.3.1   Do I own my published book or article?
Does it depend on where and when I wrote them?

As a general rule, the creator of an original work is the owner of the copyright. The application of this rule to specific circumstances comes into play most often in the context of an employer claiming ownership of works authored by an employee. An employer owns a work which is created by an employee in the scope of the employment, except where a contract expressly provides otherwise. A work is not considered to be created by the employee in the scope of the employment where it is created on the employee's own initiative and time, using the employee's own tools and resources (for example, on weekends and *not* at the employer's workplace) and is not related to their duties of employment. Another context in which this question arises is where your material is a contribution to a joint work (see 15.3.8).

It is likely that, before publication by a publishing house or reputable journal, you will be asked to assure the publisher that you hold the copyright to your material and to assign your copyright to the publisher.

15.3.2   Does my university own my thesis or do I?

In both the US and the UK, the first places to look for this information are in your contract with the university and the university's written policies on writings. These may state whether your thesis and other writings are considered works for hire (the university would own the copyright in that case) or whether there is a distinction drawn between types of writing or publication status. Many universities are now detailing things for which they will own the copyright.

A good approach, if there is nothing specified in a contract or a written policy, is to identify your work in a written agreement with your institution which states your specific work is not made for hire and that you retain the copyright.

Writings by employees of academic institutions (schools, universities) are likely to be a work made for hire if the material is teaching materials, test questions or answers.

In the US, the courts have decided cases based on similar facts in a variety of ways, causing uncertainty in this area. A thesis, for example, may seem like a work made for hire, and thus the copyright would be owned by the university, as most academics are expected, either by contract or by tradition, to produce scholarly writings as part of their employment. However, case law on this issue leans toward favouring that the work is *not* a work made for hire due to academic traditions, assumptions and practice, lack of supervision of the university over faculty writings (in time, location, format, deadlines, content and conclusions; nor does the university usually edit the work), and the fact that the university is unlikely to 'exploit' the author's writing for commercial gain. Further, the writings are not prepared for the benefit or use of the university as such, other than to enhance its academic reputation.

15.3.3   Can I publish parts of my thesis without getting permission from my supervisor or university?

As the author, you are likely to be the owner of the copyright for the thesis, not the university (see 15.3.1 and 15.3.2). In that event, you can use the materials in any way you wish. You can also share ideas or comments (such as from a supervisor) without causing any copyright to arise on behalf of the supervisor. However, if the university is the owner of the copyright (for example, by contract or written policy), you must obtain the permission of the university just as you would a third party (see 15.2.1).

15.3.4   Can I use extracts from my own thesis or book without getting permission?

You can likely use and reuse thesis materials without obtaining any additional permissions provided that the university contract or written policies did not expressly make the university the owner of those materials (see 15.3.1 and 15.3.2).

The copyright of a book published by a commercial publisher is likely to be held by the publisher pursuant to an assignment from the author. If this is the case, you should request permission from the publisher, stating how much you want to use, for what purposes, how many copies, and whether you will be selling the extracts. For use as examples, in presentations, self-marketing or even handing out copies of a full chapter in a class, the publisher will likely grant permission and ask for attribution. If you intend to sell all or a substantial portion of the book, however, the publisher is unlikely to grant permission as this will compete with the publisher's own sales.

15.3.5   Do I get royalties on my published book or article or do my employers?

The answer to this question depends on whether you own the copyright or the book/article is a work made for hire (see 15.3.1 and 15.3.2).

15.3.6   Do the funders of a research project have the right to forbid me to publish it in other forms?

The answer to this question depends on whether you own the copyright or the book/article is a work made for hire. It is best to have a written agreement with the funders concerning this matter.

If you own the copyright to the material (that is, you have not transferred or assigned your ownership rights and it is not a work made for hire), and the contract with the funders does not prohibit you from publishing your own works, you can publish the material.

However, if you have assigned your copyright to a previous publisher or to the funders, permission to publish can be withheld (see 15.1.4, 15.3.1, 15.3.2).

15.3.7   Can the funders leave out material from my findings that they don't wish to include?

If you retain the copyright (see 15.3.1, 15.3.2), then the material cannot be changed from its original format without your express permission. If you have assigned your copyright, your work can be modified without your express permission.

15.3.8   Who owns the copyright of a work if there are multiple authors? What about where there are editors who receive submissions from authors?

In the US, a joint work is defined as 'a work prepared by two or more authors with the intention that their contributions be merged into inseparable or interdependent parts of a unitary whole'. Each author of a joint work must contribute material and not just ideas. All co-authors of a work have equal shares of the copyright, regardless of their level of contribution and, if there is no agreement to the contrary, each may use or license the work without the permission of the other co-authors provided that: the use or license does not destroy the value of the work; and the profits, if any, must be shared among the co-authors.

In the UK, a 'work of joint authorship' means a work produced by the collaboration of two or more authors in which the contribution of each author is not distinct from that of the other author or authors. The 'intention' requirement of the US laws is not included in the UK statutes.

A joint owner of copyright in the UK cannot act without the consent of all of the other joint owners, and therefore one joint owner cannot transfer or license the copyright to a third party without the agreement of all other joint owners. This is different from the position in the US, but many European countries take the same position as in the UK.

If your work is part of a compilation or collection, where the parts submitted by each author are distinct, the rules of co-authorship do not apply. Your copyright extends to your own original piece of the work, but not to the whole work. Thus you may continue to license or use your material provided that you have not assigned the copyright to the editor or publisher.

15.3.9 When would I give permission to others to use my work – what should I require?

In many cases it is beneficial to you and your work to provide permission for others to reprint or extract. Consideration in general should be given to the reason for inclusion, the reputation of the publication/publisher and other author, and whether the extract or reprint would compete, either in terms of sales or in terms of audience, with your original publication.

You can limit your permission in a number of ways:

- Geographical limitations: for example, the work can only be published in countries other than where you have already published.
- Time limitations: publishable for a limited period, such as 5 years.
- Require payment, such as royalties or a one-time fee.
- Require attribution. Provide specific language, such as:

> Reprinted from [publication title], by [author name], with permission of [author(s) or other copyright owner(s)]. Copyright © [year]. For further information on this publication, please contact [insert details or, for example, web address for purchase].

> Note: the Copyright © is not necessary but often does provide a visual 'alert'.

- Media limitations, such as print but not online or electronic.
- Specify circumstances, such as extracts or amounts of material, specific uses, specifics concerning graphics.

The publisher of the article/book using your material may request your permission in writing, with your signature.

15.3.10 How do I transfer my copyright?

A transfer of copyright ownership must be in writing. A transfer can be of part or of all ownership rights and can be during the life of the creator or can continue after the death of the creator. Careful thought should be given before transferring full ownership where less than full ownership would serve the purpose.

15.4 Libel and slander

15.4.1 What is libel? What is slander?

Libel and slander are both forms of defamation, which is the act of harming someone's reputation by making a false statement to a third party.

Libel is defamation by means of writing, print, or some other permanent form, while slander is defamation by means of spoken words or gestures. Defences include proving that there was no publication, that the words were incapable of defamatory meaning, or that the words were actually true in substance and fact.

Avoidance is the best practice: review your work prior to any dissemination for statements concerning another's reputation, work or work product. Lectures, seminars and conference presentations and other public presentations are covered by the laws of libel and slander, so materials prepared for these circumstances should also be carefully reviewed.

15.5   Websites for reference

* *UK Patent Office (including Copyright): http://www.patent.gov.uk*
* World Intellectual Property Organization: http://www.wipo.int/portal/index.html.en
* US Copyright Office: http://www.copyright.gov
* US Patent & Trademark Office: http://www.uspto.gov
* General copyright links, with a section on copyright and education: http://www.kasunic.com

15.6   Authors' bio-data

Lora Siegler Thody earned her Bachelor's degree from the University of Pennsylvania, majoring in English Literature, and her Juris Doctor from Rutgers University, Camden, NJ, US. Following admission to the New York and Utah bars, she held the position of Chief of Enforcement for the Utah Securities Division in Salt Lake City and then worked in private practice there for eight years, focused primarily on securities and corporate law. Lora now works as Senior Principal Attorney Editor for Thomson West Legal Publishing based in the Rochester, NY, office and specializes in Securities Law.

Serena M. Thody graduated with an LL.B from Leicester University, UK with a specialization in Medical Law and Ethics. She then trained in Logistics Management as part of the graduate management programme at J. Sainsbury's head office in London. Moving back into the law, she joined Thomson Sweet and Maxwell legal publishing, and became the legislation manager for the development of WestlawUK. She transferred to sister company Thomson West and now works as a Senior Principal Attorney Editor on the Intellectual Property team at the Rochester, NY, office.

Part V   Valediction

16 Epilogue

CONTENTS

16.1 The debate

Relief! They're over – all those years of selecting your research topic, narrowing the scope, negotiating research funding, organizing a team, searching literature, choosing the research methodology, designing research instruments, collecting data, analysing the mountain of information gathered, checking and rechecking the outcomes, reflecting on the recommendations. All that is left is to write it up and produce a few presentations. A few months and all will be out of the way and it's on to the next project. Writing is just a task that must be done in order to disseminate the work and without which the research is incomplete. All you have to do is to 'convince others of the worth of a study in a clear and concise manner' (Cresswell, 1994: 193). Modernists view writing and presenting as reports on discoveries, in which language precision accurately conveys what happened and emotion is not a concern. Writing is an uncontentious, formulaic process (Bryman, 2001: 460).

But it's no longer seen as so simplistic, as you will have realized from this book. Postmodernists see research writing and presentation as translations of what has been discovered, a reflexive process trying to share feelings about the research. Writing up research, or its oral presentation, is a 'site of contestation' (Lewis-Beck et al., 2004: 1197), one which can be regarded as problem solving with its own subprocesses and mental events (Kellogg, 1994; Flower and Hayes, 1981). For some, it is an interpretive art which could be an integral part of the sense-making of research results (Denzin, 1998: 317).

16.2 How the protagonists line up

Since the 1980s, the trickle of spokespersons pointing out the importance of the words in reporting research results has grown to become a thin brook (Delamont, 1998) of which this book is a part. The brook has yet to babble into a mature river though its tributaries are growing (Kitchen and Fuller, 2005; Dunleavy, 2003) and there has been consensus that writing is central to the effectiveness of a research project for some time (Blaxter et al., 2001: 227; Clifford and Marcus, 1986: 2). Most writers on research methodology make at least a passing reference to the writing stage since research is nothing unless successfully disseminated (Darlington and Scott, 2002: 158; Sadler, 1990: 1).

Indicative of these developments is Holliday's (2002) *Doing and Writing Qualitative Research*, 50 per cent of which is, as the title promises, about writing. Cohen et al.'s (2000) major text on research methods for education insists that decisions on the writing and presenting should be built into project planning from its inception. Their list of the questions about research reporting, which researchers must answer, is valuable to any discipline (2000: 87). It reminds us to settle at the start who should do the writing up or presenting, through what media the research will be disseminated, whether or not there will be interim reports, and how to ensure that the anticipated readerships will comprehend the language used or the statistics presented. Knight (2002) demonstrates the importance he attaches to writing in the research process and production as he places it in Chapter 1 of his guide to small scale research.

Despite this support, there is still a very limited number of texts that allot a significant amount of attention to writing and presenting (as a casual trawl of any library's sources or the internet will demonstrate). The bibliography to this book has asterisked texts that directly discuss the writing and presenting of research; there are few asterisks. Babbie's (2001) valuable student text of 498 pages on *The Practice of Social Research* has one-quarter of a page on writing up (and yes – it's on p. 498). It is viewed as unproblematic, requiring only a few reminders of items to be included in the substantive content only. Piantanida and Garman's (1999) otherwise excellent book on all aspects of everything one might want, or even not want, to know about qualitative dissertations has no mention of how to write them up – yet surely this is the most qualitative decision of all?

Scholars themselves seem to be schizoid. Bryman, for example, reminds us that it 'is easy to forget that one of the major stages in any research project, regardless of size, is that it has to be written up … being aware of the significance of writing is crucial' (2001: 460). He then devotes only fourteen pages of his 499 page text to it, perhaps because he notes that 'good writing is *probably* just as important as good research practice' (2001: 473). In the 2004 *Sage Encyclopaedia of Social Science Research Methods*, the editors recognize that 'How one writes, what one writes, and for whom one writes are theoretical, ethical and methodological issues' (Lewis-Beck et al., 2004: 1197). They then offer only one and half pages on writing up, and one page on creative analytical practice (CAP) ethnography. Raimond (1993: 166) soundly justifies writing and presentation as 'the most important part of the project' and as constituting the second half of any research project. He then only devotes fourteen of his 188 pages to the topic.

16.3　Where you and I fit in

This book has devoted all its pages to writing and presenting research. My aims were to:

- increase awareness of the significance of writing and presenting;
- contribute to debates on writing and presentation;
- provide an introductory guide to the options available in the early 2000s and encouragement to create your own;
- show your power to influence readers and listeners through how you write and present.

I will feel that I have achieved my objectives when I read a section in a research project's methodology description that states:

> The narrative form of presenting statistics used in this e-paper is a new genre, initially suggested by Thody (2006). It builds on the pioneering work of Xu Wong (2022) who developed NASA data as poetics. While such presentation has been criticized for its 'elevation of text at the expense of data' (Abu-Azziz, 2027: 42), Jelsen (2029) has pointed out that poetics illuminates our understanding of complex scientific data by showing emphases that would otherwise remain hidden.

It's now your job to hasten the time by which statements like that will be commonplace. You, the researcher, have immense power and responsibility in creating the texts and presentations that report your work. Readers/listeners will only have your text on which to take their decisions. They cannot access the original data, or meet the respondents whom you recorded, or read all the books you read, the films you saw, the experiments you made. Nor can they travel where you went geographically, emotionally or academically. Only your words can take them there.

17 Appendix
Research Method for this Book

CONTENTS

17.1 Inception of the project

With my fellow masters degree students in the 1970s, I had to attend monthly lectures in our discipline though none was directly related to our individual research. We mainly slept politely during these irrelevant adventures until the day we faced a stern Dr John Baker of Leicester University, unusually clad in the academic gown and mortar board normally reserved for university ceremonies. He proceeded to drone through reading his lecture from the lectern. Five minutes in and he walked off the stage behind a side screen, re-emerging in the then equally unsuitable dress of jeans and T-shirt. He proceeded, without notes, to electrify us with his critique of a book on different styles of learning and teaching (Herbert Kohl's *The Open Classroom*). So engaging was this vivid, active, demonstration of different teaching styles that I even went and bought the book (and read it) although it had no relevance to my personal research.

It was regarded as a very radical presentation, so radical that the presenter was warned off doing anything like it again by his superiors. Fortunately, it inspired me into realizing that there were alternatives which needed to be considered alongside the established formats and also found myself, like John Baker, being warned off alternative presentations thirty years later.

I wanted to write this book, therefore, to make the world safer for alternatives but also to establish that either conventional or alternative can be good in the right places, the right ways and at the right times.

17.2 Sources

The research for this book has stretched over my forty years of recording and reflecting on my experiences and those of my students and colleagues. Along the way, I have tested some of the ideas through mini-surveys with my students and all of the ideas in theses, publications and presentations of my own and of colleagues. You'll find in the bibliography the sources that I used for this book specifically, but the literature and experiences that also informed it were accumulated during my many years of:

- Examining and supervising masters and doctoral theses at twelve UK universities, two in Australia, one in Malta.
- Giving lectures, devising and running programmes on research methods, including communication, writing and presentation for undergraduates and postgraduates in eight universities in England, Cyprus, Singapore and Australia.
- Making and being invited to make presentations for academic and practitioner conferences in fifteen countries and all around the United Kingdom. The range has included textile engineers in northern India, senior automotive and airline managements in the UK, school trustees in New Zealand and school principals, teachers, governors and administrators everywhere. My preference has been to find alternative ways to enliven presentations (the fairy costume was not a good idea but the alien from space was very well received) but I have also read the traditional papers.
- Facing 'lay' audiences as a volunteer for a charity supporting parents staying in hospital with their children (thus leading me into coping with unfamiliar material in front of local Rotary clubs, Women's Institutes and children's playgroups) and as a school parent-helper where I had to work out how to teach symmetry through needlework and mocked-up a 1930s classroom where I taught dessert cookery.
- Listening to other keynote speakers and presenters at conferences in England and around the world and subsequent informal discussions on what makes a good presenter. I have made a point of seeking out the experimental but I've also enjoyed learning from conventional performances. These have been as varied as the Indian professor who held a 500 strong audience in enthralled silence in Malaysia, just chatting from his armchair for ninety minutes; and the Scottish administrator with at least 120 OH transparencies, at the end of whose hour's presentation had only myself (as the chair) and twenty others left from an original audience of 200.
- Writing, reviewing and obtaining research grant applications and making the subsequent reports.
- Battling through three rounds of England's Research Assessment Exercise.
- Giving presentations, lectures, speeches in purpose-built enormous conference centres, in cathedrals and churches, a Maori meeting house, freezing cold school gymnasia, a kindergarten room with adults on mini-chairs, a TV studio, in the open air in India, in bed (by audio link to a Canadian conference during the small hours of an English morning and a Canadian evening) and in hotel dining rooms (including a memorable evening as the after-dinner speaker for a dinner that failed to arrive).

My publishing career began in 1968 through developing a first chapter from my post graduate teachers' certificate dissertation under the gentle mentorship of an established professor (as Gill, 1968). Since then I have written my masters and doctoral theses and four books, co-authored or edited five books, contributed chapters to many more, published in refereed, professional and house magazines and newspapers, produced distance learning materials, edited a journal for seven years, reviewed articles for several journals and conference committees, produced a professional association newsletter and even stretched into the Caravan Club magazine, a CD, local radio broadcasts and a programme for a TV channel for teachers.

My styles have ranged from the conventional (Thody, 2003) to academic articles written in alternative styles as short plays and novels (Thody, 1990a; 1990b).

17.3 Data analysis

For this, I used the techniques of Chapters 6 and 7.

17.4 Data presentation

I decided this from following the guiding principles of Chapters 2–4.

- *Precedent*. This must be academic textbook style following the publisher's guidelines for this series. The book is, however, about varying presentation styles so the conventions can be ignored on occasions to allow for demonstrations of alternatives.
- *Personality*. I enjoy textual experimentation but try to avoid this becoming overwhelming.
- *Practicalities*. The book had a word and time limit but I had to negotiate extensions to both. My computer literacy was limited so I had to learn some extensions to this.
- *People*. Readers were assumed to be academics though not specialists in any one field.
- *Purposes*. Overt: to add to readers' options for research writing and presentation. Covert: to increase academic debate about writing and presenting options; to produce a saleable book.
- *Planning*. An outline was agreed with the publishers in advance. This became the template for the book. All the chapters, except one, remained as originally agreed but the order altered.

Bibliography

- Entries preceded by an asterisk * are recommendations for further reading.
- The citation system for this chapter is that recommended by the publishers (12.2).
- Sources used solely *within* quoted extracts are not included in this bibliography.

Ackerman, R. and Maslin-Ostrowski, P. (1996) 'Real talk: toward further understanding of case story in teaching educational administration'. Paper presented at the Annual Meeting of the American Educational Research Association, New York.

Ahmad, W.I.U. and Sheldon, T. (1993) ' "Race" and statistics', in M. Hammersley (ed.), *Social Research: Philosophy, Politics and Practice*. London: Open University Press. pp. 124–30. Originally published in *Radical Statistics*, 1991, 48 (Spring), pp. 27–33.

*APA (2001) *Publication Manual of the American Psychological Association* (5th edn). Washington, DC: American Psychological Association.

*APA (2005) *Concise Rules of APA Style*. Washington, DC: American Psychological Association.

Arenson, K. (2004) 'Boldface professors', *Education Life: New York Times Supplement*, Section A4, 25 April: 22–4.

Arnold, R. (2001) *Fashion, Desire and Anxiety: Image and Morality in the Twentieth Century*. London: Taurus.

Babbie, E. (2001) *The Practice of Social Research* (9th edn). Belmont, CA: Wordsworth/Thomson.

Barnes, J. (2002) 'The struggle continues: *El Centro de los Trabajadores Agricolas Fronterizos*', *International Journal of Qualitative Studies in Education*, 15 (1): 55–65.

Barnett, E. and Storey, J. (1999) *Understanding Innovation through Narrative*. Human Resources Research Unit (HRRU), Working Paper 99/9, Open University, Milton Keynes.

Barone, T. (1995) 'Persuasive writings, vigilant readings, and reconstructed characters: the paradox of trust in educational storytelling', *Qualitative Studies in Education*, 8 (1): 63–74.

Bauman, R. (1986) *Story, Performance and Event*. Cambridge: Cambridge University Press.

*Bazerman, C. (1987) 'Codifying the social scientific style: *The APA Publication Manual* as a behaviourist rhetoric', in J. Nelson, A. Megill and D. McCloskey (eds), *The Rhetoric of Human Sciences: Language and Argument in Scholarship and Public Affairs*. Madison, WI: University of Wisconsin Press. pp. 125–44.

Beinhart, W. and Bundy, C. (1987) *Hidden Struggles in Rural South Africa*. London: Currey and University of California Press.

Bell, A. Oliver with McNeillie, A. (1980) *The Diary of Virginia Woolf*. San Diego: Harcourt Brace.

Belson, W.A. (1967) *The Impact of Television: Methods and Findings in Program Research*. London: Crosby Lockwood.

Bergerson, A.A. (2003) 'Critical race theory and white racism: is there room for white scholars in fighting racism in education?', *International Journal of Qualitative Studies in Education*, 16 (1): 51–63.

*Berry, R. (1994) *The Research Project: How to Write It* (3rd edn). London: Routledge.

Blaxter, L., Hughes, C. and Tight, M. (2001) *How To Research* (2nd edn). Buckingham: Open University Press.

*Bluebook (2000) *The Bluebook: A Uniform System of Citation* (17th edn). Cambridge, MA: Harvard Law Review Association (18th edn 2005).

Bossenbroek, M. (1995) 'The living tools of empire: the recruitment of European soldiers for the Dutch colonial army, 1814–1909', *Journal of Imperial and Commonwealth History*, 23 (1): 26–53.

Bovet, J. (1998) 'Long-distance travels and homing: dispersal, migrations, excursions', in N. Foreman and R. Gillett (eds), *Handbook of Spatial Research Paradigms and Methodologies. Vol. 2: Clinical and Comparative Studies*. Hove: Psychology Press. pp. 239–69.

Boyd, D.R. (2003) *Unnatural Law: Rethinking Canadian Environmental Law and Policy*. Vancouver: University of British Colombia Press.

Bradbury, M. (2001) *To The Hermitage*. London: Picador.

Bradley, W.J. and Schaefer, K.C. (1998) *The Uses and Misuses of Data and Models: The Mathematization of the Human Sciences*. Thousand Oaks, CA: Sage.

Brandon, W.W. (2003) 'Toward a white teachers' guide to playing fair: exploring the cultural politics of multicultural teaching', *International Journal of Qualitative Studies in Education*, 16 (1): 31–50.

Brundrett, M. (2003) 'School leadership: development and practice'. Unpublished PhD thesis, University of Hertfordshire (draft in the personal possession of the author).

Bryman, A. (2001) *Social Research Methods*. Oxford: Oxford University Press.

Burt, S. (2004) 'Happy as Two Blue-Plate Specials', New York Times Book Review Section, 21 November: 6.

Butts, F. (1955) *Assumptions Underlying Australian Education*. Melbourne: Australian Council for Educational Research.

Casati, R. and Varzi, A.C. (2004) 'Counting the holes', *Australian Journal of Philosophy*, 82 (1): 23–7.

Charles, C. (1988) *Introduction to Educational Research*. New York: Longman.

Chaudry, L.B. (1997) '"You should know what's right for me!": a hybrid's struggle to define empowerment for critical feminist research in education', in B. Merchant and A. Willis (eds), *Multiple and Intersecting Identities in Qualitative Research*. Mahwah, NJ: Erlbaum. pp. 33–41.

*Chicago Manual of Style (1993) *Chicago Manual of Style* (14th edn). Chicago: University of Chicago Press.

Clare, J. (2004a) 'Ministers and unruly pupils "causing collapse of schools"', *Daily Telegraph*, 27 May: 1.

Clare, J. (2004b) 'Dull, directionless and uninspiring', *Daily Telegraph*, 28 July: 19.

Clark, T.A.R. and Salaman, G. (1995) *The Management Guru as Organisational Witchdoctor*. Open Business School, Working Paper 95/3, Open University, Milton Keynes.

Clifford, J. and Marcus, G. (1986) *Writing Culture: The Poetics and Politics of Ethnography*. Berkeley, CA: University of California Press.

Cobbett, William (1818) *A Grammar of the English Language* (1823 edn reissued 2002). Oxford: Oxford University Press.

*Coghlan, D. and Brannick, T. (2001) *Doing Action Research in Your Own Organisation*. London: Sage (includes one chapter on presentation).

*Cohen, L., Manion, L., and Morrison, K. (2000) *Research Methods in Education* (5th edn). London: RoutledgeFalmer.

Collard, J. (1996) 'Leadership and gender: a conversation with Charol Shakeshaft', *Leading and Managing*, 2 (1): 70–4.

Colville, J. (1985) *The Fringes of Power*. New York, London: W.W. Norton & Company.

Conduit, E., Brookes, R., Bramley, G. and Fletcher, C.L. (1996) 'The value of school locations', *British Educational Research Journal*, 22 (2): 199–206.

Coonts, S. (2003) *Victory.* London: Orion.

Cresswell, J.W. (1994) *Research Design: Qualitative and Quantitative Approaches.* Thousand Oaks, CA: Sage.

Cutler, W.B. (2005) www.athenainstitute.com. Reference list of selected publications including Cutler, W.B. and Genovese-Stone, E. (2000) 'Wellness in women after 40 years of age: the role of sex hormones and pheromones. Part 1: The sex hormones, adrenal sex hormones and pheromonal modulation of brain and behavior', *Current Problems in Obstetrics, Gynecology and Fertility*, 23 (1): 1–32.

*Darley, J.M., Zanna, M.P. and Roediger III, H.L. (eds) (2004) *The Compleat Academic* (2nd edn). Washington, DC: APA.

Darlington, Y. and Scott, D. (2002) *Qualitative Research in Practice: Stories from the Field.* Buckingham: Open University Press.

*De Laine, M. (2000) *Fieldwork, Participation and Practice: Ethics and Dilemmas in Qualitative Research.* London: Sage (esp. Chapter 8 on textual impression management).

Delamont, S. (1998) 'Review of *Understanding Social Research*', *Evaluation and Research in Education*, 12 (3): 176–7.

Dent, T. (2001) 'Fruitbox/toolbox: biography and objects', *Auto/Biography*, IX (1 and 2): 11–20.

Denzin, N.K. (1998) 'The art and politics of interpretation', in N.K. Denzin and Y.S. Lincoln (eds), *Collecting and Interpreting Qualitative Materials*. Thousand Oaks, CA: Sage. pp. 313–44.

*Denzin, N.K. and Lincoln, Y.S. (eds) (1998) *Collecting and Interpreting Qualitative Materials*. Thousand Oaks, CA: Sage.

Dotlich, D.L. and Cairo, P.C. (2002) *Unnatural Leadership.* San Francisco: Jossey-Bass.

Dubin, S.C. (1999) *Displays of Power: Memory and Amnesia in the American Museum.* New York: New York University Press.

Dunleavy, P. (2003) *Authoring a PhD.* Basingstoke: Palgrave Macmillan.

Ellis, C. (2003) *The Ethnographic 'I': A Methodological Novel on Doing Autoethnography.* Walnut Creek, CA: AltaMira.

Evans, M.K. (2000) 'Lessons in image making: schooling through children's books', *History of Education Society Bulletin*, 65: 27–34.

Fail, H., Thompson, J. and Walker, G. (2004) 'Belonging, identity and Third Culture Kids: life histories of former international school students', *Journal of Research in International Education*, 3 (3): 319–38.

Falco, C.M. (2004) *'Errors of fact and reasoning in four papers by David Stork on "The Hockney–Falco thesis"'*, 8 January. www.stijl.tue.nl/filter22/http://www.phil.un.nl/staff/rob/texts/Storkpap,left,rightc.pdf, accessed 20 February 2006.

Fire, A., Xu, S., Montgomery, M.K., Kostas S.A., Driver, S.E. and Mello, C.C. (1998) 'Potent and specific genetic interference by double-stranded RNA in *Caenorhabditis elegans*', *Nature*, 391, 19 February: 806–11.

Flower, L. and Hayes, J.R. (1981) 'A cognitive process theory of writing', *College Composition and Communication*, I (32): 365–87.

Foreman, N. and Gillett, R. (1998) 'General introduction', in N. Foreman and R. Gillett (eds), *Handbook of Spatial Research Paradigms and Methodologies. Vol. 2: Clinical and Comparative Studies*. Hove: Psychology Press.

Frankhauser, S. (1995) *Valuing Climate Change.* London: Earthscan.

Friedman, S. (1998) *Mappings: Feminism and the Cultural Geographics of Encounter.* Princeton, NJ: Princeton University Press.

Frisch, M. (1990) *A Shared Authority.* Albany, NY: SUNY Press.

Fusarelli, L.D. (2002) 'The political economy of gubernatorial elections: implications for education policy', *Educational Policy*, 16 (1): 139–60.

Fusarelli, L.D., Cooper, B.S. and Carella, V.A. (2003) 'Who will serve? An analysis of super-intendent occupational perceptions, career satisfaction, and mobility', *Journal of School Leadership*, 13: 304–27.

Gadotti, M. (1996) *Pedagogy of Praxis: A Dialectical Philosophy of Education.* New York: SUNY Press.

Gardner, H. (1997) *Leading Minds: An Anatomy of Leadership.* London: Harper-Collins.

Gibbons, M., Limoges, C., Nowotny, H., Schwartzman, S., Scott, P. and Trow, M. (1994) *The New Production of Knowledge: The Dynamics of Science and Research in Contemporary Societies.* London: Sage.

Gibbs, G.R. (2002) *Qualitative Data Analysis: Explorations with NVivo.* Buckingham: Open University Press.

Gill, A. (1968) 'The Leicester School Board, 1871–1903', in B. Simon (ed.), *Education in Leicesteshire, 1540–1940.* Leicester: Leicester University Press.

Gomm, R. and Davies, C. (eds) (2000) *Using Evidence in Health and Social Care.* London: Sage.

Goodale, B. (2006) 'Notes and queries for the author of *Writing and Presenting Research*'. Personal document held by the author and publisher.

*Gosden, H. (1995) 'Success in research article writing and revision: a social-constructionist perspective', *English for Specific Purposes*, 14 (1): 37–57.

Graham, K. (1997) *Personal History.* New York: Random House, Vintage Books.

Griffin, G. and Chance, E.W. (1994) 'Superintendent behaviours and activities linked to school effectiveness: perceptions of principals and superintendents', *Journal of School Leadership*, 4 (1): 69–86.

*Griffith, K. (1994) *Writing Essays about Literature* (4th edn). Fort Worth, TX: Harcourt Brace.

*Griffith, K. (2002) *Writing Essays about Literature* (6th edn). Fort Worth, TX: Harcourt Brace.

Hammersley, M. (ed.) (1993) *Social Research: Philosophy, Politics and Practice.* London: Open University Press.

Hammersley, M. (2002) *Educational Research Policy Making and Practice.* London: Chapman.

Hargreaves, D.H. (1996) *Teaching as a Research-Based Profession: Possibilities and Prospects.* Teacher Training Agency Annual Lecture. London: TTA.

Harper, D. (1998) 'On the authority of the image: visual methods at the crossroads', in N. Denzin and Y. Lincoln (eds), *Collecting and Interpreting Qualitative Materials.* Thousand Oaks, CA: Sage. pp. 130–49.

Hayward, S. (1996) *Key Concepts in Cinema Studies.* London: Routledge.

Helwig, O. (1972) 'Considerations' in *The Best Name of Silence.* Ottawa: Oberon Press.

Henry, A. (1997) 'Looking two ways: identity, research and praxis in the Caribbean com-munity', in B. Merchant and A. Willis (eds), *Multiple and Intersecting Identities in Qualitative Research.* Mahwah, NJ: Erlbaum. pp. 61–8.

Ho, Sui-Chu, E. (2003) 'Teachers' views on educational decentralization towards parental involvement in an Asian educational system: the Hong Kong case', *International Studies in Educational Administration*, 31 (3): 58–75.

Hodges, H. (1998) 'Testing for spatial brain dysfunction in animals', in N. Foreman and R. Gillett (eds), *Handbook of Spatial Research Paradigms and Methodologies. Vol. 2: Clinical and Comparative Studies.* Hove: Psychology Press. pp. 189–238.

Holland, J. (2004) 'The wolf effect: Where elk fear predation, an ecosystem returns', *National Geographic*, 206 (4 October): Geographia section, pages unnumbered.

*Holliday, A. (2002) *Doing and Writing Qualitative Research.* London: Sage.

Horsley, G. (2003) Team building in schools. Unpublished thesis draft for MBA in Education Management, University of Lincoln, England (in the personal possession of the author).

Horsley, G. (2004) 'Team training for school senior leadership and governance: a possible model from a business corporation?' Unpublished MBA dissertation, University of Lincoln, England.

Hughes, G. (1998) *Swearing: A Social History of Foul Language, Oaths and Profanity in English* (2nd edn). London: Penguin.

Hughes, J. (1990) *The Philosophy of Social Research* (2nd edn). Harlow: Longman.

Hunt, C. (2001) 'Assessing personal writing', *Auto/Biography*, IX (1 and 2): 89–94.

Hytten, K. and Warren, J. (2003) 'Engaging whiteness: how racial power gets reified in education', *International Journal of Qualitative Studies in Education*, 16 (1): 65–89.

Ingersoll, R.M. (2003) *Is There Really a Teacher Shortage?* Document R-03-4, Centre for the Study of Teaching and Policy, University of Washington.

ISACS (2003) Independent Schools Association of the Central States. www.ISACS.org, accessed 16 January 2003.

Italia, I. (2005) *The Rise of Literary Journalism in the Eighteenth Century: Anxious Employment.* London: Routledge.

*Ivanič, R. and Roach, D. (1990) 'Academic writing, power and disguise', in R. Clark, N. Fairclough, R. Ivanic, N. McLeod, J. Thomas and P. Meara, (eds), *British Studies in Applied Linguistics 5: Language and Power.* London: BAAL and CILT. pp. 103–19.

*Jakobs, E. and Knorr, D.A. (1996) 'Academic writing and information retrieval', in M. Sharples and T. van der Geest (eds), *The New Writing Environment: Writers at Work in a World of Technology.* London: Springer. pp. 73–86.

James, T. (2002) 'Fruit schooners: racehorses of the sea', *Traditional Boats and Tall Ships*, 21 (August/September): 40–4.

Johnson, B.B. and Newton, R.M. (2003) 'Student willingness to enroll in a community college English course: the influence of student gender and reading assignments'. Paper presented at the Annual Conference of the Universities' Council for Educational Administration, Portland, OR.

Jones, N.B., Spurgeon, S.K., Pont, M.J., Twiddle, J.A., Lim, C.L., Parikh, C.R. and Goh, K.B. (2000) 'Aspects of diagnostic schemes for biomedical and engineering systems', *Institute of Electrical Engineers Proceedings: Science, Measurement and Technology*, 147 (6): 357–62.

Kadel, E. (2002) 'Contamination: crossing social borders', *International Journal of Qualitative Studies in Education*, 15 (1): 33–42.

Kellogg, R.T. (1994) *The Psychology of Writing.* New York: Oxford University Press.

Kelly, K. (2001) 'A maze in stories: deconstructing and confronting identity', *Auto/Biography*, IX (1 and 2): 21–31.

Kelly, L. (1999) *Domestic Violence Matters: An Evaluation of a Development Project.* London: Home Office.

Kenyon, J.P. (1963) *Pepys's Diary.* New York: Macmillan.

Kinsey, A.C. et al. (1948/1998) *Sexual Behaviour in the Human Male.* Philadelphia: W.B. Saunders; Bloomington IN: Indiana University Press.

*Kitchen, R. and Fuller, D. (2005) *The Academic's Guide to Publishing.* London: Sage.

*Knight, P.T. (2002) *Small-Scale Research: Pragmatic Inquiry in Social Science and the Caring Professions.* London: Sage.

Knorr-Cetina, K. (1981) *The Manufacture of Knowledge.* Oxford: Pergamon.

Kohl, H. (1970) *The Open Classroom* (4th printing). New York: Vintage.

Krawczyk, R. (1997) 'Teaching ethics: effect on moral development', *Nursing Ethics*, 4 (1): 56–65.

Kruger, M. (2004) 'Narrative in the time of AIDS: postcolonial Kenyan women's literature', *Research in African Literatures*, 35 (1): 108–29.

Langton, R. (2004) 'Elusive knowledge of things in themselves', *Australian Journal of Philosophy*, 82 (1): 129–36.

*Lanham, C. (1976) *Style: An Anti-Text Book.* New Haven, CT: Yale University Press.

Lawler, N., Martin, B.N. and Agnew, W. (2003) 'Leadership academies: are they an effective staff development scheme for principals? Roundtable paper presented at the Annual Conference of the Universities' Council for Educational Administration, Portland, OR.

Leading for Learning (2003) *Leading for Learning.* Centre for the Study of Teaching and Policy, University of Washington, www.ctpweb.org.

Leavens, A.D.A., Hopkins, W.D. and Thomas, R.K. (2004) 'Referential communication by chimpanzees', *Journal of Comparative Psychology*, 118 (1): 48–57.

*Lewis-Beck, M.S., Bryman, A. and Liao, T.F. (eds) (2004) *The Sage Encyclopaedia of Social Science Research Methods.* Thousand Oaks, CA: Sage.

Limerick, B., Burgess-Limerick, T. and Grace, M. (1996) 'The politics of interviewing: power relations and accepting the gift', *Qualitative Studies in Education*, 9 (4): 449–60.

Lindle, J.C. (2004) 'After-words: past editor of *Educational Administration Quarterly* attempts to unveil the journal's mystique', *UCEA Review*, XLVI (3): 1–5.

*Literati website (2003) Advice on getting published. //elvira.emeraldinsight.com/vl= 9703279/cl=59/nw=1/rpsv/literati.../publishable32.ht, accessed 23 January 2003.

Lomotey, K. and Swanson, A.D. (1990) 'Restructuring school governance: learning from the experiences of rural and urban schools', in S.L. Jacobson and J.A. Conway (eds) *Educational Leadership in an Age of Reform.* New York: Longmans.

Lord, B.R., Robb, A.J. and Shanahan, Y.P. (1998) 'Performance indicators: experiences from New Zealand tertiary institutions', *Higher Education Management*, 10 (2): 41–57.

Lott, E. (2004) 'The first boomer: Bill Clinton, George W. and fictions of state', *representations* [sic]. 84: 117, 122.

Macbeath, J. and Galton, M. with Steward, S., Page, C. and Edwards, J. (2004) *A Life in Secondary Teaching: Finding Time to Learn.* Cambridge: Cambridge Printing (Report for the National Union of Teachers).

McCall Smith, A. (2004) *The Sunday Philosophy Club.* London: Little Brown.

McCall Smith, A. (1998) *The No. 1 Ladies' Detective Agency.* Edinburgh: Polygon.

*Marsh, M. and Marshall N. (2004) *The Guardian Style Book.* London: Guardian Books.

Marshall, J. (1995) *Women Managers Moving On: Exploring Career and Life Choices.* London: Routledge.

Martel, Y. (2001) *Life of Pi.* In Canongate Edition, 2002. Edinburgh: Canongate.

Mason, J. (1996) *Qualitative Researching.* London: Sage.

Matthews, R. (2004) 'Researchers ignore "inconvenient" drug trial results', *Sunday Telegraph*, 30 May: 6.

Marx, S. and Pennington, J. (2003) 'Pedagogies of critical race theory: experimentations with white preservice teachers', *International Journal of Qualitative Studies in Education*, 16 (1): 91–119.

Mehra, B. (1997) 'Research or personal quest? Dilemma in studying my own kind', in B. Merchant and A. Willis (eds), *Multiple and Intersecting Identities in Qualitative Research*. Mahwah, NJ: Erlbaum. pp. 69–82.

*MHRA (2002) *Modern Humanities Research Association Style Guide*. Leeds: MHRA. www.mhra.org

Middaugh, M.F. (2001) *Understanding Faculty Productivity: Standards and Benchmarks for Colleges and Universities*. San Francisco: Jossey-Bass.

Middleton, S. (1986) *An After-Dinner's Sleep*. London: Hutchinson.

Middleton, S. (1995) 'Doing feminist educational theory: a postmodernist perspective', *Gender and Education*, 7 (1): 87–100.

Mies, M. (1993) 'Towards a methodology for feminist research', in M. Hammersley (ed.), *Social Research: Philosophy, Politics and Practice*. London: Open University Press. pp. 64–82. Originally published in G. Bowles and R.D. Klein (eds) (1983), *Theories for Women's Studies*, pp. 117–39.

Miller, C. (1995) 'The unhappy warriors: conflict and nationality among the Canadian troops during the South African War', *The Journal of Imperial and Commonwealth History*, 23 (1): 77–104.

Misra, R. and Panigrahi, B. (1996) 'Effects of age on attitudes towards working women', *International Journal of Manpower*, 17 (2): 3–17.

*MLA (2003) *Handbook for Writers of Research Papers* (6th edn). J. Grimaldi. New York, Modern Languages Association.

Moffett, M. (2004) 'Big Bites', *National Geographic,* 26 (1) July: 94–101. www.magma. nationalgeographic.com/ngn/0407/feature5

Mok, J.K. and Lee, H. (2002) 'A reflection on quality assurance in Hong Kong's higher education', in J.K. Mok and D.K. Chan (eds), *Globalisation and Education: The Quest for Quality Education in Hong Kong*. Hong Kong: Hong Kong University Press.

Mok, K.H. (2000) 'Impact of globalisation: a study of quality assurance systems of higher education in Hong Kong and Singapore', *Comparative Education Review*, 44 (2): 148–69.

Moore, K.A. (2001) 'Are district judges equipped to resolve patent cases?', *Harvard Journal of Law and Technology*, 15 (1): 1–39.

Mugglestone, H. (2004) 'Peer assisted learning for musical composition skills'. Unpublished draft doctoral thesis, University of Lincoln, England (in the personal possession of the author).

*Murray, A. (2001) 'On becoming a virtual editor', *Medical and Biological Engineering and Computing*, 39: 1.

Murray, A. (2004) 'In praise of referees', *Medical and Biological Engineering Computing*, 24: 1.

*Nestor, J. and Barber, L. (1995) 'Audience and the politics of narrative', in J. Amos-Hatch and R. Wisniewski (eds), *Life History and Narrative*. London: Falmer. pp. 49–62.

Neyland, D. and Surridge, C. (2003) 'Information strategy stories: ideas for evolving a dynamic strategic process', *perspectives* [sic] 7 (1): 9–13.

Oddi, A.S. (2002) 'The tragicomedy of the public domain in intellectual property law', *Hastings Communications and Entertainment Law Journal*, 25 (1): 1–64 (in offprint).

*Ó'Dochartaigh, N. (2002) *The Internet Research Handbook*. London: Sage.

O'London, J. (1924) *Is It Good English and Like Matters*. London: Newnes.

O'Neill, M. (1996) 'Prostitution, feminism and critical praxis: profession prostitute?', *Austrian Journal of Sociology*, Winter. www.staffs.ac.uk/schools/humanities_and_soc_ sciences/sociology/level3/prost3.htm.

Oster, A. (2004) 'The effect of the introduction of computers on children's problem-solving skills in science', draft article for the *British Journal of Educational Technology*, in the personal possession of the author, Dr Anat Oster, Department of Computer Science Education, Beit Berl College, Israel.

Otis Skinner, C. (1966) *Madame Sarah*. Boston: Houghton Mifflin.

*Paget, M. (1990) 'Performing the text', *Journal of Contemporary Ethnography*, 19 (1): 136–55.

Parsons, M. and Lyons, G. (1979) 'An alternative approach to enquiry in education management', *Educational Administration*, 8 (1): 75–84.

Pashiardis, P., Thody, A., Papanaoum, Z. and Johansson, O. (2002) 'European Education Leadership', seminar at the Regional Conference of the Commonwealth Council for Educational Administration, Umea, Sweden (published as *European Education Management*, CD, 2003, available from the authors at, respectively, the Universities of Cyprus; Lincoln, England; Aristotle University of Thessaloniki, Greece; Umea, Sweden).

Pettit, B. and Western, B. (2004) 'Mass imprisonment and the life course: race and class inequality in U.S. incarceration', *American Sociological Review*, 69 (2): 151–69.

Piantanida, M. and Garman, N.B. (1999) *The Qualitative Dissertation*. Thousand Oaks, CA: Corwin.

Pilling, J. (1981) *Autobiography and Imagination*. London: Routledge and Kegan Paul.

*Pirkis, J. and Gardner, H. (1998) 'Writing for publication', *Australian Journal of Public Health Interchange*, 4 (2): 71–6.

Punch, K.F. (2000) *Developing Effective Research Proposals*. London: Sage.

Punch, M. (1979) *Policing the Inner City: a Study of Amsterdam's Warmoesstraat*, Hamden, CT: Archon Books.

*Raimond, P. (1993) *Management Projects: Design, Research and Presentation*. London: Chapman and Hall (two brief chapters on presentation).

Reichs, K.J. (1989) 'Cranial structure eccentricities: a case in which precocious closure complicated determination of sex and commingling', *Journal of Forensic Sciences*, 34 (1): 263–73.

Reichs, K.J. (1990) 'Precocious and premature cranial structure union as complicating factors in the identification of skeletal remains', *Canadian Society of Forensic Sciences Journal*, 23 (1): 9–23.

Reichs, K.J. (2003) *Bare Bones*. London: BCA.

Ribbins, P. (1993) 'Towards a prolegomenon for understanding what radical educational reform means for school principals'. Keynote paper presented at the Australian Council for Educational Administration/Australian School Principals' Association National Conference, Adelaide, Australia.

Rice, A. (2004) ' "*Déchiffrer le silence*": a conversation with Germaine Tillion', *Research in African Literature*, 35 (1): 162–89.

*Richardson, L. (1997) *Fields of Play: Constructing an Academic Life*. New Brunswick, NJ: Rutgers University Press.

*Richardson, L. (1998) 'Writing: a method of inquiry', in N.K. Denzin and Y.S. Lincoln (eds), *Collecting and Interpreting Qualitative Materials*. Thousand Oaks, CA: Sage. pp. 345–71.

Ripple, W.J. and Beschta, R.L. (2003) 'Wolf reintroduction, predation risk, and cottonwood recovery in Yellowstone National Park', *Forest Ecology and Management*, 184: 299–313. Consulted online at www.sciencedirect.com.

Ritchie, D.A. (2004) 'What more's to be said? Understanding legislative bodies through oral history', *Oral History*, 32 (1): 71–8.

Roberts, V. (2003) 'Overcoming barriers to access and success in tertiary education in the Commonwealth Caribbean', *International Studies in Educational Administration*, 31 (3): 2–15.

Rusch, E.A. (2003) 'Assessing gender and race in leadership preparation: a retrospective journey along my faultlines'. Paper presented at the Annual Conference of the Universities' Council for Educational Administration, Portland, OR.

Sacco, J. (2005) 'In the milk factory', *Granta*, 89: 127–33.

*Sadler, D. Royce (1990) *Up the Publication Road* (2nd edn). Campbelltown, NSW: Higher Education Research and Development Society of Australia (HERDSA).

Saunders, D., Brake, M., Griffiths, M. and Thornton, R. (2004) 'Access, astronomy and science fiction: a case study in curriculum design', *active* learning in higher education [*sic*], 5 (1): 27–42.

Schenk, F. (1998) 'The Morris water maze (is not a maze)', in N. Foreman and R. Gillett (eds), *Handbook of Spatial Research Paradigms and Methodologies. Vol. 2: Clinical and Comparative Studies*. Hove: Psychology Press. pp. 145–88.

Schwartz, H. (2002) 'Historical memory and the importance of the Bracero Project in the struggles of *rabajadores migrantes* today', *International Journal of Qualitative Studies in Education*, 15 (1): 73–84.

Scott, D. and Morrison, M. (2005) *Key Ideas in Educational Research.* London: Continuum

Scott, D. and Usher, R. (1999) *Researching Education: Data Methods and Theory in Educational Enquiry.* London: Cassell.

Scraggs, J. (2005) *Crime Fiction.* Abingdon: Routledge.

Shah, A., Pell, K. and Brooke, P. (2004) 'Beyond first destinations: Graduate employability survey', *active* learning in higher education (sic), 5 (1): 9–26.

*Sharples, M. and van der Geest, T. (eds) (1996). *The New Writing Environment: Writers at Work in a World of Technology.* London: Springer.

Shils, E.A. and Finch, H.A. (1949) *Max Weber on the Methodology of the Social Sciences.* Illinois: Free.

Shroder, K., Drotner, K., Kline, S. and Murray, C. (2003) *Researching Audiences.* London: Arnold.

Silva, T. (1990) 'Second language composition instruction: developments, issues and directions in ESL', in B. Kroll (ed.), *Second Language Writing: Research Insights for the Classroom.* Cambridge: Cambridge University Press. pp. 11–23.

Skultans, V. (2001) 'Silence and the shortcomings of narrative', *Auto/Biography*, IX (1 and 2): 3–10.

Soth, A. with Weiland, M. (2005) 'The making of parts', *Granta*, 89: 65–96.

Staub, L. (2002) 'Photo essay: the border is …', *International Journal of Qualitative Studies in Education*, 15 (1): 67–72.

Stevenson, R. (2003) *The Last of England.* Oxford English Literary History, vol. 12. Oxford: Oxford University Press.

Stewart, J.M. and Hodges, D. (2003) 'The room that nobody wanted: an exploratory study into the importance of room quality to learning', *International Studies in Educational Administration*, 31 (3): 42–57.

Stork, D. (2004) 'Caravaggio's Leica'. http://thefilter.blogs.com/thefilter/2004/04/caravaggios_lei.html, accessed 11 January 2005.

*Strunk, W. and White, E.B. (2000) *The Elements of Style* (4th edn). New York: Macmillan.

Sutherland, J. (2004) 'Brushing up on Kinsey', *Guardian Weekly*, 19–25 November, 171 (22): 18.

Swanger, J. (2002) 'Letter from the Editor: the critical pedagogy of ethnography in the Border Studies Program', *International Journal of Qualitative Studies in Education*, 15 (1): 1–10.

Taylor, J. (2001a) 'The impact of performance indicators on the work of university academics: evidence from Australian universities', *Higher Education Quarterly*, 55 (1): 42–61.

Taylor, M., Moynihan, E., McWilliam, J. and Gresty, D. (2004) 'Teaching business IT ethics: a professional approach', *active* learning in higher education (sic), 5 (1): 43–55.

Taylor, S. (2001b) 'Places I remember: women's talk about residence and other relationships to place', *Auto/Biography*, IX (1 and 2): 33–40.

Testa, S. (2004) 'Giving children their due: an investigation into the theory and practice of leadership strategies in Maltese state secondary schools'. Unpublished International MBA thesis, University of Lincoln, England.

Thody, A.M. (1989) 'University management observed', *Studies in Higher Education*, 14 (3): 279–96.

Thody, A.M. (1990a) 'Governors of the school republic', *Educational Management and Administration*, 18 (2): 42–5.

Thody, A.M. (1990b) 'Observing a nineteenth century headteacher', *History in Education*, 23 (4): 355–73.

Thody, A.M. (1994a) 'Abroad thoughts from home: reflections on an academic visit to Australia', *Journal of Educational Administration*, 32 (2): 45–53.

Thody, A.M. (1994b) 'School management in nineteenth-century elementary schools: a day in the life of a headteacher', *History of Education*, 23 (4): 355–73.

Thody, A. (1997a) *Leadership of Schools: Chief Executives in Education.* London: Cassells.

Thody, A. (1997b) 'Lies, damned lies and … stories: principals' anecdotes as a means of teaching and research in educational management', *Educational Management and Administration*, 25 (3): 325–38.

Thody, A. (2003) 'Followership in educational organisations: a pilot mapping of the territory', *Leadership and Policy*, 2 (2): 141–56.

Thody, A.M. and Crystal, L. (1996) 'Mentoring: cultural reinforcement or destabilisation?', in L. Jacobson, E.S. Hickcox and R. Stevenson (eds), *School Administration: Persistent Dilemmas in Preparation and Practice.* Westport, CT: Greenwood. pp. 177–96.

Thody, A. and Kaabwe, E.S. (eds) (2000) *Educating Tomorrow: Lessons from Managing Girls' Education in Africa.* Kenwyn, SA: Juta.

Thody, A.M. and Nkata, J.L. (1997) 'Who is allowed to speak? Ugandan and English governance: Part I', *International Studies in Educational Administration*, 24 (1): 67–77.

Thody, A. and Punter, A. (1994) *School and College Governors from the Business Community.* Faculty of Management, University of Luton.

Thody, A., Bowden, D. and Grey, B. (2004) *The Teacher's Survival Guide* (2nd edn). London: Continuum.

Thomas, D. (2001) *Reading Hollywood.* London: Wallflower.

Thompson, A. (2003) 'Tiffany, friend of people of colour', *International Journal of Qualitative Studies in Education*, 16 (1): 7–30.

To, C.-Y. (2000) *The Scientific Merit of the Social Sciences: Implications for Research and Application.* Stoke-on-Trent: Trentham.

Tonfoni, G. and Richardson, J. (1994) *Writing as a Visual Art.* Oxford: Intellect.

Tooley, J. with Darby, D. (1998) *Educational Research: A Critique.* London: OFSTED.

Trafford, V. and Leshem, S. (2002a) 'Anatomy of a doctoral viva', *Journal of Graduate Education*, 3 (2): 33–41.

Trafford, V. and Leshem, S. (2002b) 'Questions in doctoral vivas', *Quality Assurance in Education*, 11 (2): 114–22.

Trafford, V. and Leshem, S. (2002c) 'Starting at the end to undertake doctoral research: predictable questions as stepping stones', *Higher Education Review*, 34 (1): 31–49.

Trollope, A. (1855) *The Warden.* London: Collins, 1955.

Truss, L. (2003) *Eats Shoots and Leaves.* London: Profile.

*Van Maanen, J. (1988) *Tales of the Field: On Writing Ethnography.* Chicago: University of Chicago Press.

*Vipond, D. (1996) 'Problems with a monolithic APA style', *American Psychologist*, 51 (6): 653.

Wakerlin, A. (2004) 'So, what do you think about us sharing with those rugby blokes?', *Leicester Mercury*, 27 November: 10.

Weiss, C.H. (1983) 'Ideology, interests and information: the basis of policy positions', in D. Callahan and B. Jennings (eds), *Ethics, the Social Sciences, and Policy Analysis.* New York: Plenum.

Westrick, J. (2004) 'The influence of service-learning on intercultural sensitivity: a quantitative study', *Journal of Research in International Education*, 3 (3): 277–99.

Willinsky, J. (2000) *If Only We Knew.* New York: Routledge.

Winter, R. (1989) *Learning from Experience: Principle and Practice in Action Research.* London: Falmer.

*Wolcott, H.F. (1990) *Writing Up Qualitative Research.* Thousand Oaks, CA: Sage.

*Woodley, K. (2004) 'Let the data sing: representing discourse in poetic form', *Oral History*, 32 (1): 49–58.

*Woods, P., Jeffrey, B., Troman, G., Boyle, M. and Cocklin, B. (1998) 'Team and technology in writing up research', *British Educational Research Journal*, 24 (5): 573–91.

Worster, D. (2004) *Dust Bowl: The Southern Plains in the 1930s.* Oxford: Oxford University Press.

Xu, Y., Jones, N.B., Fothergill, C. and Hanning, C.D. (2001) 'Error analysis of two-wavelength absorption-based fibre-optic sensors', *Optics and Lasers Engineering*, 36: 607–15.

*Zeller, N. and Farmer, F.M. (1999) ' "Catchy, clever titles are not acceptable": style, APA, and qualitative reporting', *International Journal of Qualitative Studies in Education*, 12 (1): 3–19.

Index